MASTER LIFE

MASTER LIFE

Developing a Rich Personal Relationship with the Master

AVERY T. WILLIS, JR.

with Sherrie Willis Brown

BROADMAN
&HOLMAN
PUBLISHERS
Nashville, Tennessee

Published by Broadman & Holman Publishers, Nashville, Tennessee
Cover & Inside Page Design: Anderson Thomas Design, Nashville, Tennessee
Typography: TF Designs, Mt. Juliet, Tennessee

Dewey Decimal Classification: 248.4
Subject Heading: Prayer
Library of Congress Card Catalog Number: 98–12670

Unless otherwise noted, Scripture quotations are from the Holy Bible, New International Version, copyright © 1973, 1978, 1984 by International Bible Society.

Other versions cited are AMP, The Amplified Bible, Old Testament copyright © 1962, 1964 by Zondervan Publishing House, used by permission, and the New Testament © The Lockman Foundation 1954, 1958, 1987, used by permission; NKJV, New King James Version, copyright © 1979, 1980, 1982, Thomas Nelson, Inc., Publishers. Phillips, reprinted with permission of Macmillan Publishing Co., Inc. from J. B. Phillips: The New Testament in Modern English, revised edition, © J. B. Phillips 1958, 1960, 1972. RSV, Revised Standard Version of the Bible, copyrighted 1946, 1952, ©1971, 1973.

Library of Congress Cataloging-in-Publication Data
Willis, Avery T.
    MasterLife / by Avery T. Willis
       p. cm.
    Includes bibliographical references (p.)
    ISBN 0-8054-0165-2
    1. Spiritual life—Christianity.
    I. Title.
      BV4501.2.W5447   1998
    248.4—dc21

    98-12670
    CIP

1 2 3 4 5 02 01 00 99 98

Contents

Table of Resources

PREFACE

Welcome to the spiritual adventure of following Christ! I invite you to experience a deepening relationship with God and others. This book is written to introduce you to the *MasterLife* discipleship process that has been experienced by more than 300,000 English-speaking people, and thousands of others in more than fifty other languages.

Why This Book?

This book will introduce you to the *MasterLife* discipleship process and give you many "how to's" of the Christian life. How much they become a part of your life will depend on you and your personal application of the truths you encounter in the person of Jesus Christ. Books don't make disciples; only Christ makes disciples. I pray that God will do a work in your life as you read this book. In addition, it will help you determine if you want to become a part of a *MasterLife* group and experience the small-group process that God has used to change many lives. Jesus and Paul demonstrate that the best disciple making takes place in a small group with a leader who is modeling the life of a disciple.

How To Become a Better Disciple

"How long did it take you to write *MasterLife*?" I am often asked. My usual answer is, "About twenty-five years because I had to learn most of what I know about discipleship through personal experience." Like many other Christians, no one systematically discipled me. I had to pick up the qualities and traits of discipleship from my own Bible study and from watching others live out its values and disciplines. My next step was to learn how to help others experience this same life-changing discipleship process.

I learned more from my mistakes than from my successes. I started by witnessing in the streets and then discipling those who came to Christ. As a pastor for ten years in the United States, I experimented with every discipleship tool I could find. By the time I went to Indonesia as a missionary, I knew how to make disciples individually and in small groups. However, I would not give them written materials for fear that we would lose the life-changing process. I did not want anyone to think that discipleship is a book or a course instead of a personal, lifelong, obedient relationship with Jesus Christ.

My experience as a missionary changed my mind about writing *MasterLife*. My wife Shirley and I experienced the Indonesian Revival in which over two million persons were baptized in six years.[1] Many churches doubled. We didn't have enough leaders for the new congregations. We began to train leaders in the discipleship process in small groups. The trained leaders were then able to make disciples and lead their churches.

That material became known as *MasterLife* when I was asked to translate and develop it for the United States. We introduced it in hundreds of five-day workshops. With the help of many other people, it was then developed for other countries.

After using *MasterLife* for fifteen years around the world, we revised it in 1997 to be more contemporary and easier to use. We made it available to the public for the first time in the form of four six-week small-group studies.

This book is another step in the process of making disciples of all nations. I am convinced that the need for discipleship in this day demands that we do more to help all Christians be better disciples. This book is an entry point for a deeper life in Christ. I have made it more personal than the other books by including fresh personal experiences and discipleship experiences of persons in many cultures. It is written in a style that flows through the processes of life—beginning with the basics and moving to fruitful multiplication.

Who Is This Book For?

This book is about your life and your relationship with the living Lord. The ideas I share with you will deepen your relationship with God and your relationships with others as you take time to incorporate them into your life. I hope that these concepts will give you a new understanding of how Christ and His Spirit want to live through you. Interspersed in the chapters are specific "how-to" resources that are step-by-step plans of action you can implement.

As I began to write, I thought of people who might be helped by this book. You will probably find yourself in one of these categories:

- A new believer who wants to become a true disciple of Jesus. Someone may have given you this book to encourage and instruct you in your Christian walk.
- A person who says, "There must be more to the Christian life than what I am experiencing!"
- A person who has been a Christian for some time but has never been discipled systematically. You are among the majority of Christians.
- Someone whose work schedule, family structure, or church affiliation has not made it feasible to join a *MasterLife* group or another discipleship study group.
- Pastors who want to preview *MasterLife* to evaluate whether to offer it to groups in their congregations or leaders of *MasterLife* groups who want to overview the content to see where the group will be going.
- Anyone who wants to grow spiritually and know Christ better.

You may want to read a chapter a day and incorporate what you are learning into your life. You may want to read this book all the way through and then return and read each chapter slowly, putting into your own life what you are learning before moving on to the next chapter. The more this book is digested, the more of it you will be able to absorb into your system of spiritual development. You may find it helpful to read this book with your spouse or a friend and encourage one another as you learn.

How Can I Use this Book to Be a Better Disciple?

The book is divided into four sections with six chapters each. Each section is built around a concept depicted in a diagram on the back of each part title page. This diagram is your map for remembering and appropriating the concepts of the sections:

Part 1: Life in Christ
Part 2: Life in the Spirit
Part 3: Life in the World
Part 4: Life for the World

You will find many "how-to" resources listed in chapters and immediately following them. They give you the opportunity to put into practice what you have been learning. Questions follow each chapter for meditation and personal evaluation. Please take the time to meditate on and answer these questions for yourself.

Who Are the Writers?

You will learn plenty about me in this book because I try to be transparent. I want to introduce my cowriter, Sherrie Willis Brown, who is my daughter. Sherrie did most of the actual writing using the *MasterLife* books, stories from participants around the world, and other content that I gave her.

Sherrie, our second child, came to me while she was in Vanderbilt University and asked, "Dad, would you disciple me?" "I would be honored and delighted to disciple you," I told her. "I have been discipling you informally in the home all your life, but that is different from systematically leading you through the discipling process." The original version of *MasterLife* was still in a trial edition, so we used it as our guide. Sherrie then discipled two friends at school and later led two *MasterLife* groups. In this book Sherrie has been able to use those experiences to make discipleship real to you.

Sherrie is married to Steve Brown and has three daughters, Stephanie, Kristine, and Lauren. They live in Kansas City, Missouri, where they are currently planting a new church. Steve was an invaluable help on the technological end of coauthoring by E-mail.

Discipleship Is Life

To give credit to all who have influenced my life and my discipleship would be impossible. I must begin with my parents, Rev. and Mrs. A. T. Willis, who lived and showed me what discipleship is. They molded my character and imparted biblical core values. I am greatly indebted to friends like Tom Elliff, Henry Blackaby, T. W. Hunt, Jerry Rankin and hundreds of others, who have helped me become a better follower of Christ. I have learned so much about discipleship and leadership from colaborers such as Marvin Leech, Jimmy Crowe, Roy Edgemon, and Howard Foshee. My mind and practice has been challenged and changed by teachers such as H. C. Brown Jr.; LeRoy Ford;

$\mathcal{P}$REFACE

Ted Ward; and Cal Guy, my seminary professor and mentor through the years. My wife, Shirley, who has walked with me all these years as helpmate and friend, has done more to make me what I am than she or others can ever know. Our children, Randy, Sherrie, Wade, Krista and Brett, have inspired me and improved my humility! I have no greater joy than to hear that my children walk in truth (3 John 3). The new generation of grandchildren encourage me.

Thanks goes to all who have worked on this book to make it effective such as my editor, John Landers, and the entire staff at Broadman & Holman.

I take responsibility for all that does not reflect the Spirit of Christ and does not edify. If this book helps anyone, all the glory goes to God.

Avery T. Willis Jr.

Introduction
A CALL TO DISCIPLESHIP

When I went away to college, I had been a Christian for several years. I had done almost everything my church had taught me. I had attended church up to five times a week, read my Bible daily, shared the gospel with non-Christians, and tithed. But when the influences of home and church were removed, I was faced with who I really was. I realized that I possessed Christ as my Savior but He did not possess me. I was not a disciple who followed Christ in everything. Jesus said, "If anyone would come after me, he must deny himself and take up his cross daily and follow me" (Luke 9:23). The Scriptures were clear about the relationship between a disciple and his Master. The Master has full reign, and the servant's responsibility is to follow and fulfill every request of the Master.

I knew I must make a decision. I had to decide whether I was going my own way or Christ's way. Intuitively, I knew that either I would become a real disciple now or I would remain a mediocre Christian for the rest of my life. I could claim Christ as Lord but the question came to me: Would Christ claim as His disciple a person who was not denying himself, taking up his cross daily, and following Him? Serving Christ must be on His terms.

I spent many nights walking through the fields near my university, talking to God and pondering whether I really meant business about being a disciple. I gave all kinds of excuses just as Moses had done. I said, "Lord, you don't need me. I am not a leader and I am a very ordinary person." In answer to my excuses, God said, "For the eyes of the LORD run to and fro throughout the whole earth, to show Himself strong on behalf of those whose heart is loyal to Him" (2 Chron. 16:9, NKJV). I remembered an anecdote about evangelist D. L. Moody. His friend Henry Varley told him, "It remains to be seen what God will do with a man who gives himself up wholly to Him." Moody responded, "I will be that man."[1]

If anyone gave himself completely to God, it was D. L. Moody. With only a third-grade education, he led hundreds of thousands of people in England and America to God. My response was, "Lord, I want to be like that. I want to have a heart committed to You. Then if You do anything with my life, everyone will know it was because You did it and not because of my abilities."

Surrendering to a lifelong, obedient relationship with Christ is crucial. Obeying whatever God tells you to do and depending on Him to accomplish whatever He wants is the focus of a disciple. Yielding to God allows Him to reveal Himself to you and teach you how to walk with Him. Once this is in place, God will receive glory for everything accomplished in your life. The commitments I made during that year set the course for my entire life. I cannot say that my heart has always been perfect before the Lord. However, since I made that commitment, God has shown me whenever my heart is not right. I confess my sin and ask Him to restore my heart so it is perfect toward Him.

What Is a Disciple?

The New Testament uses the term *disciple* in three ways.

First, it is a general term used to describe a committed follower of a teacher or a group: "Now John's disciples and the Pharisees were fasting. Some people came and asked Jesus, 'How is it that John's disciples and the disciples of the Pharisees are fasting, but yours are not?'" (Mark 2:18). Not only do we see disciples of Jesus in this passage but also followers of John and the Pharisees.

Second, the New Testament uses the term *disciple* to refer to the twelve apostles whom Jesus called. "He appointed twelve—designating them apostles—that they might be with him and that he might send them out to preach and to have authority to drive out demons" (Mark 3:14).

Third, Jesus used the word *disciple* to describe a follower who meets His requirements, forsaking all else to follow Him. "Large crowds were traveling with Jesus, and turning to them he said: 'If anyone comes to me and does not hate his father and mother, his wife and children, his brothers and sisters—yes, even his own life—he cannot be my disciple. And anyone who does not carry his cross and follow me cannot be my disciple' " (Luke 14:25–27).

Relationships of a Disciple

When I married Shirley, she did not merely top a list of girlfriends as my favorite, with whom I would spend the most time. She became the only name on the list! It is the same with Jesus. He is not just to move up to first on our list. He is to *be* our list. Jesus described the relationship He desired as a vine with branches. "I am the vine; you are the branches. If a man remains in me and I in him, he will bear much fruit; apart from me you can do nothing" (John 15:5).

Hudson Taylor once wrote a letter to his sister and described to her the magnitude he had discovered in that verse. He wrote:

> As I thought of the vine and the branches, what light the blessed Spirit poured directly into my soul! How great seemed my mistake in having wished to get the sap, the fullness, out of Him. I saw not only that Jesus would never leave me, but that I was a member of His body, of His flesh, and of His bones. The vine now I see is not the root merely, but all—root, stem, branches, twigs, leaves, flowers, fruit; and Jesus is not only that: He is soil and sunshine, air and showers, and ten thousand times more than we have ever dreamed, wished for, or needed.[2]

Scripture reveals that we are to love Christ so much more than anything else that all other love relationships would seem like hate relationships (Luke 14:26). Jesus asked His disciples to give Him supreme loyalty. He knew He must reinforce in them the need to love Him more than any other person, possession, or purpose—anything that might keep them from following Him.

Our relationship with Christ must surpass any other relationship. When Shirley and I were seriously dating and discussing marriage, I knew this relationship must be clear. I said to her one night, "Shirley, before we get married, you need to know that I loved someone else before you. That person captured my heart and will always be my first love. You will always be second."

"Who?" she asked quietly, an edge of dismay in her voice.

I said, "My Lord Jesus Christ."

She paused and then delighted me with her answer. "In that case," she said, "I would rather be second!" She knew that as long as I put Christ first in my life, I would be a better husband and father.

When we lived in Indonesia, a man named Faizal heard me speak. Afterwards, he came and asked to work for me. I knew he was educated but because of former Communist connections, he was no longer allowed to continue his teaching profession. I didn't really have work for him, but he insisted that it was very important. I offered to let him serve as our gardener and house-servant, thinking that he would not accept so menial a task. He accepted the work, and several months later he came to talk to me. He asked, "Do you know why I came to work for you?"

When I indicated that I assumed it was because he needed the money to support his wife and three children, he shook his head. "No," he replied, "My parents send me enough money every month to support my family. Yet, as I heard all those things you were saying about the good news and Christianity, I decided the only way to know if what you said was true was to be in your house and see if it really worked. I want you to know that I asked Jesus to come into my heart this morning."

Not long after that, he received a letter from his parents who were very strong Moslems. The letter stated that if he went through with his baptism, they would disown him as a son and cut off his money. He came to me asking what he should do. I showed him the passage in Luke 14:26 about leaving mother and father, but I also showed him this verse of Scripture: "But seek first his kingdom and his righteousness, and all these things will be given to you as well" (Matt. 6:33). I told him that he would have to decide who was first.

He wrote his parents, and among the things he shared with them was an Indonesian proverb which states, "I have spit on the ground, and I will not lick it up." He had made his choice.

I hope you will never have to make a choice like Faizal's, but all of us must make choices between our loyalty to our Lord Jesus Christ as His disciple and our loyalty to other personal relationships.

The Priority of Possessions

Our relationship with the Lord must mean more that any possession we own. Jesus also said, "In the same way, any of you who does not give up everything he has cannot be my disciple" (Luke 14:33). Suppose you are a pearl collector and one day you see the largest, most magnificent pearl in a store window. When you talk to the proprietor, he says he will gladly sell you the pearl for whatever you have. You readily agree, knowing that you are only a small-time collector and really do not have much. As you hand him the fifty dollars and change you have in your pocket, he asks you what else you have. "That's it! That's all I have," you answer with a shrug.

"Any investments?" he asks.

"Nothing much, a few smaller pearls, not worth much. They're at home."

"Oh, you have a house?" As he writes that down, and asks more questions, he discovers you also have a garage, furniture, two cars, a wife, and children. "That's fine," he says. "I'll take all of that and one more thing—you. Now here is the pearl."

"Again, the kingdom of heaven is like a merchant looking for fine pearls. When he found one of great value, he went away and sold everything he had and bought it" (Matt. 13:45, 46).

A pastor in Buenos Aires, Juan Carlos Ortiz, began to seek the Lord on behalf of his church. Although it had tripled in numbers, the church was not growing spiritually. The pastor committed himself to discipleship, preached on discipleship for the next year, and taught four or five men to disciple others as well. God began to move powerfully in that church. When they came to the matter of possessions, the people in the church brought the deeds to their apartments, their only commodity with real value in the rampant inflation of that economy, and gave them to the church. After about six months of prayer, the leaders of the church told those who had given over the deeds, "We accept these apartments in the name of Christ, but we believe that you should continue to live in them and be lighthouses throughout the city. However, these are still the Lord's apartments, so if we send someone to you who needs food or a place to sleep, you must welcome them as the Lord to His apartment." That is the commitment we must give to our Lord. All we own belongs to Him to use any way He chooses.

My Purpose or Christ's?

Our relationship with the Lord must be more important than any purpose we may have. Jesus said, "Anyone who does not carry his cross and follow me cannot be my disciple" (Luke 14:27). The Lord tested the depth of my commitment when He changed the focus of my life purpose. You might expect my most difficult decision would have been to take my wife and our three children to turbulent Indonesia as missionaries. However, that seemed easy compared to what God asked me to do fourteen years later.

In 1977 we returned to the United States on our third furlough. During that time I preached in many churches that were apathetic, lethargic, or dead. They showed little vitality in their worship and ministry. This was at a time when my denomination had just made a commitment to enlist fifty thousand volunteers for short-term mission trips overseas. Having seen little evidence of Christ's lordship in the churches, I said, *Surely we are not going to export this apathetic discipleship all over the world.*

God spoke to me, eventually directing me to return to the United States to write *MasterLife* and help equip His people to share the gospel with everyone in the world. Deeply committed to my work as a missionary and my role as the president of the Indonesian Baptist Theological Seminary, I struggled to understand why God would ask me to return to America. Week after week I wrote in my journal, "Lord, what are You trying to tell me?" For the next eight months I struggled with God about this matter.

As I preached from Acts 10 about Peter's being commanded to eat unclean animals, I began to see in that sheet the dead churches in which I had been preaching. Although I sensed God was saying to me, "Rise, kill, and eat," I told God, *They are already dead. I don't want to eat them. I just want to get back to Indonesia. Besides, Peter had three men at the gate telling him what to do, and I don't have anyone.* Not long after that prayer, God sent three men. Our pastor, Tom Elliff, asked me to translate *MasterLife* into English in order to train his staff. Roy Edgemon, the leader of discipleship training in our denominational publishing house, asked if I would adapt *MasterLife* for an English-speaking audience. Then Bill Hogue, our denominational director of evangelism, asked me to help design a plan to train people to witness.

I realized that if I was going to teach others to be obedient disciples, then I had to be obedient. I took a six-month leave of absence to translate and rewrite the material. During that time I heard God speak clearly about making *MasterLife* available in America and the rest of the world. He also revealed that I would share a message of revival and equip His people to be on mission with Him.

Maybe you are like I was. You are not as obedient as you should be. Perhaps you make excuses for not being obedient. Paul wrote, "For it is God who works in you to will and to act according to his good purpose" (Phil. 2:13). Christ creates in His disciples a desire and an increasing ability to obey Him. The apostles were ordinary people, but they had an extraordinary commitment to follow Christ. Jesus taught His disciples, and they obeyed. They learned what Christ was teaching them by doing what He commanded them to do. Their primary commitment was to be faithful to Jesus.

Christ's disciples learned day by day to obey Him just as we do. His followers sometimes put their own selfish needs and concerns above Him. Three of them chose sleep over honoring His request to stay awake and pray with Him in the Garden of Gethsemane. They argued about who would be most important in His kingdom. When Jesus was arrested, the disciples fled, and Peter even denied Him. Clearly, the disciples did not always have Christ as their first priority. Nevertheless, Jesus never gave up on them. After His death and resurrection, their lives changed dramatically with the coming of the Holy Spirit. Acts 4:18–37 illustrates that His disciples loved Him more than any other person, possession, or purpose in their lives. Jesus never stopped working with them to transform them into His image.

Neither will Christ cease working with you to bring you into a deeper relationship with Him. The secret of discipleship is your relationship with Jesus. When you truly acknowledge Christ as Lord of your life, His life is evidenced through you in the fullness of His Spirit. He provides what you need to be like Him and to do His will.

What is a disciple? After years of study and experience, I believe that the following definition, which I will use throughout this book, sums up what Christ means when He invites us to be His disciple. *Christian discipleship is developing a personal, lifelong, obedient relationship with Jesus Christ in which He changes your character into Christlikeness, transforms your values into kingdom values, and involves you in His mission in the home, the church, and the world.*

The Disciple's Cross

When you read the commands of Christ in the New Testament, you will realize there are basic steps of obedience required of a disciple. As my relationship with Christ grew, I began to obey Christ's commands more fully. Over time I began to develop a picture that showed the essentials of discipleship in what I call the Disciple's Cross. It is pictured on page 10 and further developed throughout the book. It incorporates all the disciplines to which Christ calls us in His commands: spending time with the Master, continuing in the Word, praying in faith, having fellowship with believers, witnessing to the world, and ministering to others. None of this can be done unless Christ becomes the abiding presence in a real and personal relationship.

Like the disciples, we are to obey Jesus' commands. Jesus provided the resources to help His disciples obey: He prayed for them, sent the Holy Spirit, and provided His written Word. You and I have those same resources available. If you obey His commands, you will experience His love and bear His fruit. You can have a lifelong, obedient relationship with Him. "Whoever has my commands and obeys them, he is the one who loves me. He who loves me will be loved by my Father, and I too will love him and show myself to him" (John 14:21).

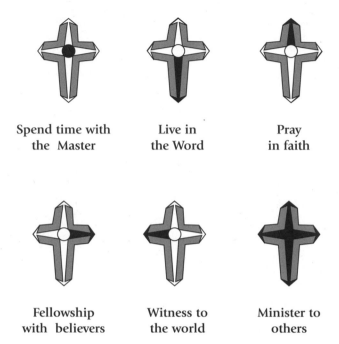

Spend time with
the Master

Live in
the Word

Pray
in faith

Fellowship
with believers

Witness to
the world

Minister to
others

You may be thinking, *Yes, I want to have Jesus at the center of my life. I want to adjust my relationship with anyone, anything, or any direction that takes priority over Him. But I get distracted. I get busy. I forget about Him. Sometimes I wait to call on Him until I'm at the end of my rope. How can I allow Him to be the priority in my life so that I can have a personal, lifelong obedient relationship with Him?* Jesus commanded us first to follow Him and to spend time with Him. In chapter 1, I will show you how to make these an integral part of your life so you may begin to develop a deeper love relationship with Christ.

Questions for Meditation and Discussion

1. Do you have any priority above Christ?
2. Has Christ called you to a deeper commitment than you have been willing to make?
3. What would you need to remove from your life in order to give Christ first place?
4. Do you feel close to the Lord throughout the day? Do you sense His leadership in your life?
5. What are you currently doing to develop your relationship with Christ?

Part 1

THE DISCIPLE'S CROSS

You will develop a deeper
relationship with Christ
as you practice
the six biblical disciplines
of a disciple.

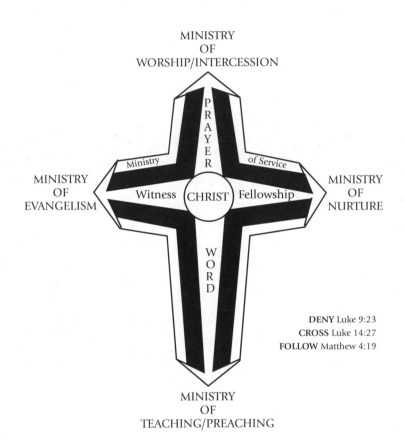

MINISTRY
OF
WORSHIP/INTERCESSION

P
R
A
Y
E
R

Ministry   of Service

MINISTRY   MINISTRY
OF   OF
EVANGELISM   Witness CHRIST Fellowship   NURTURE

W
O
R
D

DENY Luke 9:23
CROSS Luke 14:27
FOLLOW Matthew 4:19

MINISTRY
OF
TEACHING/PREACHING

Chapter 1
ABIDING
IN CHRIST

Jesus called His disciples to "come, follow me" (Matt. 4:19). More than anything else, Jesus wanted to spend time with His disciples. He knew that being with Him in all kinds of situations would equip the disciples to do that for which He had chosen them. They soon learned the truth of Jesus' declaration, "I am the vine; you are the branches. If a man remains in me and I in him, he will bear much fruit; apart from me you can do nothing" (John 15:5).

A disciple is one who follows Jesus, learns from Him, and obeys Him as Lord. God loves you and wants to have fellowship with you. Your remaining in Him is of utmost importance to God. His plans for you include spending time with Him. Only by staying in communion with Him can you be and do all for which He called you.

A disciple must deny himself (Luke 9:23) and abide in Christ (John 15:5). The empty circle at the center of the Disciple's Cross represents your life. It pictures denying all of self and letting Christ fill the entire circle as you focus on Him. He is to have priority in everything. Life in Christ is Christ living in you. This does not mean that you lose your identity but you lose your self-centeredness. John the Baptist said, "He must become greater; I must become less" (see Matt. 3:11). For Christ to increase does not depend on "trying" to deny self but on realizing, understanding, and accepting the lordship of Christ. When you fall in love with Jesus so that He becomes the number one priority in your life, "self" will begin to diminish as Christ Himself gives you the strength to obey everything He has commanded.

Spending Time with the Master

The primary motivation for spending time with the Master is so that your fellowship with Him grows deeper. For a child, love is spelled T-I-M-E. God gave you twenty-four hours a day. As His child, what portion of the day do you think He wants to spend with you? All of it! He said, "Surely I will be with you always, to the very end of the age" (Matt. 28:20). He is with you every waking and sleeping hour. Spending time with the Master is not a question of God's making time for you but of your making time for Him.

Wanting to communicate with someone you love is natural. When you love people, you want to spend time with them and get to know them more and more. You do not want to be separated from them. When you go for a while without seeing or talking to them, you no longer feel as close. You fail to share experiences, you lose intimacy, and you feel as if you are drifting apart. You long to connect with them once again. When you are a child of God, you have the same deep desire for fellowship with your heavenly Father.

We love God as a response to His love (1 John 4:19). You know that He loves you because He sent His Son to die for you. Failing to return God's love does not influence the way He feels about you. But your love for Him diminishes and grows stale if you do not have the nourishment of daily fellowship with Him. A daily time together is important so you and the Father can enjoy the close relationship made possible by Jesus' sacrifice. Paul summed up what it means to fellowship with God when he wrote to the Philippians:

> [My determined purpose is] that I may know Him—that I may progressively become more deeply and intimately acquainted with Him, perceiving and recognizing and understanding [the wonders of His person] more strongly and more clearly. And that I may in that same way come to know the power outflowing from His resurrection [which it exerts over believers]; and that I may so share His sufferings as to be continually transformed [in spirit into His likeness even] to His death (Phil 3:10, AMP).

An Appointment with God

As a young adult, I began trying to have a "quiet time," a time set apart for the Lord. I read about Christians who got up at 4:00 A.M. to read the Bible and pray for an hour or two before breakfast. I tried to do that, but I could not be consistent. Following that schedule for a day or two, I would be so tired that I could not get up and I would promise myself that I would try again the next day. I felt guilty because I was not consistent. I almost endangered my health before I realized that the Christians I was reading about were going to bed at 8:00 or 9:00 P.M. while I was going to bed at 1:00 or 2:00 A.M.!

Then I read a tract that emphasized spending seven minutes a day with God. It stressed consistency and suggested a simple plan to achieve that goal. I decided no matter what the circumstances, I could spend seven minutes with God every morning. Of course, I soon realized seven minutes was not enough and continually set the alarm earlier to have enough time with the Lord. I learned a quiet time is more than a mere habit. It was an appointment at the beginning of the day with Jesus Christ, the center of my life.

A daily quiet time helps develop your relationship with Christ. In this intimate time, He speaks with you through His Word, and you speak with Him through prayer. As you bring your needs before Him, He provides direction and guidance for your daily decisions and helps you to bear fruit for Him. If you are to have a personal, ongoing relationship with Christ, you must hear Him. The Word of God is the primary way to hear Him. Your time with Him and in His Word ensures that you have a time every day to get your orders from headquarters.

HOW TO DEVELOP A QUIET TIME

1. If you are not already doing so, find a regular time to spend with God each day that fits your schedule. Having that time in the morning begins the day with a recognition of your dependence on God and His all-sufficiency. A quiet time should be the first priority of the day. Spending time with God gives you an opportunity to yield your will to Him and consciously dedicate the day to His glory.

2. Prepare the night before.

   - If your quiet time is in the morning, set your alarm. If it is difficult for you to wake up, plan to exercise, bathe, dress, and eat before your quiet time.

   - Select a place where you can be alone. "But when you pray, go into your room, close the door and pray to your Father, who is unseen. Then your Father, who sees what is done in secret, will reward you" (Matt. 6:6). You will find that you can concentrate best when you have an established place away from noise, distractions, and other people. Wherever you choose, make sure it is a place where you can focus on the One to whom you are praying.

- Gather materials, such as your Bible, notebook, and a pen or pencil, and put them in the place you selected so you will not waste time in the morning.

3. Develop a plan. Unless you consciously follow a pattern for your quiet time, you may get off track or your mind may wander.

- Pray for guidance. During your time with the Lord, you may want to include any number of these elements: prayer, Bible reading or study, memorizing Scripture, quietly waiting on Him, worship, and intercession.

- Follow a systematic plan for your Scripture reading. For example, you may read from one of the gospels as well as another book of the Bible so that you can see Christ live out what the Scripture is teaching. You may choose to read through the Bible a chapter a day or choose one psalm, one proverb, and one chapter of the Old or New Testament each day.

- Allow enough time to read His word reflectively. Do not try to read so much Scripture at one time that you cannot meditate on its meaning and let God speak directly to you and your situation.

- Make notes of what God says to you through His Word. Your journal will become a living testimony to your relationship.

- Pray in response to the Scriptures you have read. As you pray, use various components of prayer. Using the acronym A-C-T-S—adoration, confession, thanksgiving, supplication—helps you remember the components.

- You should develop your own procedure. Choose what is helpful and manageable within the time you have. The important thing is to have a plan so you do not waste this precious time with the Lord wondering what to do or wasting time "getting started."

4. Be persistent until you are consistent.

- Strive for consistency rather than length of time spent. Try to have a few minutes of quiet time every day rather than long devotional periods every other day.

- Expect interruptions. Satan tries to prevent you from spending time with God. He fears even the weakest Christians who are on their knees. Plan around interruptions rather than being frustrated by them.

5. Focus on the person you are meeting rather than on the habit of having the quiet time. If the president of the United States was scheduled at your house at 6:00 A.M. tomorrow, would you be ready? Of course. Meeting God is even more important. He created you with a capacity for fellowship with Him, and He saved you to bring about that fellowship.

My personal procedure is to kneel first in prayer and renew my relationship with God after the night's rest. Often I incorporate adoration/worship, confession of sin, thanksgiving, and supplication (putting my requests before God). After having fellowship with God, I sit or kneel and read Scripture. I usually read a chapter a day as I read consecutively through a book of the Bible. When I have finished, I summarize in my journal what God said to me and my response to Him. Writing each day "What God Said to Me" and "What I Said to God" helps me clarify what I have read and learned, and it becomes much easier to live out that Word. Finally, I pray for those requests on my prayer list and anything else God leads me to pray about.

Being Led by the Spirit

Once you have established a daily quiet time, begin working on being led constantly by the Spirit. If you receive and meditate on Scripture daily, you will be aware of Him and His thoughts. He has constant access to you when you remain in His Word. You have constant access to Him by praying without ceasing. Imagine a husband and wife or two close friends taking a Sunday drive through the countryside. They do not have to talk constantly to enjoy each other's company. Even if others are along, they are aware of that special person's presence.

Likewise, as you go through your day with the Lord, you can have conversations about what is important to you and to Him. As you grow in maturity, you will spend more and more time with the Father, just as Jesus did, and your knowledge of Him and your intimacy with Him will deepen. You will experience the fruit of abiding in Christ.

Connie Baldwin, a schoolteacher in Virginia, gets up at 5:30 each morning to have her quiet time. She says this helps her be more like Christ throughout the day as she works with children. She also notices it helps her prepare for her job. "Getting up at 5:30 for me is quite a feat because I'm not a morning person," she claims, "but I know that God has given me the strength and determination to get up early to spend that time with Him. I know when I get to heaven, I'll never say, 'I wish I had slept more.' I'll say, 'I'm so glad I got up and spent time with my Lord!'"

Enabling sinful people to commune with God cost Him His only Son. Yet God was willing to pay that price to have a relationship with you. Part of your life in Christ is daily communication with the Father. Are you willing to pay the price of a few minutes a day to have Christ live more fully in you and reveal to you the fullness of the Father? If you do so, you will experience the endless wisdom of God. In the next chapter you will see how to keep that Word rooted in your life so that the Holy Spirit can personally apply it to each particular instance of your life.

Questions for Meditation and Discussion

1. What are the best reasons for developing a consistent quiet time with God every day?

2. Are there changes you should make to help you establish a daily quiet time? What element in this chapter could you add to your current plan for your time with the Lord?

3. Is your life characterized by love for the Lord, obedience to His Word, and demonstration of His character?

4. What price are you willing to pay to have Christ live more fully in you?

Chapter 2
LIVING
IN THE WORD

One morning a *MasterLife* group leader phoned me. A member of his group had just called him and said, "I had to tell you that God just talked to me! I read my Bible and wrote what God said to me. It is so precious." My friend reported that he went by the member's house, and the man still had tears in his eyes as he marveled that God would speak directly and personally to him through His Word.

God has revealed Himself to us through Jesus, His Living Word. "In the beginning was the Word, and the Word was with God, and the Word was God. . . . The Word became flesh and made his dwelling among us" (John 1:1, 14). "The Son is the radiance of God's glory and the exact representation of his being, sustaining all things by his powerful word" (Heb. 1:3).

He also continually reveals Himself through the Bible, God's written Word. The written Word testifies to and perfectly reflects what God has said and who Jesus is. Jesus' entire life revolved around God's Word. His ministry was a fulfillment of the Word (see Luke 24:44). He intends for the Word to be at the center of your life. After you have yielded to the call of Christ to enter into relationship with Him, you must ground yourself in knowledge of Him by spending time with Him and learning His Word. This is the first part of the vertical relationship between you and the Father.

Remaining in the Word

God's Word is the heart of a quiet time. The way to experience Christ living in you is to have His Word living in you. Jesus said, "If you hold to my teaching, you are really my disciples. Then you will know the truth, and the truth will set you free" (John 8:31, 32). The Scripture will instruct you and set you free to obey Him.

The Word of God is food for you. You cannot grow unless you regularly partake of it. Having a daily reminder of what the Bible says keeps Christ's teaching fresh in your mind. You do not have to wonder how Christ would have acted in a certain situation; those truths are hidden in your heart. Spending time in the Word will allow you to deal with the circumstances of life that come your way. Christians are not exempt from difficulties, but remaining in His Word cultivates a relationship with Christ in which you can successfully weather those storms. When you have a relationship with Christ, His Spirit uses the Scripture as the source of guidance and strength.

Several years ago God spoke specifically to me while I was preparing for a second surgery. I anticipated this operation would be similar to the first one—uncomfortable, with no lasting effects. During my quiet time I read from Psalm 116. This is what impacted me: "The cords of death entangled me, the anguish of the grave came upon me; I was overcome by trouble and sorrow" (Ps. 116:3).

The Scripture shook me! I wrote in my prayer journal, "This operation is going to be more dangerous than I thought." I prepared for the worst and then put my confidence in what God said in the later verses: "Be at rest once more, O my soul, for the Lord has been good to you. For you, O Lord, have delivered my soul from death, my eyes from tears, my feet from stumbling, that I may walk before the LORD in the land of the living" (Ps. 116:7–9).

After the surgery the pathology report showed one cancer cell. At first I was startled by the word *cancer*, but the Scripture the Lord had given me came to mind and quieted my soul. The doctor said the cancer cell might be the only one that existed, and he would monitor the situation every three months. I thanked God for His assurance. More than five years have passed since the surgery, and I have had no recurrence of cancer. However, the incident alerted the doctor to discontinue medicine that could have made the cancer cells grow faster.

God's gracious warning through His Word prepared me for the outcome of the surgery. Striving to live a life of obedience did not make me immune to cancer, but my habit of a regular quiet time made me open to a promise from God's Word that helped me get through a trying time with strength and comfort.

Finding Direction in the Word

You can discern God's will as you meditate on His Word and commune with His Spirit. David understood this as he wrote: "Let the morning bring me word of your unfailing love, for I have put my trust in you. Show me the way I should go, for to you I lift up my soul" (Ps. 143:8). Like the psalmist, you can ask God to show you the way you should walk in your life. I am often surprised by how personally God speaks to me through His Word in my time with Him and how directly it applies to problems and opportunities I face during the day.

God has used His Word to reveal His direction over and over again. Once my wife and I were in South Africa teaching *MasterLife* for leaders of nine countries. Word arrived that due to a political boycott, no passengers from South Africa would be allowed to disembark in Nairobi, Kenya, where we were to conduct training for leaders of another nine countries. We tried to get around this ruling but could find no solution. If we were not allowed to enter Kenya, we would be forced to stay on the plane and proceed to Europe without leading the training.

The day before we were to leave, we decided to go to Harare, Zimbabwe, to get new passports, visas, and tickets in an attempt to travel to Nairobi, even though we had no assurance it would be possible. On the morning we were to leave, I opened to the chapter of my regular Bible reading. God caught my attention as I read: "In my anguish I cried to the Lord, and he answered by setting me free. The Lord is with me; I will not be afraid. What can man do to me? The Lord is with me; he is my helper. I will look in triumph on my enemies. It is better to take refuge in the Lord than to trust in man" (Ps. 118:5–8).

I felt these verses were God's promise that we would be able to enter Nairobi. The next few verses offered further affirmation: "The Lord is my strength and my song; he has become my salvation. Shouts of joy and victory resound in the tents of the righteous: 'The Lord's right hand has done mighty things! The Lord's right hand is lifted high; the Lord's right hand has done mighty things!'" (Ps. 118:14–16).

We arrived in Harare, Zimbabwe, with only one hour to obtain new passports, visas, and tickets before the offices closed for the weekend. If you have ever tried to get any one of those in your own country, you know that obtaining them would be a miracle in itself—but God did it! When we disembarked in Nairobi, the officials turned back the three persons in front of us, but they examined our new passports and visas and let us walk through! Shouts of joy and victory resounded from us and from the conference participants who had prayed that we would be able to enter the country. God had performed a miracle. God had given answers from His Word. Without God's assurance, I would not have been bold enough to start the journey.

Meditating on the Word

You may think you don't have enough time to live in the Word. You may think, *Sure, it's good to read my Bible daily. I can try to establish that habit. But living in the Word sounds like something I do around the clock. Does anyone really have enough hours in the day to live in the Word continuously? I have my job, my family, and my other responsibilities. I can't walk around with a Bible in my hand all day.*

Certainly, reading your Bible regularly is a primary way to live in the Word. You need that daily obedience. However, living in the Word is not a one-time action. Have you ever read your Bible, closed it, and had a self-satisfied feeling like *Whew! Now that's done?* Living Scripture is not a task that can be accomplished and then set aside. Remaining in His Word, or holding to His teaching, means His Word is so much a part of your life that obeying is as natural to you as breathing. You respond to God's Word as immediately as your hand responds to a signal from the brain.

You can receive the Word in many ways besides reading it. These include listening to someone preach it, studying it, memorizing it, meditating on it, recalling it, and applying it. As you fill you heart and mind with Christ's words, you will be able to obey what Christ says.

In addition to the habit of daily Bible reading, the two disciplines of memorizing Scripture and meditating on it will help you grow the most as a Christian. Persons whom God has used mightily are those who have discerned God's truth and power in private worship. Joshua, who faced the seemingly impossible task of leading the Israelites to conquer the Promised Land, heard God say, "Do not let this Book of the Law depart from your mouth; meditate on it day and night, so that you may be careful to do everything written in it. Then you will be prosperous and successful" (Josh. 1:8). Memorizing puts God's Word in your head. Meditating puts it in your heart. Then God's Word can permeate your daily life. As you memorize Scripture, the Holy Spirit will bring the verses you learn to mind when you find yourself in situations that require you to apply scriptural truths. Even without an open Bible in front of you, you can meditate on verses that are in your heart and mind.

𝓜emorizing 𝓢cripture

There are several reasons to memorize Scripture. When He was tempted in the wilderness, Jesus set the example. He used Scripture as the sword of the Spirit against Satan, even when Satan tried to misuse Scripture as a part of the temptation (see Matt. 4:1–11). Memorizing verses helps us gain victory over sin. "How can a young man keep his way pure? By living according to your word. . . . I have hidden your word in my heart that I might not sin against you" (Ps. 119:9, 11).

Memorizing Scripture also helps us win others to Christ. "Always be prepared to give an answer to everyone who asks you to give the reason for the hope that you have" (1 Pet. 3:15). Once when I talked to a woman who visited our church, she made excuses for not coming to Christ. Because I had memorized many verses, the Holy Spirit led me to choose the right verse for each excuse. To each excuse I did not answer a word but asked her to read a verse I had memorized. After she read between ten and fifteen verses, she put her faith in Christ.

Being able to recite Scripture by heart helps you to meditate on it and gives you direction for your daily life at any moment. Most of all, you should memorize Scripture because God commands it. "These commandments that I give you today are to be upon your hearts" (Deut. 6:6).

HOW TO MEMORIZE SCRIPTURE

1. Choose a verse that speaks to your need or which the Lord points out to you.

2. Understand the verse. Read it in context and in different translations.

3. Develop some memory aids to help you learn the verse. For example, you might record it on a cassette tape so you can listen to it. Leave a space after each verse so you can practice quoting it. Then record the verse a second time so you can hear it again after you have quoted it.

4. Locate and underline the verse in your Bible so you can visualize it on the page.

5. Write the verse on a card, including the Scripture reference and the topic it addresses. This allows you to relate the verse to a particular subject and enables you to find it when a need arises.

6. Place the written verse in prominent places so you can review it while you do other tasks. Put it over the kitchen sink, on the bathroom mirror, on the dashboard for reviewing at stoplights, or any place you will see it often.

7. Commit the verse to memory in your favorite translation. Divide it into natural, meaningful phrases and learn it word by word. If you learn it word-perfect in the beginning, it will be set in your memory, will be easier to review, will give you boldness when you are tempted, and will convince the person with whom you are sharing that he or she can trust your word.

8. Use these activities to set a verse in your mind: see it in pictorial form; sing it, making up your own tune; pray it back to God; do it by making it a part of your life; and use it as often as possible.

9. Review, review, review. This is the most important secret of Scripture memorization. Review a new verse at least once a day for six weeks. Review the verse weekly for the next six weeks and then monthly for the rest of your life.

10. Have someone check your memorization or write the verse from memory and check it yourself. Make Scripture memorization fun. Make a game of it.

Move Past Excuses

Even though you may feel too old, too busy, or too forgetful to begin memorizing Scripture, it is a major part of remaining in the Word. Being able to recall verses as you need them is important to a Christian's daily walk. Hiding God's Word in your heart does not depend on your education; it is a work of the Spirit of God in your life. The same God who gives you strength to follow Him at all costs can also give you the ability to memorize and practice His Word.

Pearl Collinsgrove became a Christian at age seventy-nine. She began studying *MasterLife* after she heard some of her friends talk about experiencing life in Christ. Because Pearl had only a third-grade education and was blind, some church members thought she would not be able to participate in the *MasterLife* group. Nevertheless, one member recorded all the materials on tape for Pearl. She quickly memorized all the Scripture-memory verses and many more.

Furthermore, as a former entertainer, Pearl began singing her memorized Scripture verses as she played the guitar. Civic clubs around town invited her to speak and sing. When she spoke, she showed a life-size cross made for her by a group member, and sang a song based on the Scripture verse that related to the center and then each point of the Disciple's Cross. She said, "My feet are planted in God's Word; my hands are lifted up to heaven in worship and prayer; one hand reaches out to my Christian brothers and sisters in fellowship; and the other hand reaches out to the lost world that we need to tell about Jesus."

Word spread about Pearl's testimony, and to rousing applause she sang John 15:5 at a major meeting of forty-five thousand Christians in Dallas, Texas. Neither age, blindness, nor lack of education could deter this fervent woman from holding firm to the Word of God!

Obeying the Word

Discipleship is obedience to the lordship of Christ. To remain in the Word, or to hold to His teaching, means to obey Him. When you put the Word into practice, you present the strongest witness to Christ. Doing God's Word provides a powerful connection with God, making it possible for you to live in Him. God can entrust His Word to disciples who obey, and the result is a dynamic relationship.

To obey Christ's commands requires two things: knowing them and doing them. "Now that you know these things, you will be blessed if you do them" (John 13:17). "Do not merely listen to the word, and so deceive yourselves. Do what it says" (James 1:22). You can read the Word, meditate on it, pray about it, hear it preached and taught, and see it demonstrated, but if you do not obey the Word, it produces no fruit in your life. When God directs me through Scripture to forgive someone who offended me or give to someone in need, and I read it without acting on it, neither the other person nor I gain the benefit. God's glory is not revealed in me.

Jesus set the example of love and obedience. He said: "If you obey my commands, you will remain in my love, just as I have obeyed my Father's commands and remain in his love" (John 15:10). Obedience will cause you to learn His commands; love for Christ will motivate you to do them; and fruit will be the result.

Bearing Fruit

The result of obeying the Word is spiritual fruit. Jesus said: "Remain in me, and I will remain in you. No branch can bear fruit by itself; it must remain in the vine. Neither can you bear fruit unless you remain in me" (John 15:4). When Jesus emptied Himself and became a human being (see Phil. 2:6), He placed Himself in the same relationship with God that we have—that of a learner (Heb. 5:7–9). Although He was God's Son and was filled with God's Spirit, Jesus felt the need to maintain a practice of regular, private worship. He prayed early in the morning, throughout the night, and whenever He could get away from others.

"Very early in the morning, while it was still dark, Jesus got up, left the house and went off to a solitary place, where he prayed" (Mark 1:35). "One of those days Jesus went out to a mountainside to pray, and spent the night praying to God" (Luke 6:12). "After he had dismissed them, he went up on a mountainside by himself to pray. When evening came, he was there alone" (Matt 14:23). "After leaving them, he went up on a mountainside to pray" (Mark 6:46). If Jesus felt a need to spend time with the Father to prepare Himself daily for His ministry, how much greater is our need!

Jesus was prepared to bear spiritual fruit because His relationship with the Father was always up-to-date. Even when He was tired, He led the Samaritan woman to Christ (John 4). When He met the funeral procession for the widow's son, He had no time to get prepared. He immediately raised the young man from the dead (Luke 7:11–15). When He was asleep during the storm and His disciples woke Him crying, "Master, Master, we're going to drown!" (Luke 8:24), He was ready to act and brought peace to the storm.

When opportunities arise, you often have no time to prepare to meet them. But if your relationship has been renewed through your quiet time and has been kept fresh through prayer and remembering the Word through the day, you will be ready.

God does not want you to work for Him. He wants to work through you. His work is accomplished only as you yield your will to Him daily through Bible study, prayer, and meditation. In your obedience, God will continue to teach you. You can bear fruit only if you remain faithful to the Vine.

Perhaps you are wondering, *I see how I can hear from God through His Word, but isn't communication in a relationship two-way? How can I be sure God hears me?* In the next chapter, I will show you the kind of prayer God hears and delights in.

Questions for Meditation and Discussion

1. How much of your quiet time do you spend in the Word?

2. What recent experience have you had in which God gave you direction through His Word?

3. What is the last thing you know God told you to do which you have so far neglected?

4. Today, what Scriptures does He bring to mind to guide you through the day?

5. How could you invest in your "bank account" of Scripture knowledge so that the Holy Spirit has more to access and bring to your mind whenever you need it?

Chapter 3
PRAYING IN FAITH

Have you ever picked up the telephone to share exciting news with a close friend only to get the answering machine? You may have left a message anyway, but you turn from the phone disappointed. You feel the difference between giving the information and connecting with a friend.

What is the best way to talk to the Father? What prayers does God delight in? Maybe in the past you have prayed by reciting words you have memorized. Perhaps your prayers have merely been lists of requests rather than meaningful conversations with God. If you want to deepen your prayer life, you must learn to pray according to scriptural principles.

Approaching the Presence of God

The Bible teaches that prayer is actually coming into the presence of God. When you approach God, it is not proper to rush into His presence and bombard Him with your needs. Neither should you pray as if you are merely leaving a message for God and then walk away without relating to Him.

God is holy and we must approach Him with humility and a contrite heart. "For this is what the high and lofty One says—he who lives forever, whose name is holy: 'I live in a high and holy place, but also with him who is contrite and lowly in spirit, to revive the spirit of the lowly and to revive the heart of the contrite'" (Isa. 57:15).

When the prophet Isaiah received a vision of God and saw the Lord as He actually was, he was awestruck at the holiness of God: "In the year that King Uzziah died, I saw the Lord seated on a throne, high and exalted, and the train of his robe filled the temple. Above him were seraphs, each with six wings: With two wings they covered their faces, with two they covered their feet, and with two they were flying. And they were calling to one another: 'Holy, holy, holy is the Lord Almighty; the whole earth is full of his glory'" (Isa. 6:1–3).

Enter His Gates with Thanksgiving

As you pray, you can visualize the temple as a symbol of how to approach God and experience His awesome holiness. The temple in Jerusalem contained various components, beginning with the gates and culminating with the Holy of Holies. Although the Holy of Holies had limited access, the large open courtyard at the edge of the temple was open to everyone. As people came through those beautiful temple gates, they gave thanks. The psalmist encouraged worshipers to "enter his gates with thanksgiving and his courts with praise; give thanks to him and praise his name" (Ps. 100:4). King David recalled, "These things I remember as I pour out my soul: how I used to go with the multitude, leading the procession to the house of God, with shouts of joy and thanksgiving among the festive throng" (Ps. 42:4).

Your first attitude in prayer is to thank Him for all He has done for you. T. W. Hunt, author of *The Mind of Christ*, described how he became aware of his need for an expanded attitude of thanksgiving in his life. One morning as he brushed his teeth, T. W. began asking himself, "What if tomorrow I had only the things I thanked God for today?" He began to name things like his teeth, his eyes, the sense of touch, air, home, people—things he realized he sometimes took for granted. Then he changed his approach to prayer to begin with a new attitude of thanksgiving to God.

In thanksgiving, you express gratitude toward God, generally in response to His concrete acts. Psalm 69 shows you just how much God values your prayers of thankfulness. He values prayers of thanksgiving more than sacrifice. "I will praise God's name in song and glorify him with thanksgiving. This will please the LORD more than an ox, more than a bull with its horns and hoofs" (Ps. 69:30, 31). When Jesus healed the ten lepers, "one of them, when he saw he was healed, came back, praising God in a loud voice. He threw himself at Jesus' feet and thanked him. . . . Jesus asked, 'Were not all ten cleansed? Where are the other nine? Was no one found to return and give praise to God except this foreigner?' " (Luke 17:15–18).

What kinds of things do you thank God for? The psalms, in which an attitude of thankfulness is especially prominent, give examples of areas in which you can give thanks. On deliverance from a time of trouble, see Psalm 34:7, 8; on God's faithfulness, see Psalm 100:5; on forgiveness of sin, see Psalm 30:4, 5; on creation, see Psalm 92:4.

You can get so busy presenting your list of requests to God that you neglect a time of thankfulness. What about all those requests you presented Him earlier that He answered? Perhaps not everything that you asked for has been granted. You may be waiting for an answer on some issues. Sometimes the answer you wanted was not part of His plan, and He gave you an answer that was better for you than the one you desired. But He certainly answers many of them just as you asked. How many of them have you thanked Him for?

Enter His Courts with Praise

The next step in learning to pray in faith involves focusing on who the Father is and what He means in your life. Jesus did not just teach His disciples how to pray. He taught them how to know the Father through prayer. Focusing on the One whose throne you are approaching will help you tune out other distractions or demands and will help you communicate with Him.

As the people entered the courts, the first gathering place inside the temple, they would come with praise (see Ps. 100:4). Praise is pure worship and adoration of God for who He is rather than what He does. The word *praise* originates from the Latin word meaning "value" or "price." Thus, to give praise to God is to proclaim His merit or worth.

Praise is an important element of prayer. It is to be constant: "I will extol the LORD at all times; his praise will always be on my lips" (Ps. 34:1). Praise raises your prayer life beyond yourself.

Praise focuses on the person of God. The names of God that appear in the Bible reveal His character, His personality, and the ways He works in your life. You will be more able to praise God when you know the various aspects of His character that His names reveal.

As you study Psalm 91, you will discover several names of God. Each of these reveals aspects of God for which He is worthy of praise:

El Elyon. "He who dwells in the shelter of the Most High will rest in the shadow of the Almighty" (Ps. 91:1). The term *Most High* reveals the name *El Elyon,* the strongest of all gods and the possessor of heaven and earth, the strongest of the strong. You cannot win the daily battles of life in the power of your own strength. The true victory originates with El Elyon. He is capable of overcoming even the most difficult circumstances of your life.

El Shaddai. "He who dwells in the shelter of the Most High will rest in the shadow of the Almighty" (Ps. 91:1). The term *Almighty* reveals the name *El Shaddai,* the all-sufficient God. The name first appears in Genesis 17:1, where God appeared to Abraham and made great promises to Him. God promised to make of him a great nation and to give him a son at his advanced age. He is a promise-keeping God.

Yahweh. "I will say of the LORD, He is my refuge and my fortress, my God, in whom I trust" (Ps. 91:2). The term LORD, written in all capital letters, reveals the personal name of God—Yahweh or Jehovah, unlike the word *Lord* in lowercase letters, which signifies Adonai, the master, the person with authority. Yahweh signifies the God who is with you all the time. God used this name to reveal Himself to Moses when He identified Himself as "I am who I am" (Exod. 3:14). His presence with Moses was all-sufficient.

Elohim. "My God, in whom I trust" (Ps. 91:2b) includes the name for God *Elohim* which first appears in Genesis 1:1 in the creation story. It refers to the strong covenant-keeping God who is the Creator. Do you regularly approach God as the one who gave you life and created everything around you?

Some other names of God also help you focus on who He is and enable you to praise Him. God is also known as: *Jehovah Jireh,* God who provides; *Jehovah Shalom,* God who brings peace; *Jehovah Sabaot,* God who brings spiritual help; and *Jehovah Rapha,* God who heals.

You can praise Him because: He is the *living God* (Matt. 16:16); He is *holy* (Ps. 29:2); He is *Spirit* (Ps. 139:7); He is *love* (John 3:16); He is *Father* (John 14:6); and He is *glory* (Heb. 1:3). Understanding the characteristics of God will help you know how to praise Him. As you learn to praise Him, you will increasingly see how he reveals Himself to you in these same ways through your own experiences.

Come Before the Altar of Confession

After you have thanked God for what He has done and praised Him for who He is, confessing your sins to Him is a way to continue to approach His throne in prayer. As you enter into the presence of God, you continue to glorify and honor Him, but you also do another kind of praying, asking God to examine your heart. "At the sound of their voices the doorposts and thresholds shook, and the temple was filled with smoke. 'Woe to me!' I cried. 'I am ruined! For I am a man of unclean lips, and I live among a people of unclean lips, and my eyes have seen the King, the Lord Almighty'" (Isa. 6:4–6).

Isaiah became aware of the contrast between God's holiness and his own sinfulness. When you approach God's throne and become aware of His presence, your personal sin confronts you. After such a divine confrontation, it is appropriate for you to confess your sin, just as Isaiah did when he experienced the glory of the Father.

In confession, you let God examine your heart. He will show you what separates you from Him and what barriers keep you from experiencing Him to the fullest. Full fellowship with the Father is blocked if your life contains unconfessed sin. The beautiful words of Psalm 139 illustrate the proper attitude about confession. "Search me, O God, and know my heart; test me and know my anxious thoughts. See if there is any offensive way in me, and lead me in the way everlasting" (Ps. 139:23, 24).

The psalmist displays an attitude of openness: He asks God to make him aware of unrighteousness in his life so he can grow. You do not have to guess what might be sin in your life or conjure up things to confess. If you open yourself, the Holy Spirit will show you anything that is offensive to God.

To confess is to agree with God, to see sin as hideous and destructive, just as God sees it. When you confess, you not only admit your guilt but also place yourself in the hands of the only one who can forgive. In repenting of your sin, you turn away from your sin and toward God.

The Father wants you to confess sin so He can do what He has promised—to forgive you and cleanse you. As an Israelite moved past the gates and the courts of the temple, he approached the altar for burnt offerings. People offered sacrifices in an effort to atone for their sins. Animal offerings are no longer required of you because Christ has offered Himself as a sacrifice for you so that your sins may be forgiven. The Bible says, "If we claim to be without sin, we deceive ourselves and the truth is not in us. If we confess our sins, he is faithful and just and will forgive us our sins and purify us from all unrighteousness" (1 John 1:8, 9).

You only fool yourself when you claim to be sinless. The Father to whom you pray knows the sin in your heart. Confessing sin will make you feel better, but that is not the purpose. The purpose is to restore your relationship with God.

God will not listen to your prayers if you continue to cling to your unrighteous ways and refuse to acknowledge them and confess them. "If I had cherished sin in my heart, the Lord would not have listened" (Ps. 66:18). Confessing sin in your life is a crucial next step in your fellowship with the Father through prayer. (Ps. 32:1–5).

Confession is an important part of maintaining a right relationship to God. Maturity in discipleship can be thought of as the degree to which you experience harmony, or wholeness, in relationship to God and to others. You experience harmony when you have fellowship regularly with Christ. That is why a daily pattern of praying in faith is a major factor in your lifelong, obedient relationship with Christ.

Dwelling in God's Presence

Now you find yourself in the presence of God. This is a holy place. In the Old Testament, only the high priest was permitted to enter the Holy of Holies and only on the Day of Atonement. The Holy of Holies was the innermost part of the temple and the most sacred place because the presence of God dwelt there at the mercy seat of the ark of the covenant. To enter otherwise meant certain death. But Christ opened up a new way so that all people could go into the Holy of Holies and have the most intimate relationship with God through prayer. Christ's atoning death on the cross brought an end to the role of the priest. Christ Himself now serves as your great High Priest before God. (Heb. 4:14–16).

The Father wants you to approach Him with your needs. He waits to grant what you ask in His will. He delights in doing so. Now that you have thanked Him for your blessings, you have given Him the praise He is due, and you have confessed your sins, you are ready to talk to Him about your needs, both for yourself and for others. Because of Jesus Christ, you have access to God and can approach God in all His holiness with the deepest needs of your heart. You can approach His throne of grace with confidence because He is ready to grant you mercy and grace to help you in your time of need (see Heb. 4:14–16). He is pleased to hear your personal requests: "This is the confidence we have in approaching God: that if we ask anything according to his will, he hears us" (1 John 5:14–15).

Petitioning for Needs

There are two types of prayer in which we lay requests before God: petition and intercession. Petition is seeking God for your own needs. Needs and problems in your life can make you realize your dependence on God. If you are abiding in Christ, you will not wait to ask for His help as a last resort. He will be your first source of help. He wants to meet your needs: "The Lord is near. Do not be anxious about anything, but in everything, by prayer and petition, with thanksgiving, present your requests to God" (Phil. 4:5, 6).

The second type of prayer for needs is intercession—prayer for others. Jesus prayed for His disciples many times. One of the best examples is John 17, a passage which describes Jesus praying for His disciples before He went to the cross. You pray for others for the same reason you pray for yourself—

so that God can mold them into the persons He wants them to become. God uses you to accomplish His will when you pray for others.

God answers your prayers because He is your loving Father and your all-sufficient provider. He does not grant petitions that you pray for the wrong reason or that He knows would bring the wrong outcome in your life or someone else's life. How, then, do we know what to ask for? How do we know which of our requests are in His will?

The way to pray in faith rests again upon your relationship to God and your communication with Him. This is demonstrated in the vertical bar of the Disciple's Cross. First, you must continually abide in Christ. In that relationship, you can bring any matter to Him. Then you must consistently and systematically abide in the Word, allowing the Holy Spirit to lead you in truth. As you increase in your understanding of God's character, ways, and purposes, the Holy Spirit will apply the Scriptures to your particular problem. When you present your specific request to God and base it on the Word of God, then you can ask in faith, knowing that a God-revealed promise is a certainty. You can then take specific action, knowing that God will answer your prayer.

Praying for What God Wants

When I was in college, God began to teach me to pray in faith. I read a sermon by Gypsy Smith based on this Bible verse: "If you abide in Me and My words abide in you, you will ask what you desire, and it shall be done for you" (John 15:7, NKJV).

The sermon impressed me so much that I said to God, "I believe that is true, so why am I not asking for more? Lord, as best I know, I'm trying to abide in You, and abide in Your Word as I study it, memorize it, and try to apply it in my life. So I ought to be able to pray and see that prayer answered because You promised it." As I prayed I asked what I should pray for. I then felt impressed to pray that someone would trust Christ as Savior as I went out witnessing the next day. I wrote in my diary, "I believe someone will be saved tomorrow (John 15:7)."

That night I went out on the street, began sharing with a person, and within five minutes he had accepted Christ. I was walking on air and wondering why no one had told me before how to pray like this.

The next day I prayed all day, believing in my heart that God would save someone else. I was volunteering at a rescue mission at the time, so I went out on the street and began inviting people to attend the services. Two men agreed to accompany me. I said to myself, Oh, that's great. Maybe two are going to be saved. When the sermon was over, I turned to each of them and asked, "Are you a Christian?" Both responded, "Yes." I could not understand that. Hadn't I prayed that God would save someone?

After the service I looked for someone else to whom I could witness but found no one. On the way home, my mind was bombarded by questions. I prayed, "Lord, as far as I know, I am abiding in You like John 15:7 says. I know it is Your will for people to be saved. Why haven't You answered as You promised? Isn't Your Word true?"

When I got back to campus, I remembered that I had forgotten to bring home a friend's coat. I asked my roommate if I could borrow his car to retrieve it. I got the coat and decided once more to try to find someone to whom I could witness. I met a man standing on the street corner. After I explained how to be saved, he gave his life to Christ. My heart was thrilled. I praised God for the man's salvation, but even more, I praised God that His Word was true and that He did what He promised. Even before the man was baptized, he led someone else to Christ!

I was eager to press on in my new understanding of prayer and faith. I looked forward to the next Sunday night when I was to preach at the church my father served as pastor. I seldom pray for exact numbers of people to be saved, but I felt the Holy Spirit impressing me to ask that five people be converted as I preached. Now at that time, this many people had never made a decision when I preached unless it was a decision to leave!

On the way home, I witnessed to a man at the bus stop and he was converted. Eager to help the Lord out, I counted that person as the first of the five. When I arrived I asked my dad to give me some prospect cards so I could visit people, knowing that only if unsaved people were at church could they be saved in the service. When you begin to pray in faith, you begin to act in faith! During the visitation, I met an alcoholic, and he was gloriously saved. I counted him as number two. Then the Lord reminded me that I had asked for five in the service. When the night arrived and I gave the invitation, five people walked down the aisles to accept Christ and another person rededicated his life. I began to understand that God really would act if I prayed in accordance with His will.

The next week I went a step farther. I asked God, "What about ten people this weekend?" This time, however, nothing happened because God wanted me to learn an even more important lesson about prayer. This time people weren't saved because I had begun to tell God what I wanted rather than to pray on the basis of what He revealed. I learned that prayer is designed to involve me in God's purpose. Prayer is more than my calling on Him to carry out my plans.

God delights in answering prayer that is asked according to His will, but He refuses to answer prayer that is inconsistent with what He wants. We need to hear God's voice to know how to pray. The key is living in Christ, living in the Word, and living in prayer. All of these are essential for full communication with the Father.

But what checks and balances can help you to be sure that you are hearing God—not just your own thoughts? Chapter 16 of this book contains a step-by-step process for praying in faith according to a word from Scripture. But first you must learn the power of living in the "body of Christ," the church, and how relationships with other believers can help you grow in the Lord and in understanding God purposes for your life.

Questions for Meditation and Discussion

1. What has God done for you? What is the last thing you thanked God for? (Take a moment to make a list of what God has provided for you.)

2. As you look through the names of God, in what ways has He revealed Himself to you? What do you have to praise God for?

3. Is there sin in your life that remains unconfessed? (Be still before the Lord and ask the Holy Spirit to examine your heart.)

4. Are you abiding in Christ and are His words abiding in you so that you know God's will? What prayers, petitions, or intercessions can you make based on that knowledge?

5. What has the Holy Spirit led you to pray? Do you have faith that it will be answered?

Chapter 4
FELLOWSHIPPING WITH BELIEVERS

When I was in college, my friends and I decided to conduct a youth revival meeting in the hometown of my friend, Hal Brooks, of Borger, Texas. We secured the high school auditorium. We put up huge billboards, announced the event on the radio, and delivered advertisements to all the stores.

At the last minute, high school officials told us that church leaders in the community—members of our own denomination—had put pressure on the school to disallow use of the facility. Because we had not sought the local churches' involvement in advance, our plan backfired. I prayed, "Lord, You cannot let us down after we have done so much to prepare!" But He did not intervene.

The experience was a crushing defeat for me, but a lesson well learned. We left town, convinced that we would not again try to do anything without God's direct leadership and without working within the framework of local churches.

God used the experience to remind us we could do nothing without Him and should do nothing outside the fellowship of His people. My friends and I had undertaken this task on our own for God rather than asking what God wanted. We had not first prayed in faith for God's direction before we proceeded. We had not asked God to search our hearts to determine whether selfish motives and desires for success were driving our plans. We had not sought the local churches' counsel to determine their support. We had talked and prayed about the revival but had then gone ahead with our plans.

We had failed to live as part of the body of Christ.

Christ's Model for Fellowship

God has shown me many times in my Christian experience that I can do nothing without the fellowship of believers in the body of Christ. Jesus said, "A new command I give you: Love one another. As I have loved you, so you must love one another. By this all men will know that you are my disciples, if you love one another" (John 13:34, 35). Jesus demonstrates Himself through our love for others, be they neighbors, enemies, or fellow believers.

One identifying mark of a disciple is love for others. Loving others and being in harmonious fellowship with them shows the world that Christ is the center of your life. Jesus wants His followers to demonstrate the love He has modeled for them. "As the Father has loved me, so have I loved you. Now remain in my love" (John 15:9). The abundant love which God the Father has for His Son, Jesus Christ, is the source of the love the Son has for His followers and, in turn, is the model for the love you are to have toward others. The depth of Jesus' love that led Him to the cross had its basis in the love the Father has for Him.

Fellowship with believers was the centerpiece of Jesus' last message to His disciples as He was on the way to the cross. He wanted to tell His beloved all they would need to know to carry out His work on earth when He was no longer with them in a physical sense. "You are my friends if you do what I command. I no longer call you servants, because a servant does not know his master's business. Instead, I have called you friends, for everything that I learned from my Father I have made known to you"(John 15:14, 15).

Jesus wanted the disciples to know that He considered them friends, not servants. He longed for them to be in complete unity with Him and to share the fullness of His love relationship with the Father. "My prayer is . . . that all of them may be one, Father, just as you are in me and I am in you. May they also be in us so that the world may believe that you have sent me. I have given them the glory that you gave me, that they may be one as we are one. . . . May they be brought to complete unity to let the world know that you sent me and have loved them even as you have loved me" (John 17:20–23). Jesus gave us the commands, the example, and the measure of how we are to love others.

ℒove 𝒴our ℰnemies

Jesus instructed us to love our enemies as the Father loves. "You have heard that it was said, 'Love your neighbor and hate your enemy.' But I tell you: Love your enemies and pray for those who persecute you, that you may be sons of your Father in heaven. He causes his sun to rise on the evil and the good, and sends rain on the righteous and the unrighteous" (Matt. 5:43–45). We are not given the freedom to choose whom we will love. Jesus claimed that there was no reward in only loving those who love you, because even unbelievers do that (see Matt. 5:46, 47). We are called to love, pray for, bless, and treat kindly those who mistreat us. Christ is demonstrated in such behavior because only godly love loves the unlovable.

When Tony Ponceti, a print shop owner in Arlington, Texas, saw on a television newscast that deposed Panamanian president General Manuel Noriega had been arrested by the United States government for alleged involvement in the drug trade, he remarked to his wife, "They could waste a bullet on that man." Tony had a deeply personal reason for wishing ill on Noriega. Tony's own drug-addicted daughter had just returned to a normal lifestyle after her parents employed a traumatic case of tough love. Tony saw Noriega as a link to the drug traffic coming through the United States that had caused his daughter's difficulties.

Also watching the newscast about Noriega that day was Texas evangelist Clift Brannon, then in his seventies. When he saw the telecast, Clift remarked to his wife, "I need to send this man a New Testament with the plan of salvation." His wife suggested that Clift send a Spanish version so Noriega could understand it.

After receiving it, Noriega signed the card at the back of the New Testament indicating his decision to accept Christ and returned it to Clift. Clift then sought the help of Rudy Hernandez, a minister in Texas with contacts in the Spanish-speaking world, to get an opportunity to witness to Noriega personally.

Meanwhile, Tony Ponceti was in a Bible study group studying concepts that later would be published in the book, *Experiencing God*. When Tony heard the story of what Clift Brannon had done to witness to Noriega, he realized that God had been at work in that situation and also in his own life the day he had watched the newscast with bitterness in his heart. Tony was so repentant and felt so responsible for Noriega that he sold his print shop in Texas and moved to Miami, where Noriega was in custody. Tony opened a business there with the idea of trying to gain access to Noriega so he could disciple him. Although he tried every way he could, Tony could not make contact with the imprisoned general.

Tony began to ask church groups to pray for Noriega and for the opportunity to disciple him. One day, a prayer group that met at 6:00 A.M. strongly sensed God's assurance that He had solved the problem. As a result, Tony called Clift's house and discovered Clift was out of town. Upon questioning Clift's wife, he discovered he was one of three people who could be told where Clift was. Clift had been informed the night before that if he could be in Miami the next morning, officials would allow him to visit Noriega, who had been allowed to see only a few people since being brought to the United States. Tony learned that at that moment Clift was in a motel only a few blocks away. Tony contacted Clift, and although he was not able to go in with Rudy and Clift to witness to Noriega, this contact began a relationship that later opened a door. In a two-hour session that day in Noriega's tightly guarded cell, Noriega gave his heart to Christ and expressed a strong testimony of his faith. There was much evidence after that time to indicate his conversion was genuine.

Tony was later allowed to disciple Noriega, visiting him weekly in his prison cell, and using *MasterLife* to do so. Tony learned that Noriega had witnessed to his guards. He had also asked Clift and Rudy to visit his wife and daughters in the Dominican Republic, which they did. His wife and two of his three daughters became Christians at that time. Noriega also wrote a letter to Cuba's Fidel Castro, a friend of his, telling about his conversion and witnessing to Castro. He had Bibles sent to Panama so others could know about Christ. Two years later, while still in prison, Noriega was baptized before a select group of people. As of this writing, he is still incarcerated but gives a Christian witness as he appeals his sentence.

Out of an unusual set of events that only God could engineer, Tony Ponceti, the print shop owner who once held hate in his heart, became Tony Ponceti, disciple-maker. Tony allowed the unending love of Christ to flow through him to transform the despised Panamanian general who, in turn, led others to experience the love of Christ! An enemy had become a brother.

Love Your Neighbor

According to Jesus, the second greatest command after loving God is to "love your neighbor as yourself" (Matt. 22:39). In the story of the Good Samaritan, Jesus showed us that our neighbors are more than the people next door from whom you borrow tools and eggs or even the other parents at the scout meeting. Christians are to be a living demonstration of Christ's love for others, even though they may have little in common. My granddaughter Stephanie has learned to love others. She continues to invite the other children in the neighborhood to her youth group even though she knows they cause problems when they do not behave like the youth from the church.

Demonstrating love can be as simple as letting a stranger have your parking place or smiling and giving a blessing to the distraught clerk who totaled your order incorrectly. It might mean sacrificing even more and allowing a person to stay in your home when he or she needs protection and has no place to go. It includes supporting children you have never met in another part of the world. It happens whenever the love of Jesus in your heart moves you out of your self-centered nature and reaches out to meet the needs of other people regardless of whether they can return the favor or the love.

Missionary Bruce Schmidt was negotiating to buy three acres of land in a Ugandan valley to begin a new work among unreached people. He found himself face-to-face with a leader of the Karamojong, one of the most feared tribes in all of East Africa. "Why are you here and what do you want?" the chief demanded.

Bruce replied that he was in the valley because of two great things—the Great Commission and the Great Commandment. He explained, "Jesus gave the Great Commission to His disciples to go to the whole world and tell the good news of salvation to all people. Jesus gave the Great Commandment, which is to love God with all our hearts and love our neighbor as ourselves. I want to be your neighbor." To Bruce's surprise, the Karamojong leader voiced no objection and instead appeared moved by Bruce's remarks. "We can't believe you want to be our neighbor!" the man exclaimed. "Nobody wants to be the neighbor of the Karamojong. They're the most despised tribe in Uganda. There's not a neighboring tribe that borders with the Karamojong that hasn't had their cattle stolen, their women raped, and their men murdered by us."

By the time the meeting ended, God had melted hearts of stone. This feared Karamojong tribe ultimately gave Bruce thirty acres of land for new mission work—all because of the neighborly love that Bruce extended in Jesus Christ.

ℒove 𝒴our ℬrothers and 𝒮isters

Christ places a special bond of love between His followers. This love comes from the Spirit and is the same love that flows from the Father to the Son and from the Son to His followers. It is best demonstrated in the "one anothers" of the New Testament.

- "Be at peace with each other" (Mark 9:50).
- "Love one another" (John 13:34, 35).

- "Be devoted to one another in brotherly love"and "honor one another" (Rom. 12:10).
- "Live in harmony with one another" (Rom. 12:16).
- "Accept one another" (Rom. 15:7).
- "Instruct one another" (Rom. 15:14).
- "Serve one another in love" (Gal. 5:13).
- "Carry each other's burdens" (Gal. 6:2).
- "Be patient, bearing with one another in love" (Eph. 4:2).
- "Be kind and compassionate to one another, forgiving each other" (Eph. 4:32).
- "Submit to one another" (Eph. 5:21).
- "Encourage each other" (1 Thess. 4:18).
- "Confess your sins to each other" and "pray for each other" (James 5:16).
- "Offer hospitality to one another" (1 Pet. 4:9).

Jesus declared, "My command is this: Love each other as I have loved you" (John 15:12). The writer of Hebrews says, "And let us consider how we may spur one another on toward love and good deeds. Let us not give up meeting together, as some are in the habit of doing, but let us encourage one another—and all the more as you see the Day approaching" (Heb. 10:24, 25).

Fellowship with other believers allows you to show love to them, and for them to exhibit love toward you. Isolation and individualism are not Christ's ways. Christ brings believers together as a family. He provides the ideal place for you to grow—His church. The church is not a building or an organization, although it uses both of these. The church is the living body of Christ in the world today. Each local body of baptized believers is called to carry out Christ's ministry in the world. A committed Christian stays in fellowship with a local body of believers in order to grow in Christ, to worship, to use his or her gifts to serve others, and to receive instruction from God's Word. Anyone who professes to be a Christian but does not fellowship with His church is disregarding God's Word and thus is living outside His will.

Help for One Another

Jesus never intended for Christians to operate alone. You cannot be a balanced Christian if you neglect loving relationships with others. If you try to live apart from the fellowship of other believers, you will not experience the fullness of life in Christ. The Lord puts us in a body of believers because sustaining life outside the body of Christ is difficult. A lamp unplugged from its socket doesn't shed light. As we love one another and stay connected to people in fellowship, we gain strength from one another.

Many times God reveals Himself through the individuals whom He places in your church. Through that fellowship, someone may speak a God-anointed word to you that helps you see more clearly some aspect of a decision. Christian friends can help hold you accountable for times you get off course. They can remind you of what the Word says. They can hold a mirror up to you and lovingly help you see your misplaced priorities. The Father works through others in the church to accomplish His will in your life.

Furthermore, people need each other's encouragement when they try to win others. The church can keep you from feeling helpless and unsupported when you encounter people who need the Lord. Fellow church members can pray for you, encourage you, and help ground you in Scripture as you prepare to share your faith.

The easiest way to accomplish this level of relationship with other believers is in a small group. Jesus and His disciples formed the first small group as they traveled and learned together during Jesus' ministry. Groups provide an intimate setting to share what is happening in your life and what God has been saying to you. It provides access to the wisdom, counsel, and prayer of other believers. You can glean from what a number of people have learned through their own life experiences and their own study of Scripture. There is also more energy as you laugh, cry, and hold one another in tough times.

I remember my daughter remarking as she led her first *MasterLife* group, "Dad, it's a whole lot more fun with a whole group than with just you!" If you do not have such a setting in your own church, you might consider starting a group in your home. At the least, you should have some relationships that hold you accountable in your Christian walk, even if the structure for that is informal.

One of my closest prayer partners is Henry Blackaby, author of *Experiencing God*. God has led us to keep in constant contact and pray for each other over a period of several years. One day we were driving from Louisville to Nashville after having participated together in a program. I shared with Henry that I felt God was going to put me back in foreign missions. I was not sure in what capacity God would call me to serve Him, but I asked Henry to pray with me. We had conversational prayer about God's will there in the car as we drove to our destination.

That day I said, "Henry, I don't know what God has in mind for the future, but somehow I sense that you and I are to be involved with the spread of the gospel worldwide. I would like for you to pray with me about that." Eighteen months later I was elected senior vice president of overseas operations at the Foreign Mission Board (now known as the International Mission Board of the Southern Baptist Convention), and Henry was asked to work for the same mission board four months a year to minister to the overseas missionaries. God has answered our prayers as we have shared together in Christ.

Help for Struggling Christians

Sometimes you may find that you have closed yourself off from people who care about you. Do you shut out people rather than get involved in their lives? Maybe you have been hurt in past relationships and it is easier to withdraw than make yourself vulnerable again. Even if you attend church worship services, you may not allow friendships to form there. You may think you can put in your appearance, listen to the sermon, and then spend the rest of the week avoiding fellow believers who might want to get involved in your life.

If you avoid fellowship with believers because you do not want to risk relationships, you miss opportunities to serve your family in Christ. When difficulties come your way, relationships with other believers can provide resources to meet your needs.

Fellowship with other Christians will keep you from withering in your Christian life. Roy Edgemon, my longtime colleague and one of my "three men at the gate" who encouraged me to bring *MasterLife* to the United States, told me of a time when the fellowship of other Christians helped revive him in the midst of spiritual withering.

As a busy pastor in Texas, Roy was almost burned out from church building programs and heavy involvement in state denominational leadership. Then one night a missionary from Africa named Bud Frey conducted a rally at Roy's church in Odessa, Texas. As Bud Frey described his own recent period of spiritual withering and exhaustion, Roy recognized that Bud had been in the same shape he was in. Bud told how a Christian friend admonished him, "You're a Bud Frey cause, not a Jesus cause" and urged him to "find out how the Lord needs to have His way with you." Bud said from that point, he changed his lifestyle to have a more personal relationship with Christ.

Roy took out a slip of paper, wrote a note, and passed it down the aisle to Bud. The note said, "If you know how I can stop this world long enough to get off, I want to talk to you." But to Roy's embarrassment, before the note could make its way down the aisle to Bud, a friend, Bill Hogue, read the message, and wrote under Roy's comment, "Me, too."

"I didn't want anyone to know I was in this kind of shape," said Roy. But Roy, Bill Hogue, and their wives spent most of the night talking and praying with Bud Frey. The meeting resulted in a life change for Roy. "I started getting up in the morning and praying regularly," Roy recalls. "Before, if we didn't have decisions for Christ in every service, I took it as a personal defeat. I was doing the Lord's work but wasn't letting the Lord work through me."

Fellowship with other Christians who shared their own brokenness helped encourage and restore this pastor to a life of usefulness in God's kingdom. You, too, can encourage others as you become an instrument of Christ. What happens to your fellow church members is important to you: "You are the body of Christ, and each one of you is a part of it" (1 Cor. 12:27). If one member of the body withers—experiences illness, loss, or has a diminished spiritual life—the entire body suffers, and thus you suffer. The body must care for each member so together all the members become more complete in Christ's love.

What Christ Expects

Christ-honoring relationships don't just happen. They require careful cultivation and nurture. Because all of us have sinful natures, we can fall into patterns of thoughtlessness in the way we treat others. Hatred, snobbery, jealousy, and backbiting have no place in the life of a follower of Christ. The Word is filled with instructions about how Christ expects you to treat others with whom you fellowship. "My command is this: Love each other as I have loved you. Greater love has no one than this, that he lay down his life for his friends" (John 15:12, 13).

Jesus was very clear in how Christians are to resolve difficulties face-to-face. You can learn loving, diplomatic ways to communicate how you feel so that what you say strengthens rather than harms the relationship. "If your brother sins against you, go and show him his fault, just between the two of you. If he listens to you, you have won your brother over. But if he will not listen, take one or two others along, so that every matter may be established by the testimony of two or three witnesses" (Matt. 18:15, 16).

People sometimes struggle with the issue of confrontation. They believe that confronting a friend is not a Christlike thing to do because it seems to call for hostility. Actually, confronting a friend in love is a very caring act. Sometimes people tell others about a problem with a friend yet never go directly to that person. Such indirect communication can hurt the relationship. It also can hurt the body of Christ. Disagreements between individuals in the local church may fester, spreading to include others. Eventually small disputes can develop into major rifts that prevent Christ from working through His body. A church with members who squabble and fuss and do not demonstrate love to each other does not look Christlike to a lost world. In chapter 20 you will learn how to maintain right relationships and how to right wrong relationships.

People who are united in Christ can be effective witnesses for Him. Jesus wanted unity and not division in the church so others would believe in Him.

The world can mimic many aspects of the church: its traditions and rituals, its ethics and morality, and its social ministries. But it cannot imitate the love of the Spirit. True love is found only in Him who is perfect love. When you love others, you become a living expression of Christ and bring glory to God. That love will be your motivation, your method, and your goal as you learn to witness to others.

Questions for Meditation and Discussion

1. Who has Christ called you to love? Do you have any "enemies" toward whom you need to change your heart and your behavior?

2. How can you show love to your neighbors this week?

3. How are your current relationships with the other members of your church? How can you improve them?

4. Can you name a time when other believers encouraged or helped you?

5. Have you been a vessel of Christ's love to others? To whom?

Chapter 5
WITNESSING
TO THE WORLD

Bearing fruit is not optional for disciples. It is expected as part of a lifelong, obedient relationship with Jesus. Jesus told His disciples that He chose them to bear fruit that would last. (John 15:1–5, 8, 16, 27). Along with this expectation Jesus gave a promise: The disciples could pray in Christ's name and have their prayers answered.

Maybe you think that witnessing is something Jesus expects only of preachers, evangelists, or missionaries. You may have the idea that witnessing is for persons with outgoing personalities who like to talk and meet new people. But the Bible says that persons who are in Christ will bear fruit. It does not say that only a few believers will bear fruit. Nor does it say that perhaps you will bear fruit or that if you are an exceptional Christian, you will bear fruit. It says that if you remain in Christ, you will bear fruit. Christ made you clean through His Word so you can bear more fruit. You cannot bear fruit apart from Him, as I learned during my futile attempts to witness in my own strength.

Empowered by the Spirit

After I made my initial commitment as a college student to be Christ's disciple, I felt a strong need to begin to witness. About four nights a week I began going to a rescue mission operated by college students. I tried to witness week by week, but no one came to Christ. I memorized Scriptures to counter the excuses I heard when people rejected the gospel. Armed with about fifty passages of Scripture, I could answer almost any objection, but I had not discovered the real secret: The Holy Spirit is the one who empowers us to witness. He bears witness through us. When I allowed Him to fill me, the persons to whom I witnessed began to trust Christ. (I will tell you more about being filled with the Spirit in chapter 11.)

As the Holy Spirit worked through me and as I began to witness more effectively, people began to come to Christ on a regular basis. One night when I witnessed in a bar, I talked with a man who seemed to be under deep conviction about his need for salvation. As we talked, he wept, but he would not open his heart to Christ as his Lord.

At that time the bartender told me I was not welcome in his bar and made me leave. I was crushed, because the man with whom I had conversed was so burdened. When I left the bar, I went across the street to my car, knelt in the backseat, and pleaded with the Lord to lead the man to give his life to Christ. Suddenly, I heard a tapping noise and looked up. Standing beside my car was the man to whom I had witnessed. We talked for a few minutes, and he trusted Christ. I had prayed in Christ's name and kept Him as my source of power instead of relying on my own strength, and the man was saved.

The Fruit of Life in Christ

If you are Christ's disciple, you show it by bearing fruit for Him. You do this as a natural result of following Him. You do not do it in your own strength, as I tried to do at first. You allow the Holy Spirit to empower you for the task. When you bear fruit for Him, you bring glory to the Father. The Lord uses you to teach others about Himself.

What exactly does Christ mean when He speaks of bearing fruit? The apostle Paul described the fruit of the Spirit, the traits of Christ that the Holy Spirit produces in you when you abide in Him: "The fruit of the Spirit is love, joy, peace, patience, kindness, goodness, faithfulness, gentleness, and self-control" (Gal. 5:22, 23). Each of these is a desirable quality that people, with all their problems and anxieties, need and long to see. As they see them in your life, they are drawn toward you. This is your opportunity to glorify God and bear witness to His work in your life.

Consider a grapevine full of ripe grapes. You pluck a bunch from the vine and begin to eat the grapes as you walk along. As you do so, the fruit serves two purposes. The vine does not produce the grapes simply to provide food for you. Hidden in each of those sweet grapes are seeds, which you spit out as you walk along. This allows the seeds to be scattered and the vine to reproduce itself.

You are a Christian not merely to produce the sweet fruit of good deeds and godly actions. As a Christian, you live a life that reflects the characteristics of Christ and so draw others to the Vine that is Jesus Christ. For example, perhaps you have spoken kindly to a person whom you know has slandered you. You have demonstrated love. When others see you do that, they may be puzzled and ask you, "How can you love like that? How can you be kind and gentle to a person who mistreats you and lies about you?" This is your opportunity to plant a seed. You can say, "The truth is, I can't love like that, but Christ can love that person through me." Your life has been a witness, but a verbal witness is also necessary to glorify God instead of yourself. To accept credit for your good deeds would be wrong because this is your chance to give credit to Christ. Only through Christ can you love your enemy. Demonstrating the fruit of love enables you to plant a seed that may produce another disciple.

The world genuinely needs joy. You can be a joyful person who radiates joy even in the midst of difficulties. People may notice that you remain positive and thankful for the good even in a bad situation or that you always encourage others when things look bleak. When they do, you can introduce Christ as your source of joy.

Peace is another fruit of the Spirit that the world seeks and which people look for in the wrong places. When they see peace in your life that is different from the world's chaos, they may wonder what makes you different. When a person comments on your calmness in the midst of a chaotic situation, you can respond, "Can I tell you about an experience I had with Christ that helps me to respond this way?" If you confess Christ as the source of peace in your life, you produce the fruit that Christ desires for His disciples.

Bearing fruit can mean having the fruit of the Spirit in your life. Bearing fruit also includes this result: producing another follower of Christ. Jesus said, "Follow me . . . and I will make you fishers of men" (Matt. 4:19). Fruit-bearing is the normal, natural result of a life that has Christ at the center.

The Promise of Christ's Power

No branch can bear fruit by itself. The branch is part of the vine. The sap and the life-giving power that produces the fruit originate in the vine. The fruit is the part you see, but the vine is always the life-giving source. When you were saved, you were grafted into the Vine. You cannot bear fruit if you do not remain in the Vine, or stay in fellowship with Christ. If you stay in fellowship with Christ, you will be empowered to witness. In my early attempts at witnessing, I learned that I could not succeed just because I willed myself to succeed. Only when I allowed the Holy Spirit to take control of my thoughts, my words, and my actions could I witness effectively.

Jesus commanded the disciples to testify about Him because they had been with Him from the beginning; they knew about His saving truth (John 15:27). They were the ones through whom the gospel would continue after Jesus left the earth. Although you did not physically live alongside Jesus, as the disciples did, you know firsthand of His saving truth, and you experience a growing relationship with Him. You can tell others what Christ has done in your life just as the disciples did. You can tell others about Him, based on your experience. You may be thinking, *I want to do that! I know that Christ wants me to be His witness. But how will I know the words to say? How do I know I won't freeze up or embarrass myself?* In chapter 21, I will share a simple presentation of the gospel using one verse of Scripture.

Compelled to Tell

When I was six years old, I made my profession of faith in Christ while my father was attending Southwestern Baptist Theological Seminary in Fort Worth. He was preaching a revival service in a local mission and invited me to go with him. During that service, I recognized for the first time that I was a sinner and that if a trap door were under me, I would go straight to hell. Realizing that I needed to repent of my sins, I nearly ran down the aisle during the invitation. After giving my life to Christ, I felt that a burden had been lifted from me.

The next morning at breakfast, I asked, "Dad, when will I be baptized?" When he asked why I wanted to be baptized, I said, "Well, Dad, I was saved last night. Didn't you know?"

He smiled at my reminder, not realizing how many more he would receive that day. As he walked out of the house that morning, Mrs. Boyd, our next-door neighbor, called out, "I heard Avery Jr. was saved last night!" When he walked into the barbershop, the barber, Denny Moore, said, "I'm glad to hear your son was saved last night." Puzzled, my dad asked how he knew that. "Why, he was over here this morning telling me all about it!"

Later, as he walked across campus, a friend of his, Bertis Fair, said, "So good to hear about Avery Jr." A few hours later, he saw Dr. Lee Scarborough, the president of the seminary, and was greeted with, "Well, Brother Willis, I'm glad to know Avery accepted Christ." Everywhere he went, I had already been. With the enthusiasm of a new convert, I had told everyone I knew what had happened to me.

In the early days of the church, the disciples said, "We cannot help speaking about what we have seen and heard" (Acts 4:20). Has Christ ever been so real to you that you could not help testifying about what you saw and heard? Perhaps He answered a prayer in such a direct, specific, or meaningful way that you responded, "Only the Lord could have done that!" Perhaps you experienced physical or emotional healing. Perhaps He provided you special encouragement or counsel from a friend just when you needed it. You did not live at the time of Christ to observe His miracles firsthand, but perhaps you have experienced modern-day miracles. If so, how can you refrain from telling persons you encounter how awesome Christ is?

If you are in a love relationship with Jesus, you will want to talk about that relationship just as a man getting married wants to talk about his fiancée or as a pregnant woman naturally talks about babies. It is a very present part of your thinking and sharing with others.

Price of Bearing Fruit

Being Christ's disciple does not occur without sacrifice. Witnessing to the world as you bear fruit for Christ has its price. As Jesus went on to explain, when you have a relationship with Jesus, you will be persecuted, just as He suffered. Everything you endure, He also endured. He knew rejection and suffering, and so will you. "Remember the words I spoke to you: 'No servant is greater than his master.' If they persecuted me, they will persecute you also. If they obeyed my teaching, they will obey yours also. They will treat you this way because of my name, for they do not know the One who sent me" (John 15: 20, 21).

What did Christ suffer for you? The people in His hometown took offense at Him (Mark 6:1–3), a friend betrayed him (Luke 22:47, 48), and respected persons in authority rejected Him (Mark 8:31). Likewise, because of the Christ-honoring stands you take, you will sometimes experience the rejection of friends, family, neighbors, your community, and people you respect. If this frightens you, remember, "God is love" and "There is no fear in love. But perfect love drives out fear" (1 John 4:16, 18).

The disciples learned how to witness in spite of being unschooled and ignorant (Acts 4:13), being threatened (Acts 4:18), put in jail (Acts 4:3), being martyred (Acts 7), and being scattered throughout the provinces (Acts 8:1–3). Philip witnessed to the Samaritans and to the Ethiopian in spite of prejudice (Acts 8), and Peter entered a Gentile home to share the gospel with Cornelius even though it was against the Jewish tradition to do so (Acts 10).

The disciples changed from timid men who ran and hid when Jesus was arrested to bold men who could continue to proclaim Christ in the midst of persecution. This difference was due to the filling of the Holy Spirit and prayer. "On their release, Peter and John went back to their own people and reported all that the chief priests and elders had said to them. When they heard this, they raised their voices together in prayer to God. . . . Now, Lord, consider their threats and enable your servants to speak your word with great boldness. . . . After they prayed, the place where they were meeting was shaken. And they were all filled with the Holy Spirit and spoke the word of God boldly" (Acts 4:23, 24, 29, 31).

After the apostles had been flogged for continuing to preach, they "left the Sanhedrin, rejoicing because they had been counted worthy of suffering disgrace for the Name. Day after day, in the temple courts and from house to house, they never stopped teaching and proclaiming the good news that Jesus is the Christ" (Acts 5:41, 42). It was during this time that they began to perform great miracles and many were added to the church. In spite of their difficulty, the apostles had cause to rejoice! The price was high but great was the reward!

A high school principal, John Eluru, was rehearsing to play the role of Jesus in the Ugandan translation of the "Jesus" film, a riveting movie about the life of Christ. The film has brought countless people to Christ in every corner of the globe. As crews carried John and other film personnel from their Ugandan village to the production site, guerrilla fighters burst onto the road and fired. John was shot in the heart.

That night as John lay dying, he urged the film technician, "Don't stop the dubbing. Uganda needs this film. I have done my part, but don't stop the work, and don't ever be afraid." The next morning John died, but today every time the completed film is shown in Uganda, John's voice as Jesus tells hundreds of people how to know Christ.[1]

Sometimes the cost of discipleship is high and the disciplines you have learned are difficult to maintain. Yet the Holy Spirit continues to empower you to abide in Christ, to hear God through His Word, to pray according to God's will, to fellowship in love with God's people, and to proclaim God's message of salvation. It is also the Holy Spirit who uses all of these in balance in your life to enable you to minister to others. When you see the fruit in the lives of others, your heart becomes like that of the Father, and you rejoice in His rewards.

Questions for Meditation and Discussion

1. Which of the fruit of the Spirit are evidenced in your life?

2. Are you bearing witness to Christ when people notice the fruit of the Spirit in your life?

3. Is your life bearing fruit in the form of new disciples for Christ?

4. What fears keep you from witnessing to others?

5. What more do you need to learn to witness more effectively?

6. What cost or what rewards have resulted from your sharing of the gospel?

Chapter 6
MINISTERING TO OTHERS

When I led a *MasterLife* training seminar in Kenya in 1983, I met Seleshi Kabede, a Christian Ethiopian who shared with me his story. Four years earlier, when Communists had taken control of Ethiopia, they had banned worship in churches by ordering that no more than five persons could meet at any time without a permit. Naturally, the Communists did not grant permission for worship services. The pastor had to flee for his life when caught baptizing a convert. Many in this eight-hundred-member church stopped practicing their faith because the circumstances were so difficult.

"Seven other men and I decided that we must do something to carry on the work," Seleshi told me. They approached missionary veterinarian Jerry Bledsoe, who was allowed to stay in Ethiopia because he took care of the animals at the palace. Jerry began to disciple these Ethiopian Christians secretly at his house, using *MasterLife*. Later, each man discipled four other persons. "We could not meet at the same place or time each week; we could not take Bibles to a meeting; and we had to pray with our eyes open, using conversational prayer, so that we would not be discovered," the man said. Because the Ethiopian Christians feared that the Communists would soon confiscate their Bibles, they devised a plan for each person to memorize a portion of the Bible so they could reproduce it.

"Oh yes, we know we will be put in jail. Some of us already have been, but the government doesn't know what to do with us once we are behind bars. We witness and win the other prisoners, so they kick us out," he said. Eventually, Seleshi began underground discipleship groups in 170 places around the country.

Fourteen years later, after the Communists had been overthrown, I made a trip to Ethiopia to see him. This irrepressible man was still on fire for Christ—this time without an oppressive government to restrain him. He reported that his church had reopened with 2,500 members and had started 7 new churches in Addis Ababa and 150 more throughout the country. Another group of churches had just inquired about purchasing 100,000 sets of *MasterLife* to train more Ethiopians to be disciples.

From Personal Growth to Effective Ministry

What if you did not have a church in which to worship? What would you do if you could not sing praise to God? What if the government took away your Bible and prohibited your witness? What if you could not meet or pray with others? Would your personal growth suffer? How would it affect your ministry to others?

So far, you have been learning how to grow as a disciple and deepen your walk with Christ through the resources He has given you. Look again at the circle in the center of the Disciple's Cross on page 10. As you continue to abide in Christ, to learn of Him through His Word and prayer, and as you touch others in fellowship and witness, your life in Christ should continue to grow and expand. As the fruit of the Spirit grows in your life, that expanding center which is Christ will begin to affect others around you. Your service and ministry to others will impact them and begin to produce fruit in their lives. Through ministry, you expand your influence and your own growth.

TAKE UP YOUR CROSS

Jesus said, "If anyone would come after me, he must deny himself and take up his cross daily and follow me" (Luke 9:23). For Jesus, "taking up his cross" meant giving Himself to redeem the world. "Being found in appearance as a man, he [Jesus] humbled himself and became obedient to death—even death on a cross!" (Phil. 2:8). Jesus was obedient to God's will for His life even when it meant dying. We learn from Jesus' example that a Christian's cross has two characteristics: It is a voluntary commitment, and it is an act of obedience. For believers, cross bearing is voluntary, redemptive, sacrificial service for others. Self-denial emphasizes turning from commitment to self to commitment to Him. Taking up your cross involves turning with Christ to a world in need. The first result is a new vision of self; the second result is a new vision of the world's need.

THE MINISTRIES OF THE CROSS

In the last four chapters, we have discussed four resources to help you grow in Christ: the Word, prayer, fellowship, and witness. A growing disciple uses his or her growth in each of these areas to help others in Christ's name. Each of these disciplines can result in a type of ministry as you pass on to others what the Holy Spirit is producing in you.

THE WORD

Study of the Word can lead to a ministry of teaching and/or preaching. God calls some people to be preachers, evangelists, and teachers to lead the church. You may discover that this is His will for your life. However, you do not need a position in the church to share with others the truths that the Holy Spirit has revealed to you. Jesus commanded us to "go and make disciples of all nations, baptizing them in the name of the Father and of the Son and of the Holy Spirit, and teaching them to obey everything I have commanded you" (Matt. 28:19, 20). Most people who stay in the Word have the opportunity to share in a variety of contexts what God has said to them. People are eager to know the truth, and if the Word abides in you, you can share with them Scriptures that apply to their situation.

When I was the president of the Indonesian Baptist Theological Seminary, I hired a former lieutenant colonel in the Indonesian army to manage the seminary property and the employees who took care of it. Although he had been a Christian for only about six months, he was very committed to the Lord. The problem was that he tried to manage the seminary property and its employees as he would manage an army. Time after time I had to intervene to keep war from breaking out between the employees and this supervisor. Praying for God's guidance, I decided to disciple this man and to teach him to be an effective and Christlike manager. Using the Scriptures, I taught him how to relate to his employees with patience, kindness, and self-control. This man effectively served at the seminary for more than ten years.

A teaching opportunity that is very close to you is your own family. Parents are commanded in Scripture to tell their children about God's mighty acts and to instruct them in God's commandments: "These commandments that I give you today are to be upon your hearts. Impress them on your children. Talk about them when you sit at home and when you walk along the road, when you lie down and when you get up. Tie them as symbols on your hands and bind them on your foreheads. Write them on the doorframes of your houses and on your gates" (Deut. 6:6–9). Clearly, the Lord meant for you to use every available opportunity to teach God's Word.

Teaching is also part of sharing your faith. To witness to others, believers must first understand the gospel and then be able to present it to others so that their lives are changed. This is the essence of teaching: communicating to others what you know so they can apply it in their own lives, whether you teach from a pulpit, in a classroom, in a small-group study, or one-to-one.

PRAYER

The more you get involved in prayer, the more you worship. Worship is ministering to the Lord (see 1 Chron. 23:13). It is bowing before God and worshiping Him through praise, adoration, and devotion. Prayer enables you to develop a closer relationship with the Father. The ministry of worship can take the form of individual worship during your quiet time. But it goes beyond private prayer. You also worship as you fellowship with the body of Christ, gathered as His church. Worship is the primary way you glorify the Lord, and it is God's primary reason for creating and redeeming you. All Christians have a responsibility for worship, whether they are participants or leaders. It is a choice to give your heart and your devotion to fellowship with God.

A second ministry that develops through spending time in prayer is a ministry of intercession. In this ministry, you bring the needs of the church and of the world before the throne of God. Intercession can result in changed lives and changed churches. It is one thing to care deeply about the hurts of others; it is an even greater thing to pray earnestly and sacrificially for God to meet those needs. To pray effectively, you must stay alert, spend time listening, write down concerns, and then pray earnestly, keeping a record of God's activity. "The effectual fervent prayer of a righteous man availeth much" (James 5:16, KJV).

Evangelist Luis Palau says that he takes seriously all prayer requests that he receives. When he and his team gather for prayer, he says they pray earnestly. "Because," he says, "when my wife had cancer, and I asked people to pray for her, I wanted them to pray with all their heart. Her life depended on it!"

Intercession is also vital to the ministry of others. Before I became a missionary, I heard many missionaries say that their greatest need was prayer, even more than finances. I made a commitment to God that before I began to serve as a missionary, I would enlist as many prayer partners as possible so

He could do more than I could do as a missionary. I enlisted about two thousand people to pray daily. Over the years that list grew to six thousand. I wrote to them every month to give them prayer requests and to report answers to prayer. I believe God's work through us in Indonesia was a direct answer to the prayers of our prayer partners. Their ministry was as vital as ours!

FELLOWSHIP

The believers in the early church in Jerusalem grew in Christ by spending time together and encouraging one another in their new faith. "They devoted themselves to the apostles' teaching and to the fellowship, to the breaking of bread and to prayer. . . . Every day they continued to meet together in the temple courts. They broke bread in their homes and ate together with glad and sincere hearts" (Acts 2:42, 46). As they met on a daily basis in their homes, they learned together the same disciplines you have studied: the Word, prayer, fellowship, and how to share their faith. They encouraged one another to live godly lives. They comforted and strengthened one another.

Fellowship also leads to a ministry of nurture. A normal outgrowth of being part of the body of Christ is discipling new believers. A ministry of nurture involves taking care of spiritual infants and helping them grow into mature Christians. God gives some persons special gifts that enable them to counsel and train others in the various stages of spiritual growth. In the Bible, this happened several times. Jesus saw Simon's potential and helped him grow into the rock called Peter (see Matt. 16:16–19 and John 21:15–17). Barnabas encouraged Paul, the apostle, and also John Mark, who later wrote one of the Gospels.

As other Christians spend time with you, they will model their walk after yours. The apostle Paul was not afraid to be a model. He said, "Follow my example, as I follow the example of Christ" (1 Cor. 11:1) and also, "Whatever you have learned or received or heard from me, or seen in me—put it into practice" (Phil. 4:9). He was able to make such a claim because he walked in deep fellowship with Christ. As your fellowship with Christ and His body deepens, you will continue to learn from the model of others even as you become a model yourself. Fellowship brings Christians close enough to benefit from one another's growth.

WITNESS

The well-known evangelist D. L. Moody had a personal commitment to witness to someone every day of his life. Even if he had already gone to bed when he remembered that he had not witnessed that day, he would get up and tell someone about Christ.[1]

The fourth resource you have for living the Christian life is the resource of witness. Many believers do not think of witness as a resource. However, nothing encourages Christians more than bearing witness, especially when they see someone accept Christ. From the resource of witness grows a ministry of evangelism. Evangelism is the proclamation of the good news of salvation in Christ. Evangelism is a means the Holy Spirit uses to convert the lost. It is one method the Lord uses to teach others about Himself.

The ministry of evangelism may be expressed in several ways. Long before D. L. Moody became a preaching evangelist, he witnessed to one person at a time. Evangelism may occur through lifestyle—living such a godly life that it attracts a lost person's attention and provides an opportunity to witness. It may occur through participation in small groups gathered around similar interests, where sharing Christ is a natural part of the conversation. Church evangelism may include visiting homes, taking a religious survey, or using another method to ensure that every person in your church's range of influence hears the gospel message. You may help your church gather people for a community-wide revival in a church building or stadium. Perhaps you will enter another culture to tell others about Jesus as a career, short-term, or bivocational missionary. You may contribute money or prayer for mission causes. All of these are forms of evangelism.

SERVICE

Fellowship and witness lead to a ministry of service: "Greater love has no one than this, that he lay down his life for his friends" (John 15:13). Service is rendering for someone else what he or she cannot readily do for themselves. It can be as simple as raking the leaves for an elderly neighbor, changing a baby's diaper, or going grocery shopping for a family in need. It may be visiting prisoners, playing the piano at a nursing home, or vacuuming the church building. The task may be tedious and time-consuming. It may seem simple and unworthy of notice, but if it helps someone else and brings glory to Christ, then you have honored Christ.

Jesus said, "I tell you the truth, whatever you did for one of the least of these brothers of mine, you did for me" (Matt. 25:40). Your service may require a great deal of you. It may require many sleepless nights sitting up with an invalid or hours of counseling on the phone. It may even involve risking your life for another.

A Christian relief worker in central Asia, who must remain nameless for security reasons, was ministering when some people rushed into the room. They pleaded, "Please come help this old man, or he will die!" In this war-torn country, mine fields were plentiful. The people had found a shepherd injured by a mine. The relief worker knew he must decide immediately what to do. "I knew it was not wise to enter a mine field, but I felt that the Lord wanted me to help this person in need," he told me. "As I crossed the field, I noticed that everyone following me was walking single file in my footsteps."

They located the man, carried him to the road, and flagged down a passing truck. The relief worker begged the truck driver to carry the injured shepherd to a hospital, but no one in the crowded vehicle would give up his seat. He then asked a man who spoke English, "Tell the truck driver I will pay twice what any rider has paid if you will take this man to the hospital." As he translated, the man commented to the truck driver, "This Christian is going to pay the man's way when we Muslims won't do anything." At that point, the truck driver refused the money and made a place for the injured man.

In this country of central Asia where Christianity is not accepted, this modern-day Good Samaritan story spread all over the countryside with the message, "This is what a Christian does. This is the kind of service a Christian does in Jesus' name."

How do you serve others? What does being a disciple of Christ lead you to do? Your opportunities for sacrificial service to others are endless. Every Christian is a minister if he or she follows Jesus and serves others as He did.

Bringing It Together

These five ministry areas compose the ministry of a disciple and of Christ's church. The goal of discipleship is expressed like this: "If a man cleanses himself from the latter, he will be an instrument for noble purposes, made holy, useful to the Master and prepared to do any good work" (2 Tim. 2:21). You need to grow in all spiritual disciplines and ministries to master life and to be prepared for the Master's use. If you develop all of these disciplines, your life will be balanced and fruitful.

If your church includes all of these disciplines, your church will be balanced and fruitful. Walker Moore was serving as associate pastor in charge of youth ministries at the First Baptist Church of Tulsa and also leading the congregation between pastors. As they considered inviting someone in to lead them in revival meetings, Walker led the church to focus on having revival using their own people. In order to do that, they took Acts 2:41–47 which described the behavior of the New Testament church (and the same disciplines described in the Disciple's Cross) and divided the church into groups for each of these five disciplines: the Word, prayer, praise and worship, fellowship, and evangelism.

Each discovery group was given three weeks to study and prepare for the week of revival, which they named "AWE Week" after Acts 2:43, "Everyone was filled with awe." They were asked to study what it meant to be a disciple in the first century, in terms of their respective discipline, to share what they had learned with the church, and to report how their church compared with what they had studied.

Each group prepared its own program for one night of AWE week. On the first night, the group studying the Word began the program with a little girl singing, "The B-I-B-L-E." She was joined by a young adult singing, "Yes, that's the book for me," and then a senior adult with a cane came on stage singing, "I stand alone on the Word of God, the B-I-B-L-E." Then the group shared what they had learned. On Tuesday night the church focused on fellowship. The people met by zip codes, in homes within a square mile of one another, and shared their testimonies. On Wednesday they spent the entire service in praise and worship. On Thursday they divided into groups and went into classrooms and had long sessions of prayer. On Friday they went out to evangelize. Some went house to house, and others went to visit friends, family members, or coworkers who needed a witness for Christ. Each night, as the church experienced the fullness of what they had studied, the meetings went for two or three hours. Time was not a factor. It truly was an awesome experience!

A Summary

You can learn an easy way to remember what you have learned so far in this book. Summarizing what it means to be a disciple is as simple as 1-2-3-4-5-6. There is:

- One Lord as the first priority of your life.
- Two relationships: The vertical crossbar represents your relationship with God and the horizontal crossbar represents your relationship with others.
- Three commitments: Deny yourself, take up your cross, and follow Christ.
- Four resources to center your life in Christ: the Word, prayer, fellowship, and witness.
- Five ministries that grow from the four resources: teaching/preaching, worship/intercession, nurture, evangelism, and service.
- Six disciplines of a disciple: spending time with the Master, living in the Word, praying in faith, fellowshipping with believers, witnessing to the world, and ministering to others.

Questions for Meditation and Discussion

1. Have you been willing to take up your cross and serve others sacrificially?

2. Are you useful to the Master and prepared to do any good work?

3. What ministries have you been involved in? Have you been effective and brought glory to God?

4. Which ministries would you like to explore? Who could you learn from?

5. When you look around, whose life do you want to model? Who is watching you?

6. Are the six disciplines balanced in your own life, or are you lopsided? What do you need to change, if anything?

HOW TO EVALUATE YOUR SPIRITUAL GROWTH

As we finish this first section of the book, you may wish to stop and do the inventory below. This inventory, based on observable characteristics of a disciple, can help you determine where you are in your growth as a disciple. Even though the inventory will help you to look at yourself in terms of behavior and attitudes, the most important questions you can ask yourself are:

- Where am I in my relationship with Christ?
- How far am I from the lifelong, obedient relationship with Him that I desire?
- If He desires to transform my values into kingdom values, have I learned to submit?

In the next section of chapters, I will introduce you to life in the Spirit in which submission to the work of the Holy Spirit will transform your personality.

Personal Spiritual Inventory

	ALWAYS	USUALLY	SOMETIMES	SELDOM	NEVER
ABIDING IN CHRIST					
• I have a daily quiet time.	❑	❑	❑	❑	❑
• I try to make Christ Lord of my life.	❑	❑	❑	❑	❑
• I feel close to the Lord throughout the day.	❑	❑	❑	❑	❑
• I try to discipline myself.	❑	❑	❑	❑	❑
• I am aware that the Lord disciplines me.	❑	❑	❑	❑	❑
LIVING IN THE WORD					
• I read my Bible daily.	❑	❑	❑	❑	❑
• I study my Bible each week.	❑	❑	❑	❑	❑
• I memorize a verse of Scripture each week.	❑	❑	❑	❑	❑
• I take notes at least once a week as I hear, read, or study the Bible in order to apply it to my life.	❑	❑	❑	❑	❑
PRAYING IN FAITH					
• I keep a prayer list and pray for the persons and concerns on the list.	❑	❑	❑	❑	❑
• I have experienced a specific answer to prayer during the past month.	❑	❑	❑	❑	❑
• Each day my prayers include thanksgiving, praise, confession, petition, intercession.	❑	❑	❑	❑	❑
FELLOWSHIPPING WITH BELIEVERS					
• I am in a small group or some form of accountable relationship with other Christians.	❑	❑	❑	❑	❑
• I seek reconciliation with those who have a problem with me or with whom I have a problem.	❑	❑	❑	❑	❑

- Others know I am a Christian by the way I love God's people. ☐ ☐ ☐ ☐ ☐
- I live in harmony with other members of my family. ☐ ☐ ☐ ☐ ☐

WITNESSING TO THE WORLD

- I pray regularly for lost persons by name. ☐ ☐ ☐ ☐ ☐
- I share my testimony with others when an appropriate opportunity arises. ☐ ☐ ☐ ☐ ☐
- I share the plan of salvation with those who are open to hear it. ☐ ☐ ☐ ☐ ☐
- I witness for Christ each week. ☐ ☐ ☐ ☐ ☐
- I follow up and encourage persons whom I have won to Christ. ☐ ☐ ☐ ☐ ☐

MINISTERING TO OTHERS

- I serve Christ through a job in my church. ☐ ☐ ☐ ☐ ☐
- I give at least a tithe through my church. ☐ ☐ ☐ ☐ ☐
- At least once a month I do kind deeds for persons less fortunate than I. ☐ ☐ ☐ ☐ ☐
- I have goals for my life that I keep clearly in mind. ☐ ☐ ☐ ☐ ☐

Subtotals	—	—	—	—	—
	x4	x3	x2	x1	
Totals	—	—	—	—	—
Score	—	—	—	—	—

When you have finished checking each item, add each column except the *never* column. Each check in the *always* column is worth four points; the *usually* column, three points; the *sometimes* column, two points; the *seldom* column, one point. Add these four totals together to get your overall score out of a possible 100.

Part 2
THE DISCIPLE'S PERSONALITY

You will develop a Christlike
character as you learn
to live in the Spirit.

The Spiritual Christian

Gal. 2:20
1 Thess. 5:23-24

GOD

Eph. 5:18

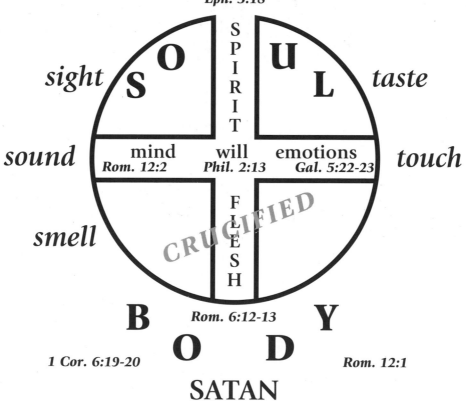

Chapter 7
DOING GOD'S WILL

The whole spring of my freshman year in college was a marvelous time for me as I moved from mediocre Christianity to white-hot fervency, was filled with the Spirit, saw thirty or more people saved through my personal witness, and was involved in a revival happening on our campus. A few of us who had begun to pray regularly began to dream together of going on an evangelistic tour. We were greatly disappointed when no one would sponsor or invite us and we couldn't secure a tent.

We decided, then, to be a part of the "tentmaker" program through the mission board, which used college students to start churches in the West and Northwest, mainly among the workers in the logging industry. We hitchhiked out to California, thinking we would help start a church. When we arrived, we found ten of us had been assigned to the small town of Fortuna which already had a church with a seminary-trained pastor. That church had not planned to start other churches; they wanted us to build their building, all out of donated two-by-fours! We would work eight hours a day at the logging mill and build this building after our shift. We only got to preach one time the whole summer. We were so immature that we did not handle our frustration and disappointment very well. Our fervor began to cool, we spent less time reading our Bibles and praying, and we rarely witnessed. We squandered our extra time in resentment.

After about three weeks, Hal Brooks and I lost our jobs in the mill because of a truckers' strike and eventually had to return home. It was then that we planned to have the revival services in the high school and were turned away. My summer seemed a waste.

When I returned to school for my sophomore year, the students asked if I would be the director for the rescue mission. Although I was officially "in charge," I felt very empty and dry. I prayed, "Oh, Lord, will I ever again know the joy of your Spirit? Will you ever use me again? I don't feel the way I did. I've asked forgiveness and I've tried to repent but nothing is like it was before."

I knew what to do. I knew I needed to move past my feelings and return to the Scripture, prayer, witnessing, and other disciplines which I have discussed in this book. As I did so, the joy began to return and the Lord began to overflow in my life again. If I had known what I will share with you in this part of the book about the disciple's personality, I would not have had to experience that long drought. I would have known how a Christian who has moved out of the will of God could return to Christ and be led by the Spirit.

About Your Personality

Do you wonder why you often try to carry out your own will instead of seeking God's will first? Do you ever wonder why you have thoughts, feelings, and behaviors that do not honor Christ? As I share with you about life in the Spirit over the next few chapters, I'd like to use a simple illustration, which demonstrates the biblical teachings about your personality. It will show you how to make Christ the master of your life and how to master life. It will help you submit to God's will instead of your own. It will demonstrate how God transforms your personality by His Spirit so that you can be His disciple.

God created you as a physical and spiritual being. The physical part came from the earth. The spiritual part originated in God's spirit. The circle in the illustration represents you—your total personality. The Bible describes you as a unity of body, soul, and spirit. When you understand each element of your personality and how it functions, you will discover how to integrate your personality under the lordship of Christ.

BODY

The Bible pictures you as a body. God made your body from the earth to serve several functions. Through your body you are able to participate in the

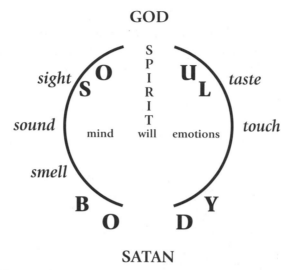

physical world. Your five senses relate you to the rest of God's creation. Your body makes it possible to communicate with the world around you and with other living creatures. Your body gives you a physical identity that makes you a distinct and unique personality. God created your body "good."

SOUL

The Bible also pictures you as a soul. You do not just have a soul; you are a soul. The first human being became a living soul when God breathed into his nostrils the breath of life (see Gen. 2:7). God imparted His life to the person He had made. The words for "soul" in the Bible generally mean life or the total self. When the Bible says a person's soul is saved or lost, it refers to the total person. "Do not be afraid of those who kill the body but cannot kill the soul. Rather, be afraid of the One who can destroy both soul and body in hell" (Matt. 10:28).

Sometimes the word for "soul" means "heart" or "the seat of the will, desires, and affection"; that is, the inner human being. The word *psyche* originates from the Greek word for "soul." The soul's ability to think, to will, and to feel is additional evidence that human beings are created in the image of God. These three elements—mind, will and emotions—form your distinctive personality.

SPIRIT

The Bible also pictures you as spirit. Your spirit directly relates you to God's image. "The Spirit himself testifies with our spirit that we are God's children" (Rom. 8:16). It gives you self-awareness and makes it possible for you to fellowship and work with God. God communicates with you through your spirit. "Who among men knows the thoughts of a man except the man's spirit within him? In the same way no one knows the thoughts of God except the Spirit of God" (1 Cor. 2:11). According to Genesis 1:31, when God finished creating the first person, "God saw all that he had made, and it was very good."

The Natural Person

Soon after the creation of man, another spiritual being, Satan, interfered with God's good creation. Adam and Eve succumbed to Satan's temptation and disobeyed God. A different aspect of the spiritual nature entered the personality of human beings. That aspect is called "the flesh." The Bible uses the word *flesh* in two ways. The general meaning is "body" and refers to the physical body. The other meaning is symbolic and refers to the lower nature. It refers to the human capacity to sin and to follow Satan instead of God.

Notice the two open doors inside the circle on the diagram on page 69. The top door, "the door of the spirit," allows you to relate to God. The bottom door, "the door of the flesh," allows you to relate to Satan. God created human beings with a free will. Note that the will stands between the door of the spirit and the door of the flesh. Unfortunately, when Satan tempted Adam and Eve, they chose to turn from God's leading to follow Satan's leading. At that moment the human being's ego, the big "I," took over. The door of the spirit closed, and humanity died spiritually. The door of the flesh was opened, and sinful nature became the spiritual part of the human personality. The results were terrible. The flesh came alive and caused the mind, will,

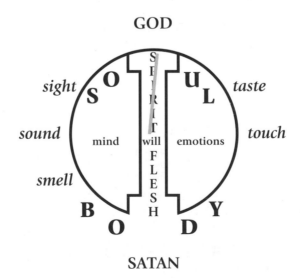

and emotions to degenerate. The entire personality—body, soul, and spirit—was infiltrated by evil and death.

Through the temptation of Satan, humanity transgressed the command of God and fell from its original innocence. Consequently, the descendants of those first sinful human beings inherit a nature and an environment inclined toward sin. As soon as they are capable of moral action, they become transgressors and are responsible to God for closing the door of the spirit and shutting Him out.

The Condition of the Natural Person Today

The natural person is centered in himself or herself and is open to the temptation and power of Satan. The natural person is in the process of dying and cannot reverse it. This person is not able to relate to God properly. "The man without the Spirit does not accept the things that come from the Spirit of God, for they are foolishness to him, and he cannot understand them, because they are spiritually discerned" (1 Cor. 2:14).

Your thoughts are influenced by evil; your emotions control you; your will is weak. Even strong-willed and disciplined persons are not able to overcome the effects of the flesh. No matter how many good things you do, the Bible says that a natural person cannot please God: "Those controlled by the sinful nature cannot please God" (Rom. 8:8). Without the Holy Spirit intervening, this person will continue in the type of life that separates him or her from God. People can come to God only as the Holy Spirit draws them. If you have not come to Christ by repentance and faith, you are estranged from God for eternity.

God loves you even though you have sinned. He sent His only Son to pay for your sins so that you would not perish but have eternal life. Jesus died on the cross to save you from sin and death and to bring you to God. After His resurrection, He sent the Holy Spirit to earth to draw you to God. The Holy Spirit can speak to a natural person even though the door of the spirit is closed. When you open the door of the spirit, the Spirit of God enters your personality, and your spirit is born again.

As you take on the disciple's personality, you will see your life change the more you come to know Christ. You are no longer the natural person, so you will want to do God's will and become like Christ and have Christ's character. The Scriptures say God provides you with exactly what you need to achieve His will: "And my God will meet all your needs according to his glorious riches in Christ Jesus" (Phil. 4:19). Extraordinary knowledge or intellect is not required to know God's will. He will supply your need and will work all things together for good. But doing God's will on your own is impossible.

Only God has the capacity to do exactly what He intends and purposes. Doing God's will involves a process whereby God uses the provisions He has given you to accomplish His work: "May the God of peace, who through the blood of the eternal covenant brought back from the dead our Lord Jesus, that great Shepherd of the sheep, equip you with everything good for doing his will, and may he work in us what is pleasing to him, through Jesus Christ, to whom be glory for ever and ever" (Heb. 13:20, 21).

Ask yourself: What vision do I have of God's purpose for my life? If I were to say, "I commit my whole personality to God," what would that mean for me? Because I know that God will provide for me when I do His will, what action will I take?

Who's in Charge?

One day my sixteen-year-old sister, Norma, asked me about the will of God. I told her that God has a purpose for every person. To make my point, I used several illustrations. "Do you know how many sections are usually in an orange? Ten. On a stalk of bananas, each hand has one less banana than the hand before it. A watermelon usually has an even number of stripes. Grains like wheat, barley, millet, and rye have an even number of grains on a stalk. In a fully developed ear of corn, an even number of rows are on each ear, an even number of grains are in each row, and an even number of silks are in the tassel." I asked her, "Do you think it's just an accident that so many things God has made have a symmetry about them?"

She asked, "No, but does that mean that I have to do whatever God wants me to do?"

I answered, "Although God has a perfect will for your life that He wants you to follow, He does not force you. He leads you to do His will, but He gives you the freedom to make your own choice." I went on to explain, "It's as if God has a blueprint for your life. Although He may desire to build a beautiful mansion of your life, you can still choose to draw your own plans and build a shack. But God's intent is that you build according to His will. Make sure that Christ is the foundation of your life. Let the Holy Spirit be the builder. He can design and build far better than you can."

I watched to see how God worked in her life. She later became a pastor's wife, and currently she and her husband, Ernie Whitten, serve God as missionaries in Argentina. The key to finding God's will in her life was making Christ the foundation and allowing the Holy Spirit to guide her instead of acting on her own will. When she submitted her own desires and allowed the Holy Spirit to lead her, He directed her to the center of God's will.

$\mathcal{Y}$ou $\mathcal{C}$an $\mathcal{C}$hoose

"This day I call heaven and earth as witnesses against you that I have set before you life and death, blessings and curses. Now choose life, so that you and your children may live and that you may love the LORD your God, listen to his voice, and hold fast to him. For the LORD is your life, and he will give you many years in the land he swore to give to your fathers, Abraham, Isaac and Jacob" (Deut. 30:19, 20).

God has a purpose for you, but He leaves the ultimate choice up to you. In making your choice, you can choose good or evil. God wants you to choose His way, and His heart breaks when you choose ways that turn you away from Him. "Be very careful, then, how you live—not as unwise but as wise, making the most of every opportunity, because the days are evil. Therefore do not be foolish, but understand what the Lord's will is" (Eph. 5:15–17).

For Jesus, doing God's will was like food—a constant part of His obedient life and purpose. "My food," said Jesus, "is to do the will of him who sent me and to finish his work" (John 4:34). You can find God's will when you are willing to obey Him. "Do not conform any longer to the pattern of this world, but be transformed by the renewing of your mind. Then you will be able to test and approve what God's will is—his good, pleasing and perfect will" (Rom. 12:2).

$\mathcal{C}$haracteristics of $\mathcal{G}$od's $\mathcal{W}$ill

God's will and the human will are vastly different. They differ in capacity and purpose. Your capacity to carry out your own will is limited. "I know that nothing good lives in me, that is, in my sinful nature. For I have the desire to do what is good, but I cannot carry it out" (Rom. 7:18). Even good purposes can be corrupted and motivated by the wrong things. For example, you could desire to win people to the Lord just so others will think you are a great Christian.

Unlike your frail, human capacity, however, God's capacity to carry out His will is unlimited. His purpose is always holy, upright, and constant. He does not change His mind on a whim or when the way is difficult. He always wants His will to be done, and He sends His Holy Spirit to help accomplish it. "It is God who works in you to will and to act according to his good purpose" (Phil. 2:13).

God does not omit anyone from His will. When a person becomes a Christian, the Holy Spirit begins revealing to that person God's will for his or her life. "For this reason, since the day we heard about you, we have not stopped praying for you and asking God to fill you with the knowledge of his will through all spiritual wisdom and understanding" (Col. 1:9).

Yet, when you think about finding God's will for your life, you may feel lost. You may wonder how to grasp God's will. You may feel that you cannot possibly think God's thoughts or get inside His mind to see what He has in store for you.

Fulfilling God's Purpose

God wants to reveal to you His will *and* how you can accomplish it. Doing the will of God begins when you have a vision of God's purpose for your life: to bring glory to God so that His name will be praised.

> He predestined us to be adopted as his sons through Jesus Christ, in accordance with his pleasure and will—to the praise of his glorious grace, which he has freely given us in the One he loves . . . in order that we, who were the first to hope in Christ, might be for the praise of his glory. And you also were included in Christ when you heard the word of truth, the gospel of your salvation. Having believed, you were marked in him with a seal, the promised Holy Spirit, who is a deposit guaranteeing our inheritance until the redemption of those who are God's posses-sion—to the praise of his glory (Eph. 1:5, 6, 12–14).

Jesus' life brought glory to God because Jesus lived to do God's will. Jesus said all of these words: "For I have come down from heaven not to do my will but to do the will of him who sent me" (John 6:38). "By myself I can do nothing; I judge only as I hear, and my judgment is just, for I seek not to please myself but him who sent me" (John 5:30). "I have brought you glory on earth by completing the work you gave me to do" (John 17:4).

Jesus did not seek His own will. Would a person deliberately wish humil-iation, anguish, and death upon Himself? If Jesus could have had His way, would He have chosen for friends and family to reject Him and for crowds to mock and scorn Him? He experienced these things because they were part of His Father's perfect will, not because He wanted them. Jesus' commitment to God's purpose made His ministry on this earth effective.

Your development in every part of your Christian life and ministry depends on your commitment to God's purpose. God's purpose and will for you are that you bring glory to Him by becoming like Jesus. "Those God foreknew he also predestined to be conformed to the likeness of his Son, that he might be the firstborn among many brothers" (Rom. 8:29). Therefore, if God's will is accomplished in your life, you will be conformed to the likeness of Jesus. You will act like Him, think like Him, and have the same kind of relationship with God and with others as Christ did. You will have Him at the center of your life, and you will yield to the Holy Spirit's leading in your life.

Committing Your Personality

Doing God's will depends on a commitment of your whole personality to God. *Discipleship is developing a personal, lifelong, obedient relationship with Jesus Christ in which He transforms your character into Christlikeness; changes your values to Kingdom values; and involves you in His mission in the home, in the church, and in the world.* Transforming your character into Christlikeness means that the Holy Spirit helps you increasingly become like Christ in every character trait.

Even when you commit yourself to God, you soon discover that doing His will is not easy. Many factors influence you. Your sinful nature is the primary culprit that causes you to refuse to listen to the Holy Spirit and decline to do God's will.

Scripture indicates that your sinful nature and love for the things of this world inhibit you from doing the will of God. "Do not love the world or anything in the world. If anyone loves the world, the love of the Father is not in him. For everything in the world—the cravings of sinful man, the lust of his eyes and the boasting of what he has and does—comes not from the Father but from the world. The world and its desires pass away, but the man who does the will of God lives forever" (1 John 2:15–17). Other factors may hinder you from doing God's will. You may live in an environment in which sin is rampant. You may come from a family that did not honor Christ. Even so, you still have a choice about whether or not you do God's will.

How do you commit your whole personality to God? Does that mean losing your identity, so that you become passive and simply let life roll over you? No. Does it mean you will never again struggle with what God wants you to do? No. Even Jesus struggled when He was tempted. "During the days of Jesus' life on earth, he offered up prayers and petitions with loud cries and tears to the one who could save him from death, and he was heard because of his reverent submission. Although he was a son, he learned obedience from what he suffered" (Heb. 5:7-8). When struggles occur, God provides a way to accomplish His will in you when you commit your entire personality to Him and to the leading of the Holy Spirit.

The Scriptures show several ways in which God enables you to commit yourself fully to Him, each of which will be discussed in the upcoming chapters. God works in you to provide the will and the ability to do His good pleasure (Phil. 2:13). God renews your mind so that you can prove that His will is good, pleasing, and complete (Rom. 12:2). God tells you to present your body as a living sacrifice to Him as your reasonable service (Rom. 12:1). The Holy Spirit produces the fruit of the Spirit in you to replace evil emotions and actions (Gal. 5:18–24). Finally, Christ lives in you when you are crucified with Him, and He provides the power to do His will. "I have been crucified with Christ and I no longer live, but Christ lives in me. The life I live in the body, I live by faith in the Son of God, who loved me and gave himself for me" (Gal. 2:20).

Doing God's will requires a vision of God's purpose for your life; commitment of your whole personality to God; and action(s) based on God's provision for doing His will. When mankind was in fellowship with God after creation, this process was natural and easy. I'm sure you do not feel that being wholly submitted to God is either natural or easy. Because you have opened the door to the flesh and God has opened the door to the spirit, there is a continual struggle between flesh and spirit. In the next two chapters, I will share more about this struggle and how God would lead you to close the door to the flesh and remain open to the Spirit.

Questions for Meditation and Discussion

1. What roles do your body, soul, and spirit play in forming your total personality? Which currently has the greatest control in your life?

2. What role does the flesh play in your personality to undermine your good intentions?

3. Does God give us all we need to overcome the desires of the flesh and submit to the will of the Spirit? Does your behavior reflect that ability?

4. Instead of seeking what you want, do you strive to do God's will and to have Christ's character?

5. Is seeking God's will in decisions a major part of your life in the Spirit?

Chapter 8
RENEWING YOUR MIND

Your mind is much like a video recorder. You record events and thoughts and then rehearse them in your mind. Usually these images and thought patterns help you make sense of life around you, but sometimes they are incorrect or self-destructive. Replaying harmful messages may lead you to repeat the same wrong choices over and over.

Paul described his situation like this: "I do not understand what I do. For what I want to do I do not do, but what I hate I do. . . . I know that nothing good lives in me, that is, in my sinful nature. For I have the desire to do what is good, but I cannot carry it out. For what I do is not the good I want to do; no, the evil I do not want to do—this I keep on doing. Now if I do what I do not want to do, it is no longer I who do it, but it is sin living in me that does it" (Rom. 7:15, 18–20).

Some commentators believe that when Paul said, in a subsequent verse, "What a wretched man I am! Who will rescue me from this body of death?" (Rom. 7:24), he was referring to a practice of that day in which a murderer's punishment was to have the body of his victim chained to him so he would have to pull it along with him as it decayed. I'm sure there are times you feel like Paul, that somehow you're trapped with a sinful nature that does not want to do the will of God. You drag around with you the effects of past sins, internal messages and lies from Satan, and a record of past behavior.

Paul provided an answer to his own dilemma when he said, "Thanks be to God—through Jesus Christ our Lord!" (Rom. 7:25). He added, "Therefore, there is now no condemnation for those who are in Christ Jesus, because through Christ Jesus the law of the Spirit of life set me free from the law of sin and death" (Rom. 8:1, 2). That Spirit of life is the Holy Spirit who takes God's Word and the words spoken by Christ, makes them real, and applies them to your life.

Jesus told the disciples He was sending the Holy Spirit to provide the same kind of help, comfort, and teaching that He had provided them while He was on earth. He said they would know the Holy Spirit because He would live within them (see John 14:16–20). Once you have received Christ as your Savior, the Holy Spirit is actually in your heart and life and not just one who merely walks beside you. "But the Counselor, the Holy Spirit, whom the Father will send in my name, will teach you all things and will remind you of everything I have said to you" (John 14:26). In doing so, the Holy Spirit renews your natural mind.

The Natural Mind

When I speak of the "natural mind," I'm referring to the thinking process that is limited to human reason and resources. Human history shows that the natural mind becomes progressively self-destructive if left to its own desires. People who are directed by their natural minds walk in darkness and have incorrect thinking. "So I tell you this, and insist on it in the Lord, that you must no longer live as the Gentiles do, in the futility of their thinking. They are darkened in their understanding and separated from the life of God because of the ignorance that is in them due to the hardening of their hearts" (Eph. 4:17, 18).

The Scriptures call the mind of the natural man "blinded" (2 Cor. 4:4); "depraved" (Rom. 1:28); "corrupt" (1 Tim. 6:5); and "unspiritual" (Col. 2:18). The natural mind thinks from a humanistic, sin-debased viewpoint. The viewpoint of the flesh directs its thoughts. The sinful mind is under the control of Satan and can never please God because it concentrates on things of the world and not things of the Spirit. The natural mind walks a path of hopelessness and self-destruction.

The natural mind inevitably becomes enslaved to other masters: "Furthermore, since they did not think it worthwhile to retain the knowledge of God, he gave them over to a depraved mind, to do what ought not to be done. They have become filled with every kind of wickedness, evil, greed and depravity. They are full of envy, murder, strife, deceit and malice. They are gossips, slanderers, God-haters, insolent, arrogant and boastful; they invent ways of doing evil; they disobey their parents; they are senseless, faithless, heartless, ruthless" (Rom. 1:28–31). The natural mind in turn enslaves a person's personality by reducing it primarily to the world of the senses and of evil. Meditate on the words above. Can you identify with any of these masters?

Yet the person who sets aside worldly ways and turns his or her life and thoughts over to Christ can know forgiveness and joy. You can have a spiritual mind even if a worldly mind has ruled you in the past. The natural mind and the renewed mind have the same basic functions: thinking, judging, reasoning, and evaluating, but the mind ruled by the Holy Spirit is in stark contrast to the worldly mind. The renewed mind is able to know with certainty how trustworthy and correct the will of God is (see Rom. 12:2). The primary difference is who is in control.

The renewed mind is obedient to Christ. It thinks from Christ's viewpoint, as the Holy Spirit directs. The renewed mind frees the personality by enlarging it to encompass the world of the Spirit in addition to the senses. When the Holy Spirit rules your mind, you obey Christ. You think, *What would my Lord have me to do in this situation?* You try to understand what the Holy Spirit is leading you to do.

Ruled by the Flesh

When you read about the natural person in the preceding chapter, you probably realized that this person did not know Christ. He or she was living the natural, unregenerate life. This is the way you lived before you personally came to know Christ in salvation. "As for you, you were dead in your transgressions and sins, in which you used to live when you followed the ways of this world and of the ruler of the kingdom of the air, the spirit who is now at work in those who are disobedient. All of us also lived among them at one time, gratifying the cravings of our sinful nature and following its desires and thoughts. Like the rest, we were by nature objects of wrath" (Eph. 2:1–3).

Before you knew Christ, you were dead in your transgressions and sins. When you repented of your sinful nature and way of life and asked Jesus to be your Savior and Lord, God made you alive with Him. By His grace, God saved you and raised you up with Christ. You are now God's workmanship, created in Christ Jesus to do good works (see Eph. 2:10).

However, many persons who have received Christ and have the Holy Spirit living in their hearts still do not live as God intended. That is why Paul told the Ephesians that, as Christ's disciples, they should move away from the world's way of living: "You were taught, with regard to your former way of life, to put off your old self, which is being corrupted by its deceitful desires; to be made new in the attitude of your minds; and to put on the new self, created to be like God in true righteousness and holiness" (Eph. 4:22–24).

If a Christian lives like the unbelieving world, this person is a worldly Christian. The King James Version calls this person "carnal," meaning "fleshly." It refers to a person governed by human nature instead of the Spirit of God. Paul contrasts spiritual people—those who are under the control of the Holy Spirit—with those who are carnal—those under the control of the flesh. Let's look again at the illustration of the Disciple's Personality. It will help you visualize what I've shared regarding the worldly mind.

The Worldly Christian

I will use the same circle to illustrate the Worldly Christian. The difference between this picture and the one of the natural person is that this person has opened the door of the spirit but has left open the door of flesh. The worldly person still lives in the flesh, even though he or she has been born again.

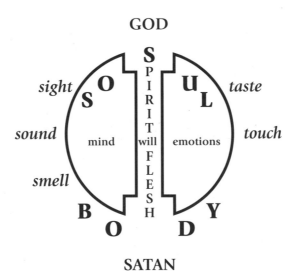

This Christian was made alive and became a partaker of the divine nature but failed to grow as he or she should: "His divine power has given us everything we need for life and godliness through our knowledge of him who called us by his own glory and goodness. Through these he has given us his very great and precious promises, so that through them you may participate in the divine nature and escape the corruption in the world caused by evil desires" (2 Pet. 1:3, 4). This passage then lists character traits which the Christian needs to add as he or she grows.

> For this very reason, make every effort to add to your faith goodness; and to goodness, knowledge; and to knowledge, self-control; and to self-control, perseverance; and to perseverance, godliness; and to godliness, brotherly kindness; and to brotherly kindness, love. For if you possess these qualities in increasing measure, they will keep you from being ineffective and unproductive in your knowledge of our Lord Jesus Christ. But if anyone does not have them, he is nearsighted and blind, and has forgotten that he has been cleansed from his past sins (2 Pet. 1:5–9).

If you do not possess these qualities, then you have the characteristics of a worldly person. A worldly person is ineffective and unproductive. He is sluggish and does not grow in faith. Such a person is nearsighted and blinded to the Holy Spirit's truth and listens to the lies of Satan. He or she is not sensitive to sin and does not appreciate the forgiveness of God.

Christians who are not taught how to grow and live in the Spirit live much as they did before they were born again. They are babies in the faith, still showing traits of the worldly nature, although they may have been believers for many years: "Brothers, I could not address you as spiritual but as worldly—mere infants in Christ. I gave you milk, not solid food, for you were not yet ready for it. Indeed, you are still not ready. You are still worldly" (1 Cor. 3:1–3).

In the diagram of the Worldly Christian we replace the letter "s" in spirit with a capital "S" to show that the Holy Spirit is eternally part of your spirit when you are born again. He does not leave. However, the worldly Christian's big mistake is leaving open the door of the flesh. Satan still has access to this person, allowing the flesh to dominate this worldly Christian's thoughts, will, and emotions. The word *worldly* means "fleshly" or "carnal," and this type of Christian is more likely to follow the physical senses and fallen nature rather than the spiritual nature that he or she received at conversion.

No doubt you sometimes feel conflict in your heart when you try to have the mind, attitudes, and actions of Christ. Why does such conflict occur? If, as a disciple, you do not allow Jesus to continually be master of your life through His Spirit, you will be a worldly Christian. Although you have allowed Christ to enter your life, you still struggle to control your own life. The big "I" of the old, natural person is still dominating you. Worldly

Christians continually allow the old nature to determine what they think, do, and feel rather than to follow the Spirit of God.

Competing influences cause this conflict in your personality. You hear Satan's voice through your flesh, the voice of the world through your senses, the voice of self through your mind, will, and emotions, and God's voice as His Spirit speaks to your spirit. You are a battleground. How can you have victory in this kind of situation? Do not despair. Christ wants to be your Lord and to give you daily victory.

You may be struggling with the terms I have used. Some people believe that the soul and the spirit are the same rather than being two distinct aspects of your personality. The function is the same whether you think of your soul as having three parts (body, soul, and spirit) or two parts (body and soul, with the spirit being seen as part of the soul). Although people who hold to each viewpoint have a biblical basis for their position, it does not affect the result. You are dealing with the battle between the flesh and the spirit, not between the soul and the spirit.

The Mind of Christ

In the preceding chapter I talked about how to surrender your will to God to let Him work in you to will and to do His good purpose (see Phil. 2:13). In this chapter I want to show you how to take the next step in becoming a spiritual Christian—by renewing your mind to think the thoughts of Christ. As a Christian, your goal is to personify the "mind of Christ," which you have received. Paul said, "Let this mind be in you, which was also in Christ Jesus" (Phil. 2:5, KJV). He also said, "'For who has known the mind of the Lord that he may instruct him?' But we have the mind of Christ" (1 Cor. 2:16).

Every Christian has the mind of Christ, but he or she doesn't always choose to engage it. To do so, you must allow Christ to guide your thoughts. You make Christ the master of your mind by removing all obstacles to your knowledge of God and by making every thought obedient to Christ (see 2 Cor. 10:5). You possess the mind of Christ and He continually renews your mind.

Perhaps you have sought to renew your mind by trying to put worldly thoughts out of your mind. But does it happen easily? Try this experiment. Think about an elephant. Visualize it. Now, use your willpower to stop thinking of the elephant. Were you able to do it? Probably not, because you were concentrating on not thinking about it. Have you ever been hungry for a chocolate sundae? Try to stop thinking about that sundae, and you'll probably find yourself checking the freezer because you've thought about it all the more. You do not rid yourself of worldly thoughts by trying not to think about them. Renewing your mind is accomplished by filling your mind with Christ's thoughts.

Mastering Your Mind

The Holy Spirit wants to be to your mind what a rudder is to a ship. A rudder keeps the ship on course so it arrives at its destination. Paul described a two-step plan for mastering the human mind: "For though we live in the world, we do not wage war as the world does. The weapons we fight with are not the weapons of the world. On the contrary, they have divine power to demolish strongholds. We demolish arguments and every pretension that sets itself up against the knowledge of God, and we take captive every thought to make it obedient to Christ" (2 Cor. 10:3–5).

Paul described an offensive/defensive game plan. In the defensive game plan, you are to defeat worldly ideas that obstruct the knowledge of God. In the offensive game plan, you are to keep Christ in control. When a thought which would rob God of His glory enters your mind, should you continue to think about it, wonder what to do with it, or ask Christ to remove it? Paul chose to surrender every thought and put it under Jesus' control. Let me give you more specific ways to renew your mind by defeating worldly ideas and making every thought obedient to Christ.

The Renewal Process

In the experiment in which we visualized the elephant, the only way not to think about an elephant was to think specifically about something else. The Scripture says to give attention to things of the Spirit: "Those who live according to the sinful nature have their minds set on what that nature desires; but those who live in accordance with the Spirit have their minds set on what the Spirit desires. The mind of sinful man is death, but the mind controlled by the Spirit is life and peace" (Rom. 8:5, 6). Set your heart's desire on heavenly things: "Set your minds on things above, not on earthly things" (Col. 3:2). Think on praiseworthy things: "Finally, brothers, whatever is true, whatever is noble, whatever is right, whatever is pure, whatever is lovely, whatever is admirable—if anything is excellent or praiseworthy—think about such things" (Phil. 4:8).

Meditate on God's Word: "But his delight is in the law of the LORD, and on his law he meditates day and night" (Ps. 1:2). Let the Holy Spirit reveal truth: "But when he, the Spirit of truth, comes, he will guide you into all truth. He will not speak on his own; he will speak only what he hears, and he will tell you what is yet to come" (John 16:13). Living in God's Word, the

Bible, is the primary source of your knowledge about Christ. As you spend time reading the Word, He speaks to you through the Holy Spirit. One of the Holy Spirit's roles is to show you the truth. His truth will set the enslaved mind free.

HOW TO RENEW YOUR MIND

To renew your mind, you must replace ungodly thoughts with Scriptures or Christlike thoughts. When impure thoughts run through your head like an old tune you cannot stop humming, try some of these activities. (You may want to keep this list in a handy place for quick reference.)

1. Sing songs of praise.

2. Start quoting Scripture. Use this time to review past verses or memorize a new one that addresses the problem.

3. Pray. Commit yourself as a living sacrifice. Claim the mind of Christ. Demolish Satan's strongholds.

4. Set your mind on things above. Count the blessings God has given you.

5. Talk to a friend. Ask him or her to pray with you even over the phone.

6. Help someone in need. Begin thinking of a way to surprise or bless someone.

Read what the Bible says about how your thoughts shape your desires and your actions: "As he thinketh in his heart, so is he" (Prov. 23:7, KJV). For example, when you replace harmful thoughts with thoughts that honor Christ, your entire concept of yourself can change. If you constantly tell yourself, *I'm no good,* you may begin to act out those thoughts as a self-fulfilling prophecy. If you remind yourself about how much Christ loves you and how worthy you are in His sight, you will begin to act like a person of worth. You can renew your mind by replacing negative thoughts about yourself with the reminder that Christ died for you. You can renew your mind by remembering who you are and whose you are. This is much more than "positive thinking." It is scriptural meditation and application.

What areas of your thought life need to be renewed? What things do you need to put away so that you are no longer tempted? The psalmist declared, "I will be careful to lead a blameless life—when will you come to me? I will walk in my house with blameless heart. I will set before my eyes no vile thing" (Ps. 101:2, 3). If your temptation is viewing pornographic material, you need to destroy it. You may need to turn off the television when a program comes on that is not proper for you or your family to watch. You may

need to spend less time with a person who is always negative or who gossips about others. You may have to avoid situations that cause you to covet or envy someone else.

HOW TO RESIST TEMPTATION

Here are some simple, practical steps to allow the Spirit to activate the mind of Christ when you are tempted to act in harmful ways:

1. Remember that Jesus was tempted in every way you are tempted, yet He overcame the temptation (Heb. 4:15). Temptation itself is not sin, unless you dwell on it or act on it.

2. Pray for grace in your time of need (Heb. 4:16).

3. Express humility and your dependence on God by kneeling in prayer (James 4:10).

4. Adopt God's attitude and choose His response toward the temptation (Prov. 3:5, 6).

5. Ask the Holy Spirit to impress you with a way to deal with the temptation (1 Cor. 10:13).

6. Ask for God to walk with you past the temptation (James 4:7, 8).

7. Look for a Scripture to claim during the temptation (Ps. 119:9–11).

8. Ask God to help you focus on His will (Phil. 2:13).

9. Acknowledge and ask forgiveness for thinking about the temptation (1 John 1:9). Repent as many times as necessary through the day.

10. Obey God's commands, knowing that you are in spiritual warfare (2 Cor. 10:3–5).

I hope that the Worldly Christian part of the Disciple's Personality will help you identify areas of weakness or compromise in your life. The ability to think Christ's thoughts is crucial to your life in the Spirit. Allowing Christ-honoring thoughts to replace worldly, fleshly thoughts is a challenge for most disciples. The Holy Spirit is with you to help you renew your mind. You do not have to be a victim of Satan's efforts to have you adopt his destructive attitudes. Satan is defeated when you push his thoughts out of your mind and replace them with those that please Christ.

Even if your mind thinks rightly, your emotions may interfere and lead you to think wrong thoughts. We will discuss how to master your emotions in the next chapter.

Questions for Meditation and Discussion

1. How much does your life reflect characteristics of a worldly Christian? Of a spiritual Christian?

2. Do you spend a greater percentage of time operating with your natural mind or your renewed mind?

3. Can you explain the reason for the struggle between the flesh and the Spirit? Do you know how to obtain victory?

4. Name a specific temptation you have in the area of the mind. What Scriptures apply to your situation?

5. What other means might you use to replace the temptation with beneficial thoughts?

Chapter 9
MASTERING YOUR EMOTIONS

My father had a terrible temper when he was young. Even after becoming a Christian at age nineteen, he often exploded in anger. He struggled over and over again to remain calm and to have an attitude that would honor Christ.

After much prayer and Bible study, my father began to notice a change in his responses to situations. One night a man stuck his fist in my dad's face and threatened to fight him over a remark in his sermon. But Dad refused to fight. He later related, "I knew I had won the battle over my temper when I felt the hair on his knuckles and I did not respond as I had in the past."

Almost everyone has had experiences in which controlling emotions has seemed like an overwhelming battle. The self-centered philosophy of "if it feels good, do it!" surrenders the will to emotions. Emotions make good servants but dreadful masters. Christ is to be your Master, even of your emotions. He wants to help you use your emotions in a responsible way. The Bible has a plan to help you deal with your emotions. In this chapter you will learn how the Holy Spirit can help you gain victory over your emotions.

What Are Emotions?

Emotions are God-given feelings of pleasantness or unpleasantness. They are reactions to internal or external stimuli. Emotions are not good or bad; they just spontaneously occur. You make the choice of whether you use emotions to honor Christ or to harm yourself or others.

Emotions are an essential part of your personality. Life without them would be dull. If you did not have emotions, you would not experience anger or anxiety, but you also would not experience joy or love. God created you to experience a variety of emotions.

Because Jesus was fully human, He experienced the whole range of human emotions. He experienced anger with the Pharisees who judged Him for healing the man with the shriveled hand on the Sabbath (Mark 3:5) and with the money changers in the temple (Matt. 21:12–16). He loved not only his disciples (John 13:34) but he loved Martha, Mary, and Lazarus (John 11:5) and wept with grief when Lazarus died (John 11:35). He wanted His disciples to have the full measure of His joy (John 17:13). The difference between Jesus and us is that He never acted on His emotions in a sinful way.

Emotions are spontaneous responses to your values and beliefs. Over the years your emotional responses have been either affirmed or challenged. Because your values and beliefs are not exactly the same as any other person's, you react to the same circumstances differently than someone else.

While the chief priests proudly or indifferently saw the money changers as a service to the temple worshipers, Jesus felt anger because He knew His Father designed the temple to be a house of prayer. While the chief priests felt suspicious and antagonistic toward Jesus' healing on the Sabbath, the healed man knew great joy. Children felt joy when they recognized Jesus as the Messiah during the triumphal entry, while the chief priests and teachers of the law felt indignation and hatred that Jesus was proclaimed the Son of David (the Messiah).

I once learned the hard way how emotional responses can differ. What I thought would be humorous was devastating for my wife. At that time, we were in our second term of missionary service to Indonesia. I was very busy sharing the gospel around the city of Jember in Java, where approximately eight to nine million people lived without a missionary of any denomination. In addition, I was helping lead a strategic church study for our denomination in Indonesia. I had received an invitation to go to the Philippines to lead a youth camp, and I had accepted.

Meanwhile, my wife Shirley was teaching our three oldest children in the third, fifth, and seventh grades as well as taking care of our two children still in diapers. To compound that, we were living in a house for eight months while workers remodeled it, so we had people around us at all times. We were a four-hour drive from the nearest missionaries, so Shirley had no other American adults with whom she could relate.

On April Fool's Day I did a very foolish thing. As we ate lunch, I said to my wife, "Oh Shirley, I almost forgot to tell you. I got a letter saying that you could go with me to the Philippines. Then we could go on and visit Hong Kong after the camp is over." She began to brighten up and get very excited, until I said, "April Fool!" That definitely was the wrong thing to do. She burst into tears. Then the Holy Spirit convicted me of how insensitive I had been to her needs during the previous months. I began to spend time with her and made permanent changes in how I related to her and in the amount of time that I gave her versus my work.

Your values help determine whether you make the correct emotional response in a given situation. Too many people are glad, sad, or mad about the wrong things for the wrong reasons. If you can discern what makes you feel a certain way, you will understand your true values. Often, a person cannot control emotions because the emotions are narrowly focused on himself and arise from a worldly nature. Paul said of the Christians controlled by jealousy and strife, "You are still worldly. For since there is jealousy and quarreling among you, are you not worldly? Are you not acting like mere men?" (1 Cor. 3:3).

Spiritual Christians also have strong emotions, but they have learned to master them. They control the responses to their emotions instead of letting the emotions control their responses. A growing disciple learns more and more to rely on the Holy Spirit instead of the flesh. When the Holy Spirit transforms you, He is present in your life to give you the ability to control your emotions.

The Spiritual Christian

Let's use the illustration of the Disciple's Personality once more to demonstrate the Spiritual Christian. In this illustration, a cross in the center represents the crucified life of a disciple. Once again, the will is located between the door of the spirit and the door of the flesh. For the spiritual Christian, the door of the spirit is open because this person has opened his or her heart and spirit to follow God. The door of the flesh is closed because the flesh has been crucified with Christ. The mind, will, and emotions are submitted to the Spirit. You can say, as the apostle Paul did, "I have been crucified with Christ and I no longer live, but Christ lives in me. The life I live in

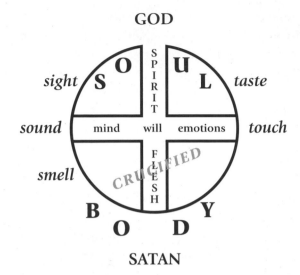

the body, I live by faith in the Son of God, who loved me and gave himself for me" (Gal. 2:20).

The way to have victory is to consider your flesh crucified. Because this is an ongoing act of your will, the indwelling Christ helps you keep the door of the spirit open and the door of the flesh closed. As you put your old self to death, the Spirit of God gives you new, victorious life. When you do this, you are filled with the Spirit of God. You are able to live in the Spirit. God takes control of your mind, will, emotions, and therefore, your soul and body.

Now you can see the contrast between the natural person, the worldly Christian, and the spiritual Christian. You can also see that the spiritual Christian walks in the Spirit so that he or she will not yield to the desires of the flesh. A spiritual Christian sets aside old ways and fleshly lusts as though he or she has buried them. If you are a spiritual Christian, you can do this because God promised victory over the world, flesh, and the devil and God promised to indwell you with His Holy Spirit.

The encouragement to crucify the flesh and surrender to the Spirit became almost a motto for the Kagiso Baptist Church in Johannesburg, South Africa, while Christians there completed *MasterLife*. It was amazing how they learned to use aspects of the Disciple's Personality in their conversations as they held each other accountable," reported the pastor, Zachariah Mataung. "If a brother did something questionable, another would urge him to 'Shut the door to the flesh and keep it closed' until we meet (for *MasterLife*) tomorrow," the pastor recalled.

$\mathcal{S}tepping\ into$ A-C-T-I-O-N

Sometimes you may believe that your emotions are so strong that you cannot master them. You may feel that when they sweep over you like a giant tide, you have no choice but to drift along with them. However, you are not helpless in learning to control your emotions. The Holy Spirit can help you when you are tempted to give in to your emotions.

A specific course of action can help you master your emotions. I have made a simple acrostic A-C-T-I-O-N to help you recall it. Emotions are closely tied to actions. Your emotions cause you to act, but you can also act your way into an emotion. Here is what ACTION means:

     A cknowledge the emotion.

     C onsider why you have it.

     T hank God that He will help you master it.

     I dentify the biblical response to it.

     O bey the Holy Spirit's leading.

     N urture the appropriate fruit of the Spirit.

ACKNOWLEDGE THE EMOTION

The first step is to acknowledge the emotion. Denying or suppressing your feelings does not help. Have you heard someone shout through clenched teeth, "I am not angry!" The words are entirely different from the emotion communicated. You can deal with an emotion only if you recognize it and admit it.

Jesus did not try to deny or suppress His grief as He faced the cross but admitted that He was distressed. "He took Peter and the two sons of Zebedee along with him, and he began to be sorrowful and troubled. Then he said to them, 'My soul is overwhelmed with sorrow to the point of death. Stay here and keep watch with me' " (Matt. 26:37, 38).

Burying an emotion can cause it to emerge in an unhealthy way later. Suppressing emotions can make you physically ill as well as add to the emotional load you carry. Learning to identify your exact emotion will help you acknowledge your feelings. For example, you may think you are just feeling sad when a closer look reveals that you actually feel lonely, abandoned, helpless, or overwhelmed. Giving an exact name to an emotion helps with the later steps of this action plan.

CONSIDER WHY YOU HAVE THE EMOTION

A second step toward mastering an emotion is to consider why you have it. After you have acknowledged a feeling, it is important to understand why you are experiencing it. Doing this may not be as simple as you think. Sometimes an event that occurred hours or days before is still in your subconsciousness, causing an emotional reaction. Identifying the underlying cause of an emotion is a big step toward mastering your reaction to that emotion.

Sometimes you may be able to identify the feeling but when you try to determine the cause of it, you are clueless. Or perhaps you sense that your emotion is out of proportion to the event that caused it. For example, you may know that you feel a deep sense of anger because your boss overlooked your name in your company's awards ceremony, but you are puzzled about why an oversight like this should evoke such strong feelings. Or you may know that you feel rejected and hurt when a friend forgets a luncheon engagement with you, but you do not understand why you have such difficulty accepting her apology for her absentmindedness.

If this is your situation, you may want to talk to your pastor or a professional Christian counselor, or you may choose to participate in a Christ-centered support group that helps people understand their emotions. A person can take big steps toward mastering his or her emotions by discovering the deeper issues behind the strong feelings.

The person who reacts strongly to a boss who forgets to announce an award may learn that he or she feels victimized when relating to authority figures because of a painful childhood relationship with a parent. The person who feels lonely and abandoned after an appointment falls through may still be struggling unconsciously with childhood feelings of abandonment.

THANK GOD

Whether or not you can identify the cause of your emotion, you can take the third action step: Thank God that He will help you master it. In grief about the death of his son and about his own spiritual condition, King David took these same action steps. He admitted that he was downcast, analyzed why he felt this strong emotion, and thanked God because he believed God would help him (see Ps. 42).

You do not have to understand a situation to believe that God will work in it and to be grateful that He will. According to Scripture, you are to give thanks in all things, not just the ones you understand or the ones that please you. "Give thanks in all circumstances, for this is God's will for you in Christ Jesus" (1 Thess. 5:18). If you are a person of faith, you can do this because you believe that God will work all things together for good. "We know that in all things God works for the good of those who love him, who have been called according to his purpose" (Rom. 8:28). When by faith you trust God to work in a situation and when you thank Him for doing so, your mind is open to consider the benefits that may result.

Even though you may not like to think about feeling fear, anger, loneliness, or jealousy, these emotions can have good results. Fear may keep you from taking unnecessary risks or may prompt you to take extra precautions in a situation. Anger might lead you to right a wrong or an injustice. A person who is lonely may learn to rely on God to fill the emptiness in his or her life. Jealousy can make you realize that you need to work more diligently in a relationship or to strive harder toward a goal.

IDENTIFY THE BIBLICAL RESPONSE TO THE EMOTION

The fourth step in your A-C-T-I-O-N plan to master an emotion is to identify the biblical response to it. Although emotions are spontaneous, the actions they produce do not have to be. The Bible teaches that you are responsible for how you behave. You cannot escape responsibility by blaming your behavior on a negative feeling or on the person or circumstance stimulating that feeling.

You may believe that someone wronged you or that your family background programmed you or predisposed you to act a certain way. You may think, *I can't help that I act this way. He made me angry when he criticized me.* But can someone really make you angry or make you respond improperly? Regardless of what precipitates the event, the choice of how to respond is yours. You can sin in that response, or you can choose to honor Christ. One sin does not justify another.

The Bible gives principles for responding to emotions. The better you know the Bible, the more easily you can apply it to deal with your emotions. Read the following biblical responses to the emotions of hate, anxiety, joy, anger, and envy.

For hate, the biblical response is to do good to those who hate you (Luke 6:27–28). For anxiety, you are to pray to God rather than be anxious (Phil. 4:6, 7). When you are joyful, you are to acknowledge the source of goodness (Phil. 4:4). If you are angry, you are to avoid sin and to settle matters quickly (Eph. 4); and if envious, you are to lay it down and to love others (1 Cor. 13:4).

Another way to determine a Christ-honoring response is to think about how Jesus did or would respond. As you think about ways Christ would have you master your emotions, you can remember His example on the cross—the ultimate example of a person's control of emotions. Think of the ways Christ could have responded to this event. He could have raged, threatened, blamed, or scolded. He could have called on angels to protect Him. Instead, He sought God's will in His responses, even to the end. Certainly, He expressed His sorrow and His concern for His mother. He expressed His human physical need. But the ultimate mastery occurred when He surrendered everything to God's will, even when that meant suffering and dying on the cross.

OBEY THE HOLY SPIRIT'S LEADING

The fifth A-C-T-I-O-N step is to obey the Holy Spirit's leading. Natural and worldly persons want to do what their emotions, mind, or will tell them. In contrast, spiritual persons obey the higher call to do what the Holy Spirit reveals. Doing what God says is right, rather than what you want to do, is a conscious act of the will. Christians must understand their obligation to act rightly toward others even if they do not feel like doing so. If you wait to do right until you feel like it, you may never act at all.

Not only do your feelings influence the way you act, but the way you act also determines how you feel. You can change your feelings by changing your actions, as the adage states, "Act your way into a new feeling." Jesus' solution for many emotional responses was to command an action rather than a feeling. "Therefore, if you are offering your gift at the altar and there remember that your brother has something against you, leave your gift there in front of the altar. First go and be reconciled to your brother; then come and offer your gift" (Matt. 5:23, 24).

When the Bible tells you to love your fellow Christians, love is described as a way of behaving, not as an emotional feeling. "Love is patient, love is kind. It does not envy, it does not boast, it is not proud. It is not rude, it is not self-seeking, it is not easily angered, it keeps no record of wrongs. Love does not delight in evil but rejoices with the truth. It always protects, always trusts, always hopes, always perseveres" (1 Cor. 13:4–7). Love is something you do. Love manifests itself in the way you act. Acting lovingly toward someone when it goes against your nature to do so is the essence of love. The Holy Spirit can help you do this.

Proverbs 16:32 says that a person who remains in control of himself is stronger than the strong and mightier than the mighty. A person who declines to reply in anger, conquering his or her emotions, demonstrates more strength than does a person who conquers a city. "He that is slow to anger is better than the mighty; and he that ruleth his spirit than he that taketh a city" (Prov. 16:32, KJV).

NURTURE THE APPROPRIATE FRUIT OF THE SPIRIT

The sixth A-C-T-I-O-N step in mastering your emotions is to nurture the appropriate fruit of the Spirit. "But the fruit of the Spirit is love, joy, peace, patience, kindness, goodness, faithfulness, gentleness and self-control" (Gal. 5:22, 23). Each fruit of the Spirit is more than an emotion. Each is an enduring character trait. You develop spiritual fruit by having a close relationship with Christ through the Holy Spirit and by growing in maturity through experience.

One of the most amazing stories of an individual who mastered the Disciple's Personality occurred in prison. A man named J. D., an inmate in a state prison in Texas, told Don Dennis—a former-inmate-turned-preacher who pioneered using *MasterLife* in prisons—that concepts of the Disciple's Personality now keep him from reacting violently when people's actions arouse anger within him. "My old way was to react from my emotions," J. D. told Dennis. "When J. D. was in control, if someone got in my face, I would go off. I would shoot him, stab him, whatever was convenient. Part of the game I would play was to be a tough guy, a bad guy. It's one way you think you win respect, but people don't respect you. They fear you. Respect is something you get from people when you show love and kindness and consideration."

I hope that you feel more confident in your ability to act in Christ-honoring ways as the Holy Spirit helps you bring your emotions under control. You may not be able to achieve the ideal results instantly. Changing old patterns takes practice. Do not be discouraged if you occasionally revert to former out-of-control behaviors. When you do, ask forgiveness and ask God to make you aware of the Holy Spirit's presence in your life to help you make better choices. Some of those choices are physical as well. God calls us to submit our bodies as well as our emotions and our will.

Questions for Meditation and Discussion

1. What emotions do you experience frequently? Which ones are desirable and which ones undesirable?

2. How are your emotions reflected in your behavior? Do you sin with your emotions?

3. What behaviors or emotions does Christ desire to produce in your life to better display Himself through you?

4. Name again the six A-C-T-I-O-N steps. Which of them do you have the most difficulty implementing?

Chapter 10
PRESENTING YOUR BODY

I once heard Bill Tisdale, a missionary to the Phillippines, give an illustration about surrendering his physical body to the Lord. He described presenting the parts of his body one by one for Christ's use through a prayer like this:

"Lord, here are my eyes. I give them to you. I want them to see only the things you want them to see. Help me to always look at the things you want to look at and avoid the things you do not want to look at. Here are my hands. Work through my hands to do what you want to do. Here are my feet. Guide them to go where you want them to go. I give you the lordship of my body."

That illustration helped me with my difficulty in presenting my body to Christ as a living sacrifice through which He could work. Each time I was tempted to let a part of my body dominate me, I offered that part of my body to Christ so that He could master it and use it for His glory.

The stomach is a means He has provided for me to live but I am not meant to overeat or to eat unhealthily or excessively. He can help me control my eating. "The tongue also is a fire, a world of evil among the parts of the body. It corrupts the whole person, sets the whole course of his life on fire, and is itself set on fire by hell" (James 3:6). But if I present my tongue to God, I do not say anything He does not want me to say. I choose my words carefully to speak kindly and truthfully. If I give my ears to God, I decide to listen only to those things that honor Him.

God's Intentions for Your Body

God created Adam's body from the dust of the earth. "The LORD God formed the man from the dust of the ground and breathed into his nostrils the breath of life, and the man became a living being" (Gen. 2:7). God intends for the body to perform three essential functions:

- Your body identifies you as a unique person. It provides you with individual features so that others can recognize you.
- Your body allows you to participate in the world. You can experience the world through your senses, move about and interact in the physical dimension.
- Your body helps you to communicate with others. Being able to touch, speak, and express yourself physically makes you able to relate to others.

God expected His creation to be fruitful and multiply, to subdue the earth and make it useful, and to master or have dominion over living creatures (see Gen. 1:27, 28). Your body allows you to influence the created order. Because you have mobility, you can move from place to place to perform God's tasks. Because you have strength in your body, you can fulfill assignments for Him.

But the first human beings failed to do what God asked. Instead of being partners with God in ruling the world, they selfishly decided to do things their own way. The result was chaos. When they sinned, their good bodies were invaded by a sinful nature.

Your body can still be used for good. The fact that Jesus was incarnated in a human body testifies to the fact that God looks with favor on the physical body. (see John 1:14). God intends for you to have a high regard for your body because it is the dwelling for His Spirit. "Do you not know that your body is a temple of the Holy Spirit, who is in you, whom you have received from God? You are not your own; you were bought at a price. Therefore honor God with your body" (1 Cor. 6:19, 20). You will not always have your earthly body but someday it will be redeemed for the spiritual body that Jesus wants you to have in heaven (see Rom. 8:23). Christ's incarnation in a human body shows its potential for being restored to its original condition when Christ returns again and gives you a spiritual body like His. In the meantime, you have a responsibility to provide the best dwelling for the Spirit of God.

The Struggle for Control

The potential for your body to be used in positive, Christ-honoring ways is tremendous. However, in reality, your body is still subject to sin and death. Although the body is not evil in itself, it is weak and susceptible to the flesh. God expects you to honor Him with your physical body and to decline to let the flesh, or the sinful nature, take over. The body has the capacity to do good if the flesh is not in control.

Being self-disciplined is not in my nature. I have found that Spirit-control, not self-control, makes the difference. The Holy Spirit can control what I cannot. I must say again and again, "Lord, I can't control this; will you control it?" Then He takes over and controls the part of my life that my physical body might lead me to misuse or misapply. When the Spirit of life is at work in my body, I can make the following commitments.

- I will watch my intake of empty calories that do not add to my nutrition.
- I will exercise regularly.
- I will give my body the amount of rest it needs each day.
- I will examine my eating patterns and find an alternative approach when I realize that I am eating from anxiety or tension rather than from hunger.
- I will monitor my intake of substances, like caffeine, which do not nourish me and may make me irritable.
- I will not use substances like nicotine, alcohol, or other drugs that harm my body.

Becoming an Instrument of Righteousness

How do you realize this potential for righteous living? It is through your identification with Christ in His incarnation, crucifixion, and resurrection. Christ's coming to earth as a human being—His incarnation—condemns sin (see Rom. 8:3), His crucifixion frees you from sin's bondage, and His resurrection gives you life through the Spirit. "We know that our old self was crucified with him so that the body of sin might be done away with, that we should no longer be slaves to sin" (Rom. 6:6).

"In the same way, count yourselves dead to sin but alive to God in Christ Jesus. Therefore do not let sin reign in your mortal body so that you obey its evil desires. Do not offer the parts of your body to sin, as instruments of wickedness, but rather offer yourselves to God, as those who have been brought from death to life; and offer the parts of your body to him as instruments of righteousness. For sin shall not be your master, because you are not under law, but under grace" (Rom. 6:11–14).

Because your old self is crucified with Christ, you are no longer a slave to the body of sin. You can act as the new creation you are in Christ. You can consider your sinful nature, with its lusts and desires, dead; and so you can walk in the Spirit as He directs your thoughts and actions.

"Those who belong to Christ Jesus have crucified the sinful nature with its passions and desires. Since we live by the Spirit, let us keep in step with the Spirit" (Gal. 5:24, 25).

A Living Sacrifice

You are to present your body as a living sacrifice: "Therefore, I urge you, brothers, in view of God's mercy, to offer your bodies as living sacrifices, holy and pleasing to God—this is your spiritual act of worship" (Rom. 12:1). What does that mean? Christ came to change the old practice of offering animal sacrifices for sin when He died on the cross as the ultimate sacrifice. Christ wants you in His service not as a dead sacrifice but as a living one. He wants a life fully given to Him. It means that you do more than give lip service to your faith. It means you will sacrifice every area of your life to Him and will commit your body to holy, righteous living.

Presenting your body to God can be the most freeing, gratifying, and joyful feeling in the world. You have a choice about how your body responds to situations. The decision to present your body as a living sacrifice means that you close the door of the flesh. With the Holy Spirit's help, you can change harmful habits and yield all of your life, not just part of it, to the Master.

The Spiritual Christian

Stop a moment and think about the various parts of your body. Think about your eyes, hands, ears, stomach, sex organs, or tongue. In which of these do you feel you need the most help surrendering to God? Ask Him to help you by making you aware of His presence when you are tempted to use that part of your body in wrong living. Then ask Him to give you victory over that temptation.

Your victory is not automatic. As long as you live in your body, you continually fight the good fight of faith. But God promises you victory. Let me explain in practical terms how to let Christ master your total personality and to enable you to live in the Spirit.

HOW TO LIVE VICTORIOUSLY

1. Ask God, through the Holy Spirit's guidance, to help you to will to do the right thing. "For it is God who works in you to will and to act according to his good purpose" (Phil. 2:13). God helps you to want to do His will and then gives you the ability to do it.

2. Open the door of the spirit to the Spirit of God by asking Him to fill you. "Be filled with the Spirit" (Eph. 5:18). Ask the Holy Spirit to fill your personality and to keep on filling you so He can guide you, teach you, and give you power to be a spiritual person.

3. Close the door of the flesh to Satan by confessing your sins and claiming Christ's crucifixion of the flesh. "I have been crucified with Christ and I no longer live, but Christ lives in me. The life I live in the body, I live by faith in the Son of God, who loved me and gave himself for me" (Gal. 2:20).

4. Renew your mind by saturating it in the Word of God. "Do not conform any longer to the pattern of this world, but be transformed by the renewing of your mind. Then you will be able to test and approve what God's will is—his good, pleasing and perfect will" (Rom. 12:2). As you listen to God and His Word and obey Him, your mind is renewed. You experience the mind of Christ helping you know and understand the will of God.

5. Allow the Holy Spirit to master your emotions by producing the fruit of the Spirit in you. "The fruit of the Spirit is love, joy, peace, patience, kindness, goodness, faithfulness, gentleness and self-control. Against such things there is no law" (Gal. 5:22, 23). As you allow the Spirit of God to fill you, He produces in you the fruit of the Spirit. The fruit of the Spirit helps produce the right emotions in you and helps you control your emotions.

6. Present your body to Christ as an instrument of righteousness. "Therefore do not let sin reign in your mortal body so that you obey its evil desires.

> Do not offer the parts of your body to sin, as instruments of wickedness, but rather offer yourselves to God, as those who have been brought from death to life; and offer the parts of your body to him as instruments of righteousness" (Rom. 6:12, 13). Your body is God's gift to you so you can have an identity, participate in this world, and communicate with others. It is not evil in itself; only the flesh, or your sinful nature, is evil. Jesus came to live in your body and to make it an instrument of righteousness instead of an instrument of sin. Present your body and all of its members to God.

7. Love the Lord your God with all your heart, and with all your soul, and with all your mind, and with all your strength. As you yield yourself to God fully, the Holy Spirit helps you to master your mind, your will, your emotions, your body, and your soul through the power of Christ. As you obey Christ and His commands, He lives in you and you in Him. Christ lives in the world through you. Your inner self is integrated, and you experience peace. You are being filled continually with the Holy Spirit, and you overflow with joy, love, peace, praise, and thanksgiving. Rivers of living water flow out of you to other people as a witness to Christ who lives within you through the Spirit. "May God himself, the God of peace, sanctify you through and through. May your whole spirit, soul and body be kept blameless at the coming of our Lord Jesus Christ. The one who calls you is faithful and he will do it" (1 Thess. 5:23, 24).

The Disciple's Personality presentation has been used many times to win someone to faith in Christ and to help others better understand how to live the Christian life more victoriously. David Carter, while serving as a pastor in Florida, was visiting a couple he had visited several times before. The wife was a Christian, but the husband, an unbeliever, had always been unwilling to listen to a traditional gospel presentation. This time David decided to use the Disciple's Personality to confront the man with his spiritual condition. Drawing the Natural Person and Spiritual Christian diagrams, he asked the man, "Which are you?" The husband pointed to the Natural Person. David asked, "Which would you like to be?" The man pointed to the Spiritual Christian diagram and replied, "I've always wanted to be a Christian." David then led the man to pray to receive Christ as Savior and Lord.

After the prayer, the wife spoke up. "I am not either one." David replied, "I may have a diagram that represents you." When he drew the Worldly Christian diagram, she immediately said, "That's me!" David then led her to rededicate her life to Christ.

Who Are You?

Now, evaluate your own life.

- Are you a natural person whose spirit is dead? Do your bodily senses and your natural desires control you?
- Are you a worldly Christian who has allowed Christ to enter your life but is still being mastered by the desires of the flesh? Is the big "I" still in control?
- Are you a spiritual Christian who has been crucified with Christ and is being controlled by the Holy Spirit?

Spiritual Christians are not perfect, but daily they crucify the flesh and consciously allow the Holy Spirit to fill them. When they are tempted, they invite Christ to fill their lives, and they close the door of the flesh. When they sin, they ask for God's forgiveness and strength to help them overcome the next temptation. They continually seek to offer themselves—mentally, emotionally, and physically—to Christ to be used for His purposes.

Only through the power of the Holy Spirit can this occur, and only when He is invited to come in His awesome presence and power. In the next chapter, I will share with you my life-changing experience of being filled with the Spirit.

Questions for Meditation and Discussion

1. Do you see your body as good or evil? How do you feel about it? What does the Scripture say?

2. What areas of your physical life do you need to surrender to God?

3. Is there a particular body part that causes you the most temptation or struggle? What Scripture could you memorize to apply to this situation?

4. Which of the seven steps to victorious living do you need to learn most?

Chapter 11
BEING FILLED
WITH THE SPIRIT

After I made the decision to follow Christ with all of my heart during my freshman year in college, the Holy Spirit created in me an overwhelming desire to bear witness to Christ. His presence overcame my natural shyness and thrust me several times each week into the streets and bars to witness. However, I was not successful in leading persons to Christ. I memorized Scriptures, studied soul-winning books, and prayed. But something was missing.

One day I received a booklet that told about the experience of D. L. Moody, R. A. Torrey, Billy Sunday, Billy Graham, and others whose ministries had been transformed when they experienced the filling of the Holy Spirit. I had a burning desire to be used by God, but I could find no one who knew how to lead me into such an experience. One day I found a classroom on the third floor of a nearby church and committed myself to pray until I was filled. I chose that room because I didn't know what happened to a person who was filled with the Spirit.

For two hours I prayed, cried, and sought God to be filled, but nothing happened. I went in search of a book that a friend had recommended, *The Holy Spirit: Who He Is and What He Does,* by R. A. Torrey. As I read it, I began to understand that the Holy Spirit is a person who possesses us—not just a power, an influence, or an attitude we possess. I learned that the Holy Spirit, who lives in me, wants to fill me for service.

By the next evening I had finished the book and was ready to follow its instructions to be filled with the Spirit. I confessed all my sins, presented myself fully to God, and asked in faith for the Holy Spirit to fill me. As I confessed my sin, I realized how much the Holy Spirit loved me and had been grieved by my ignoring Him. Then I presented my body, will, emotions, mind, and spirit to be used by God in any way He chose. I accepted by faith the filling of the Holy Spirit. I told God, "I will accept the fact that I am filled with the Spirit on the basis of faith in the Word, no matter what happens afterward." I immediately sensed a deep awareness of the Spirit's love. This sense of the Spirit's presence has grown stronger through the years as my relationship with God has deepened.

The next morning when I went to class, I was so aware of the Spirit's presence that I wanted to move over on the sidewalk to let Him walk beside me. That evening I witnessed to a boy on the street, and he accepted Christ as his Savior. Two nights later, two teenagers received Christ. The following night, a man professed faith in Christ; the night after, another man did.

I remarked to a friend: "I don't see how this can continue. Every night I go out to witness, someone accepts Christ." That night no one did. I asked forgiveness for daring to think I had won those people to Christ myself. God refilled me with His Spirit when I was willing to confess my sin, yield myself to Him, and ask in faith. Once again the people to whom I witnessed accepted Christ. I learned that I must be refilled for each act of service if I expected God to use me.

About a month later, I met a man named Curly Clark in the mission. During the invitation time, I asked him if he wanted to become a Christian, and he said that was why he had come. We went back to the counseling room, and he told me he had been working as a roustabout on an oil rig. Then he said the Lord had been working on him for seventeen days and he knew he needed to come to Christ. "But," he said, "I can't be saved. I was a member of 'Pretty Boy' Floyd's gang and I have killed so many people, both in the war and as a member of this gang, that I'm not even sure how many I've killed. In fact, I've been on death row three times. Each time the governor has pardoned me for different reasons so I've not been executed. But I know I can't be saved because I've killed all those people."

I shared with him that the apostle Paul had killed people and that God had forgiven him. Curly then prayed to give his life to Christ. He was so thrilled his sins had been forgiven that he wanted to tell the world. He said we could even call the police, and he would tell them. Then he looked up and said, "Hey, I want you to pray for my arm! I hurt it on the oil rig, and I'm not able to lift it. Pray that it will be healed!"

I stuttered around and assured him that we would pray but that I was not sure what God would do about it. By that time, some others had joined us in the prayer room. While one of them was praying for him, Curly began to move his arm around, saying, "Hey, I'm healed." (It was surely not my faith that had healed him.)

"Oh," he said, "I need to tell my mother. She has prayed for me for so long." Since she lived only about ten miles away, we offered to drive him there. On the way, Curly wanted to stop at one of the creeks by the road so we could baptize him, but we assured him he could wait until a church could baptize him. It was quite late at night when we arrived and knocked on the farmhouse door. His mother's weak, plaintive voice said, "Oh, Curly." It was evident he had come home many times before drunk and in trouble. When she came to the door, he said, "Mom, I've been saved!" She began praising God, and heaven came down to that little house as we rejoiced.

We were so moved by the experience that four of us stayed up all night praying. God's presence was so powerful that we agreed to pray again the next night. As we did so, another student came in and asked what we were doing. When we shared how God was leading us to pray and confess our sins and seek the filling of the Spirit, the student wanted the same experience in his own life. This was repeated night after night until we had about thirty students gathering in our small dorm room, without our inviting any of them. This started a revival on that campus, and several of those young men became pastors, ministry leaders, and missionaries.

The most important manifestations of the filling of the Spirit in my life have been a deep awareness of the love and presence of God and an increased effectiveness of my ministry. Over the years, the Holy Spirit has repeatedly filled me for each task of service. Whenever I have sinned, I have asked Him to refill me, and He has done so. The filling of the Spirit energizes and empowers different gifts in different persons, but in every case the result brings glory to Jesus and attracts others to Him.

$\mathcal{W}$hat $\mathcal{I}$t $\mathcal{M}$eans to $\mathcal{B}e$ $\mathcal{F}$illed

Every person who has been born of the Spirit has the Holy Spirit living in his or her heart. Paul told us, "It is God who makes both us and you stand firm in Christ. He anointed us, set his seal of ownership on us, and put his Spirit in our hearts as a deposit, guaranteeing what is to come" (2 Cor.

1:21–22). "The Spirit himself testifies with our spirit that we are God's children" (Rom. 8:16). "And if anyone does not have the Spirit of Christ, he does not belong to Christ" (Rom. 8:9). If you have given your life to Christ, He lives in you through His Spirit. The Holy Spirit is God's down payment, His earnest deposit. God intends to demonstrate the full sum of Himself in you and through you.

A distinct difference exists between having the Spirit of God in you and being filled with the Spirit—just as there is a difference between a small amount of water in a cup and a cup overflowing with water. The disciples were examples of this difference. Before Pentecost they had the Spirit of Christ; before His ascension, Jesus had breathed on them and said "Receive the Holy Spirit" (John 20:22). This allowed them to take up His mission, which they could accomplish only under the Spirit's leadership. Still, Jesus instructed them to wait for the outpouring of the Spirit. Up until this time, the disciples had sought their own good first (Mark 10:35–41), had been cowardly and had run away when their lives were threatened (Mark 14:50). They were still looking for Jesus to establish God's kingdom on earth in a human sense (Acts 1:6).

At Pentecost a major change occurred in their lives. When the Holy Spirit came in His fullness on the church, the disciples were filled with the Spirit. They preached boldly with faith and authority, allowed God to work miracles through them, proclaimed Christ at the risk of their lives, and were even martyred for the sake of the gospel.

God wants you to be filled and overflowing with His Spirit too. "Do not get drunk on wine, which leads to debauchery. Instead, be filled with the Spirit" (Eph. 5:18). As you yield yourself to God, He takes control of every facet of your personality. Your inner self is integrated, and you experience constant fellowship with Him. Jesus spoke of the Spirit's overflowing you: "'Whoever believes in me, as the Scripture has said, streams of living water will flow from within him.' By this he meant the Spirit, whom those who believed in him were later to receive" (John 7:38, 39).

The Holy Spirit wants to flow through you like the living water Jesus mentioned. Whenever the disciples in the book of Acts encountered believers who were not filled with the Spirit (and they could tell the difference), they prayed for them to be filled.

Many of today's Christians face the same problem as the "unfilled" believers—trying to fight spiritual battles with human resources. Most Christians live and serve as if Pentecost never happened. They try to obey the commands of Christ in their own strength, yet they wonder how Satan so often outsmarts and overpowers them. They ignore the mission of the Holy

Spirit, who came to continue Jesus' role of inspiring, empowering, and guiding them. For them, the third member of Trinity—the Holy Spirit—is almost "the unknown God." They think of Him only as an influence, an attitude, or a way to express the fact that God is everywhere.

You may have tried to witness or teach a Bible study without relying on the Holy Spirit's power. You may have tried to solve a problem in your personal life, such as dealing with a rebellious child or improving an estranged relationship, without asking God to fill you with His Spirit. If so, it was probably a frustrating situation and may have left you feeling empty and ineffective.

Let me give you another way to visualize the difference between operating in the power of the Spirit and operating in your own power. The Christian life is like trying to cross a lake in a boat. You can grab the oars and row hard. You may make it across, but it will involve great effort and perseverance. Or you can hoist the sail, and let the wind of the Spirit carry you across that lake. The power and direction, then, come from a source outside you. If you submit to that power, the crossing will be much quicker, more successful, and more fun!

You can participate in many of the disciplines taught in this book through self-discipline and willpower. However, the infilling of the Holy Spirit will cause you to desire, even to thirst after, these things. I have seen many disciples who have been filled with the Spirit craving the Word of God, praying unceasingly, and eagerly sharing the gospel. Ministering to people and spending time with other believers becomes an opportunity and a joy, and they experience a power and giftedness to do so that is beyond their own ability.

The secret lies in experiencing the Holy Spirit's presence and power as the disciples did at Pentecost. The event of Pentecost cannot be repeated even as Calvary cannot be repeated. Yet Christians can lay hold of the power of Pentecost just as surely as they can experience the redemption of Calvary.

The Work of the Spirit

When you are born of the Spirit, your spirit is made alive, and you are able to respond spiritually. The Holy Spirit helps you understand spiritual things. "The man without the Spirit does not accept the things that come from the Spirit of God, for they are foolishness to him, and he cannot understand them, because they are spiritually discerned" (1 Cor. 2:14). Without the Spirit, a person can understand nothing of God. The Holy Spirit helps you understand the truths of God and recall Jesus' teachings. Jesus said, "The Counselor, the Holy Spirit, whom the Father will send in my name, will teach you all things and will remind you of everything I have said to you" (John 14:26).

Another responsibility of the Holy Spirit is to convict the world. According to John 16:8–11, the Holy Spirit convicts people of sin because they do not believe in Jesus. He convicts the world of unrighteousness as measured by the sinless life of Jesus, and judges and condemns Satan and anyone who follows Satan.

Not only does the Holy Spirit make you aware of the truth, but He also does God's work through you and other believers. He enables you to be Christ's witness. "You will receive power when the Holy Spirit comes on you; and you will be my witnesses in Jerusalem, and in all Judea and Samaria, and to the ends of the earth" (Acts 1:8). It was by the power of the Holy Spirit that the apostles were able to continue the miracles of Jesus: teaching, healing, even raising people from the dead! "'Not by might nor by power, but My spirit says the LORD Almighty" (Zech. 4:6).

Filled without Limit

A true disciple lets the Spirit of God continually fill and control his or her entire personality. You have the Spirit of God dwelling in you if you belong to Jesus. You may treat Him as a guest, a servant, a tenant, or as Lord and Master—the owner of the property. But the Spirit will not fill you completely until you acknowledge Christ's lordship and submit to His personal and divine authority. Then your entire personality is cleansed as God's Spirit controls your spirit. As God sanctifies your personality (1 Thess. 5:23), He and you enjoy mutual fellowship.

In his book *The Full Blessing of Pentecost*, Andrew Murray presents seven powerful observations about a Christian's being filled with the Holy Spirit.

1. It is the will of God that every one of His children should live entirely and unceasingly under the control of the Holy Spirit.

2. Without being filled with the Spirit, it is utterly impossible that an individual Christian or a church can ever live or work as God desires.

3. Everywhere and in everything we see the proofs, in the life and experience of Christians, that this blessing is but little enjoyed in the Church, and alas! is but little sought for.

4. This blessing is prepared for us and God waits to bestow it. Our faith may expect it with the greatest confidence.

5. The great hindrance in the way is that the self-life, and the world, which it uses for its own service and pleasure, usurp the place that Christ ought to occupy.

6. We cannot be filled with the Spirit until we are prepared to yield ourselves to be led by the Lord Jesus to forsake and sacrifice every thing for this pearl of great price.[1]

Now read the following quotation by L. L. Letgers. As you read, think about how your life resembles or does not resemble this description. "Your evidence that you are filled with the Spirit is that Jesus becomes everything to you. You see Him. You are occupied with Him. You are fully satisfied with Jesus. He becomes real, and when you witness about Him, the Holy Spirit witnesses with you regarding the truth about Him. Jesus is your Lord and Master and you rest in His Lordship. . . . The real evidence of a Spirit-filled life is first, that others see the fruit of the Spirit, and second, that you in your own private life see in the Book the things of Jesus and that you are personally rejoicing in Him, and are occupied with Him."[2]

Be Filled

Ephesians 5:18 commands us to "be filled with the Spirit." God's purpose is to fill you continually and to flow through you to others. You are not to be a container but a conduit or a channel for Him. The filling of the Spirit enables God to communicate His message to others through you. If we examine the meaning of this verse in the original language, we learn four important facts about how to be filled with the Spirit. The phrase "be filled" is:

- Passive voice. Passive means that you yourself can do nothing. Someone has to do it to you. Only God can fill you. You cannot cause yourself to be filled.
- Present tense. You are to be filled now.
- Continuous action. Present tense in Greek indicates continuous action. It means to keep on being filled. Although your conversion was a one-time experience, the filling of the Spirit is not. You need to be continually filled. Envision a pipe through which water passes at all times. If the Spirit is filling you, He is always operating through you as He ministers to others.
- Imperative mood. "Be filled" is an order, a command to all Christians. It is not just an option or something you can dismiss because you do not understand it. It is a teaching of God's Word.

In his sermon on the day of Pentecost, Peter responded to the question, "Brothers, what shall we do?" with this admonition, "Repent and be baptized, every one of you, in the name of Jesus Christ for the forgiveness of your sins. And you will receive the gift of the Holy Spirit" (Acts 2:37–38). To repent is to confess your sin, disobedience, emptiness, and need for God's cleansing. "If we confess our sins, he is faithful and just and will forgive us our sins and purify us from all unrighteousness" (1 John 1:9). He exhorted them to be baptized by water as a submission of every part of themselves to the lordship of Christ. Then God's response would be to pour Himself out upon them in the person of the Holy Spirit.

You may not feel that you have experienced the full measure of God's Spirit in your life. If you will surrender your life to Him, He will gladly come and move through you. Ask God to fill, control, and empower you. "If you then, though you are evil, know how to give good gifts to your children, how much more will your Father in heaven give the Holy Spirit to those who ask him!" (Luke 11:13). Believe God has answered your prayer.

My initial experience of being filled with the Spirit came as I was alone in prayer. I believe God was faithful to fulfill the desire of my heart. I can sum up how one is filled with the Spirit in three steps:

1. Confess your sin, disobedience, emptiness, and need for God's cleansing (1 John 1:9).

2. Present every member of your body to be made a righteous instrument in God's hands (Rom. 12:1).

3. Ask God to fill, control, and empower you and believe that God has answered your prayer (Luke 11:13; 1 John 1:9).

In Scripture, we see additional models for the filling of the Spirit. The Spirit was poured out in the midst of believers who were praying together (Acts 2:1–4), during a sermon (Acts 10:44), and through the presence, prayers, and laying on of hands of other believers (Acts 8:15–17). Only God does the filling, not other believers. But like many of our growth experiences, receiving the Spirit often happens within the context of the body of Christ, the fellowship of believers.

God's Purposes in Filling You

God has a double purpose for filling you with His Spirit. First, God wants to develop Christlike character in you. Galatians 5 indicates that we are to walk, to "keep in step" with the Spirit (vv. 16, 25), be led by the Spirit (v. 18), and live by the Spirit (v. 25). This is achieved through the fruit of the Spirit and as God replaces the natural tendencies of the flesh with the godly responses of the Spirit. We will discuss this further in the next chapter.

The Holy Spirit accomplishes the second purpose, equipping you for ministry, by bestowing spiritual gifts. He empowers you to minister to others through the gifts He has given you. When you see people who are filled with the Spirit, you immediately sense that they want to minister. They want to join God in His work and let Him work through them. Only the continual filling and refilling of the Holy Spirit can produce this desire. Every believer should know his or her spiritual gifts and should allow the Holy Spirit to develop them.

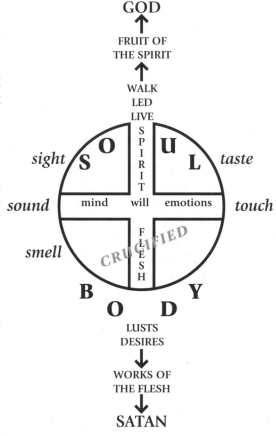

What Are Spiritual Gifts?

Spiritual gifts are spiritual abilities given to believers by the Holy Spirit to equip them to carry out God's work in the world. "There are different kinds of gifts, but the same Spirit. There are different kinds of service, but the same Lord. There are different kinds of working, but the same God works all of them in all men. Now to each one the manifestation of the Spirit is given for the common good. . . . All these are the work of one and the same Spirit, and he gives them to each one, just as he determines" (1 Cor. 12:4–7, 11). "We have different gifts, according to the grace given us" (Rom. 12:6).

The word *gifts* in these verses is a translation of the Greek word *charismata*, which means "gifts of grace." It refers to gifts based on the love of the giver, not on the merit of the ones who receive them. Just as you are saved by God's grace, you are also given spiritual gifts by God's grace. He gives them to you not for your personal benefit but to equip you for His service.

Spiritual gifts differ from spiritual fruit. The fruit of the Spirit, listed in Galatians 5:22–23, are character traits of the Disciple's Personality. Although no Christian is expected to possess all spiritual gifts, every Christian should seek to develop and exhibit all the fruit of the Spirit. These Christlike qualities are to characterize your life, while spiritual gifts enable you to serve God with your life. Spiritual fruit represents the kind of person you are to be, while spiritual gifts emphasize what you are equipped to do. While spiritual fruit is developed within, spiritual gifts are given from without.

Spiritual gifts also differ from talents. Talents are natural abilities; gifts are spiritual abilities. Talents depend on genetics; gifts, on spiritual endowment. Talents inspire or entertain; gifts are used to build up the church. You receive your talents when you are born physically. You receive your spiritual gifts when you are born-again spiritually. Both Christians and non-Christians possess talents. A spiritual gift is a spiritual ability that only Christians possess.

For example, faith is a gift; the ability to sing is a talent. Although talents and spiritual gifts are not the same, both are God-given. Christians should develop their talents fully and should use them in God's service. You may be able to use your talent in combination with your spiritual gift. For example, the gift of encouragement or evangelism may be exercised through the medium of music.

To Whom Are Spiritual Gifts Given?

"Now to each one the manifestation of the Spirit is given for the common good" (1 Cor. 12:7). "All these are the work of one and the same Spirit, and he gives them to each one, just as he determines" (1 Cor. 12:11). "Each one should use whatever gift he has received to serve others, faithfully administering God's grace in its various forms" (1 Pet. 4:10).

Every believer has been given at least one spiritual gift. In God's family of grace, everyone is important. Every child of God has the ability and privilege to exercise his or her spiritual gifts in ministry. You cannot choose your own spiritual gifts. God distributes them as He thinks best. The gifts of the Spirit are just that—gifts. Because you do not earn them or work for them, you have no grounds for bragging about them. God knows how each part can best be used in the body of Christ to help the whole operate effectively and efficiently.

First Corinthians 12 and Romans 12 list some of the spiritual gifts. Read through them. Do you recognize any that you believe the Holy Spirit has given you? If so, to what extent have you developed your gifts? In the final chapter of this book, I will share more with you about discovering and developing your spiritual gifts and how gifts function together within the church.

Fruit produces character, and gifts produce effectiveness in ministry. Trying to achieve either one by your own efforts is an exercise in futility. God never meant for you to produce these good works in or of yourself. Jesus commanded the disciples not to leave Jerusalem until they had been filled with the Spirit because He knew their mission and ministry would be hopelessly ineffective in their own strength. "I am going to send you what my Father has promised; but stay in the city until you have been clothed with power from on high" (Luke 24:49). "Do not leave Jerusalem, but wait for the gift my Father promised, which you have heard me speak about. For John baptized with water, but in a few days you will be baptized with the Holy Spirit" (Acts 1:4, 5).

The way to walk and live in the Spirit is to be continuously led and filled by the Holy Spirit, allowing Him to walk and live through you. Then you will begin to experience the victorious life of a disciple.

Questions for Meditation and Discussion

1. What are the steps to being filled with the Spirit?

2. Have you experienced the filling of the Holy Spirit? If so, do you regularly seek to renew that filling by confessing any known sin and yielding yourself anew to the Spirit of God?

3. What evidence exists to demonstrate the filling of the Holy Spirit in your life?

4. How is the Holy Spirit within you currently motivating and equipping you to minister to others?

Chapter 12
LIVING VICTORIOUSLY

Once as my wife and I were flying home from speaking to missionaries overseas, a young woman who attended the conference sat down next to us and told one of the most amazing stories of victorious living I have ever heard. She will remain anonymous to protect her security since she continues to serve Christ in a non-Christian country.

Her life began anything but victoriously. The young woman was one of six children of an alcoholic father. By the age of thirteen she was living on the street on her own. From there her life spiraled downward. Yet through determination she went to college, got a degree in elementary education, and started teaching. She noticed that one of her students, a nine-year-old girl, seemed different. The girl helped erase the chalkboard and clean the room after school, and the two became good friends.

One day the student asked whether the woman went to church. The teacher answered that she used to go to confession with her mother. The girl asked the teacher to help her study some Scriptures she wanted to learn before being baptized. The first Scripture was John 3:16. As the woman read it, she cried, unable to imagine that God loved her after all she had done.

The woman then attended a church service and cried all the way through it. "I talked to my live-in boyfriend and told him that we needed to change," she said. One day when he was away, she returned home to find a man ransacking her apartment in search of money. When she could give him no money, the man raped her. The woman recounted what happened next: "After it was over, I opened the Bible to John 3:16, which was the only verse I knew. Then the man, who was deaf, wrote on a piece of paper that he knew what he had done was wrong but his mother was sick and needed money. He wrote asking if I could forgive him. I responded, 'If God is willing to forgive me for all I've done, how can I refuse to forgive you?' We knelt, and he asked God for forgiveness. Asking forgiveness for my sinful lifestyle, I turned my life over to Christ. Two weeks later I went back to church and shared my decision to follow Christ. My boyfriend would not change, so I moved out."

The woman then began praying for her parents' salvation. Six years later they gave their lives to Christ following a Bible study she had begun in their home. She began serving at church, then went on mission trips to Mexico and Belize. Now she serves as a missionary in a country that allows little access to the gospel. She concluded her story: "I praise God for His goodness and His love. I am thankful I can show His love to people who don't know anything about Him."

As she returned to her seat on the plane, I said to myself, "O the depth of the riches both of the wisdom and knowledge of God! how unsearchable are his judgments" (Rom. 11:33, KJV). I understood even more clearly the victory we have in Christ.

Alert to the Enemy

A Spirit-filled life leads to a victorious life. The spiritual Christian is not perfect. But daily this disciple crucifies the flesh and consciously allows the Spirit to fill him or her. When tempted, he or she opens the door to Jesus and closes the door to Satan. "Thanks be to God that, though you used to be slaves to sin, you wholeheartedly obeyed the form of teaching to which you were entrusted. You have been set free from sin and have become slaves to righteousness" (Rom. 6:17, 18).

By learning how your personality works, you can know how to live a victorious life. But understanding these concepts does not stop sin in the world. Satan is seeking to devour anyone he can: "Be self-controlled and alert. Your enemy the devil prowls around like a roaring lion looking for someone to devour" (1 Pet. 5:8). Victorious living involves being aware of Satan's potential hold on you and keeping the enemy at a distance. Satan's weapons are powerful. Only a foolish Christian fails to take him seriously. Even though the human personality is God's highest creation, that personality is damaged when a person chooses the way of sin. The enemy is alive, vigilant, and eager to destroy you. He constantly looks for a weak point in your personality so he can cause you to stumble. He sees moments of distress, doubt, fear, and pain as golden opportunities to erode your trust in God.

Victory in Jesus

Your sinful nature, the world, and the devil are forces that fight against the Spirit of God within you. Yet, the Spirit is always stronger. The Holy Spirit can help you rest in the Lord and exercise self-control while you wait for God's help. When Jesus died on the cross and rose from the grave, He won the victory over sin. He promised His disciples would share in His victory. "Everyone born of God overcomes the world. This is the victory that has overcome the world, even our faith. Who is it that overcomes the world? Only he who believes that Jesus is the Son of God" (1 John 5:4, 5).

Jesus told his disciples, "I have told you these things, so that in me you may have peace. In this world you will have trouble. But take heart! I have overcome the world" (John 16:33). You are not alone when you resist Satan's attacks. Christ has gone before you to provide a victory for you. In His death on the cross He condemned sin in the flesh, He overcame the world, and He destroyed the work of Satan. "The reason the Son of God appeared was to destroy the devil's work" (1 John 3:8). He has also given you the Holy Spirit to strengthen you in times of temptation.

Resisting Temptation

To understand how to experience victory in the heat of daily struggles, first understand how sin takes root in your life. Sin begins with temptation. The Bible says that Jesus was tempted in every way you are tempted; yet He did not sin. "We do not have a high priest who is unable to sympathize with our weaknesses, but we have one who has been tempted in every way, just as we are—yet was without sin" (Heb. 4:15). Furthermore, "Because he himself suffered when he was tempted, he is able to help those who are being tempted" (Heb. 2:18). For every temptation, God provides a way of escape. "No temptation has seized you except what is common to man. And God is faithful; he will not let you be tempted beyond what you can bear. But when you are tempted, he will also provide a way out so that you can stand up under it" (1 Cor. 10:13).

When Jesus was in the Garden of Gethsamene with His disciples the night before His death, He said, "Watch and pray so that you will not fall into temptation. The spirit is willing, but the body is weak" (Matt. 26:41). He knew that they would need more than willing spirits to withstand the temptation ahead of them. He knew that they needed to be fortified with prayer. Prayer does not prevent temptation. Temptation will always occur. Prayer can give you the spiritual strength to resist it.

Evil thoughts and desires may pass through your mind. That is temptation. Temptation itself is not sin. Dwelling on those thoughts, letting the mind entertain the idea, is sin. If you "window shop" for sin, the devil will invite you to buy. Even if you say, "Oh, no, just looking," the openness to temptation often leads to sin. That is the reason Timothy was encouraged to run away from sin: "Flee the evil desires of youth, and pursue righteousness, faith, love and peace, along with those who call on the Lord out of a pure heart" (2 Tim. 2:22). Read James 4:1–8. The first four verses list the source of

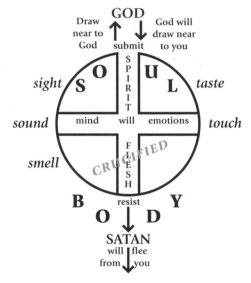

our problems in living the Christian life. They are the desires that battle within us, our wrong motives, our pleasure-seeking lusts. Verse 5 claims that "the Spirit Whom He has caused to dwell in us yearns over us—and yearns for the Spirit (to be welcome)—with a jealous love" (AMP). The Spirit is aggressively concerned about your victory. Verses 7 and 8 give us the key to gaining victory. "Submit yourselves, then, to God. Resist the devil, and he will flee from you. Come near to God and he will come near to you."

First, we must submit to the Spirit. As we draw near to God, He draws near to us. Then, in the power of the Spirit, we can resist Satan and Satan will flee from us. If we attempt to resist Satan in our own strength, we will fail.

But if we send Christ to the door when Satan knocks, Satan will back out quickly, knowing he has the wrong house!

Examining the warring components of your personality is challenging, often requiring that you admit your weaknesses and temptations even though you like to think of yourself as someone who does not easily stumble. Sometimes submitting your weaknesses to the life-changing power of the Spirit requires changing an unhealthy habit and sometimes it means rearranging your entire lifestyle.

Bob and Janie Garrett, missionaries to Argentina, shared this story about Richardo, one of the members of their *MasterLife* group. Richardo had inherited his family's meat-packing business. In the cattle lands of Argentina, that made him a wealthy man. One night Richardo invited the Garretts over for dinner. As they sat around enjoying the meal and company, Richardo said, "Bob, I want to ask you some questions about my business life. There is no way I can turn in the right tax forms and keep my books the way they ought to be kept and still make money. I tried to do it one time and the government inspector told me I should change it. So we changed it the way he said, but I don't feel right about it. What should I do?"

Bob knew it would be too easy to condemn and perhaps too difficult to help so he suggested only that they pray and ask the Holy Spirit to guide Richardo into all truth and reveal how he could be more upright in his business dealings. They took the situation to the group and began to pray. Richardo also shared his concern that since he was on the job morning to night, he had little time for his family or church. As they prayed, Richardo became convicted that he should sell the family business. His parents who were not Christians did not understand this at all, but Richardo felt at peace about it. In fact, it was during one of the group sessions when a man came by and he and Richardo went into a back bedroom and closed the deal.

Richardo was able to sell the business for a good price. Then he reinvested the money in a parking garage, realigned his personal priorities, and is now leading his church to plant a church in another neighborhood of Buenos Aires. In an added blessing, the parking garage provided a job for one of the unemployed men of the church and became the site of the men's prayer meeting each week.

$\mathcal{I}n$ the $\mathcal{C}arpenter's$ $\mathcal{S}hop$

What happens when you set aside your natural inclinations and seek to become increasingly more Christlike? The Holy Spirit will develop your character. It is much like buying a "fixer-up" house, that "handyman's dream home." When Jesus purchased you with His blood, He bought you and has now brought you into His carpenter's shop. In order to make you into a dwelling that is holy and inhabitable by the Holy Spirit, He must remodel. The first step in remodeling is always tearing down and getting rid of what you do not want. Only when the old is removed can you build in the new and desirable characteristics.

What kind of character will you have? You have learned about the difference between the old person and the new person. Now you will want to focus on specific ways you can develop your character with the help of the Holy Spirit. Galatians 5:16–25 is one of three similar Bible passages that illustrate what it means to leave the old life behind, or tear it down, and to take up, or build, the new life. Read the passages below that describe the various behaviors that a Christian will want to be rid of and will want to acquire.

So I say, live by the Spirit, and you will not gratify the desires of the sinful nature. For the sinful nature desires what is contrary to the Spirit, and the Spirit what is contrary to the sinful nature. They are in conflict with each other, so that you do not do what you want. But if you are led by the Spirit, you are not under law.

The acts of the sinful nature are obvious: sexual immorality, impurity and debauchery; idolatry and witchcraft; hatred, discord, jealousy, fits of rage, selfish ambition, dissensions, factions and envy; drunkenness, orgies, and the like. I warn you, as I did before, that those who live like this will not inherit the kingdom of God.

But the fruit of the Spirit is love, joy, peace, patience, kindness, goodness, faithfulness, gentleness and self-control. Against such things there is no law. Those who belong to Christ Jesus have crucified the sinful nature with its passions and desires. Since we live by the Spirit, let us keep in step with the Spirit (Gal. 5:16–25).

In the following passage, compare the statements that describe the tendencies of the old life before Christ with those that describe the tendencies of the new life after Christ.

Put to death, therefore, whatever belongs to your earthly nature: sexual immorality, impurity, lust, evil desires and greed, which is idolatry. Because of these, the wrath of God is coming. You used to walk in these ways, in the life you once lived. But now you must rid yourselves of all such things as these: anger, rage, malice, slander, and filthy language from your lips. Do not lie to each other, since you have taken off your old self with its practices and have put on the new self, which is being renewed in knowledge in the image of its Creator.

Therefore, as God's chosen people, holy and dearly loved, clothe your-selves with compassion, kindness, humility, gentleness and patience. Bear with each other and forgive whatever grievances you may have against one another. Forgive as the Lord forgave you. And over all these virtues put on love, which binds them all together in perfect unity (Col. 3:5–10, 12–14).

Now read Ephesians 4:17 through 5:10. Hear the words to the old per-son: "No longer live as the Gentiles do," "Put off your old self," "Get rid of . . . ," "Do not give the devil a foothold," or "Do not grieve the Holy Spirit." Hear also the commands to the new person: "Be made new in the atti-tude of your minds," "Put on the new self," "Be like God in true righteous-ness and holiness," "Live a life of love," "Live as children of light," or "Find out what pleases the Lord." As you learn to live more like Jesus, you will dis-cover the stark contrast between the ways of the world and the lifestyle of the Christian.

𝓑uilding 𝓒hristlike 𝓒haracter

As you read these passages, identify any specific behavior(s) you want to be rid of. Look for a trait or action to replace it. Then ask the Holy Spirit to reveal to you each time you begin to act in the old way and to show you His desired response. If you take time to meditate on these passages on a regular basis, the Holy Spirit will begin to develop the character of Jesus in you. It will take time to listen to the conviction of the Spirit, to let Him teach you the better way, and to formulate a plan of growth.

For example, perhaps you use impure language. You read in the Scripture, "Among you there must not be even a hint of sexual immorality, or of any kind of impurity, or of greed, because these are improper for God's holy peo-ple. Nor should there be obscenity, foolish talk or coarse joking, which are out of place, but rather thanksgiving" (Eph. 5:3, 4). The Holy Spirit helps you see that your profanity or "dirty jokes" shock people and that it impacts your Christian witness. You agree with the Holy Spirit that you have sinned in your speech and that, beginning today, you will ask Him to help you speak and choose words that honor Christ and reflect a thankful heart.

You might have a quick temper demonstrated in fits of rage. In your quiet time, you read that "the acts of the sinful nature are obvious: . . . hatred, dis-cord, jealousy, fits of rage" (Gal. 5:19, 20) but that one of the fruits of the Spirit is self-control (Gal. 5:23). You ask the Holy Spirit to help you deal with your anger. You decide to receive prayer in your small group about this issue.

You may choose to see a counselor to work on the root of the anger. You could also agree to be accountable to one or more believers and to call them each week with your progress.

Developing Christlike character does not happen overnight. It is a life-long process of spiritual transformation. Having the new character as your natural, first response may take weeks or months but as you submit to the Spirit each day, you will see daily improvements. Do not give up. Remember, one of the fruits of the Spirit is patience!

Questions for Meditation and Discussion

1. Do you usually have a victorious lifestyle? How can you experience victory instead of repeated defeat?

2. What areas of behavior has the Holy Spirit indicated He needs to remodel in your life?

3. How can you learn to resist temptation in these areas?

4. How has what you have learned about the Disciple's Personality made a difference in your life?

HOW TO WRITE YOUR TESTIMONY

One of the members of a church I served as pastor told me of a tragic experience. She and her sister got together around the piano at a reunion and began to sing songs they had learned as children. After singing a song about heaven, the sister asked how she could be saved and go to heaven. Carrie couldn't tell her. Not long after, the sister died—without Christ. Carrie said, "Oh, Brother Avery, if I had just known how to tell my sister how to be saved like I am, she would be in heaven today."

God intends for you to participate with Him to communicate His good news to the world. One of the ways He wants you to do that is by bearing witness to His work in your life. To "witness" means to give evidence. You have evidence of a changed life through the indwelling Christ. You need to verbalize that witness—to tell others who Christ is, what He has done, and how much He means to you. The following guidelines will help you prepare a basic testimony of your salvation experience and then help you to enlarge or adapt it to meet the needs of a particular witnessing opportunity. I have discovered that when people write a brief account of their personal testimony for Christ that can be given verbally in about three minutes, God will give them opportunities to witness, and they will be able to expand their testimony to any length needed.

I am going to ask you to follow the instructions below as you read them. You will be tempted to skip the exercise. Don't yield to that temptation. It may take you several hours or you may write your testimony over several days. Regardless, don't let Satan cheat you out of a deep spiritual experience and keep you unprepared to witness. Finish writing your testimony before reading the next part of the book. Satan will do all he can to hinder you. Recognize this as a spiritual battle and ask God to give you the victory (see Eph. 6:11–18).

WHAT ARE THE ESSENTIALS?

The apostle Paul knew how to verbalize his witness. Furthermore, he did so at every opportunity to everyone who would listen. The Scriptures provide at least two detailed records of Paul giving his personal testimony: Acts 22:1–15 and Acts 26:9–20. In both cases, he included four facts in the same order: (1) He had not always followed Christ; (2) God had begun to deal with Paul's rebellion; (3) Paul received Christ as Lord; (4) Paul's new life was centered on Christ's purposes.

You may be amazed to discover that most unbelievers have never heard anyone share information of the type Paul shared in his testimony. Each conversion experience is different. Therefore, your testimony of how you came to know Christ is personal and unique. It is evidence that only you can give. No one else can duplicate it.

Although your conversion experience is unique, it can probably be outlined in much the same way Paul outlined his, especially if you became a Christian as an adult. In verbalizing your witness, share the same four types of information that Paul shared, even though the story itself will be quite different. Even Christians who are skilled in giving their testimonies and in adapting them to specific situations begin with the basic testimony of conversion. Regardless of how they enlarge it or adapt it, their testimonies follow this basic outline.

- My life and attitudes before I followed Christ
- How I realized that God was speaking to me
- How I became a Christian
- What being a Christian means to me

EXPANDING THE BASIC OUTLINE

As you become more skilled at witnessing, various situations will call for you to give your testimony differently. Because each situation will be unique, your testimony will be unique to each situation. You will nearly always follow the basic outline, but a particular situation may call for you to say more about one point than the others. Or you may discover that the person to whom you are witnessing identifies more closely with different illustrations and examples.

It is helpful to gather and write down background material for each point in your testimony to provide for the diverse situations. Use the following steps to write your own testimony. It is helpful to do this in several sittings. First, write the basic outline. Then come back and fill in more details. Do this as many times as you need. If you spend time over several days thinking through your testimony, you will be surprised at all that God will show you. This exercise may stir deep emotions as you think back over your life. You may understand for the first time how God has been working in your circumstances to help you grow in Him. There may be themes and patterns you have never recognized before. Be prepared! Even while you are just working on this, you may see God give you opportunities to begin giving it!

One of the most common approaches to writing your testimony is to do it chronologically. This approach is better when enough significant experiences happened before your conversion to distinguish clearly between your life before and after conversion. If you choose the chronological approach, skip to the next heading.

CHRONOLOGICAL

1	2	3	4

If, however, you were saved as a child and/or do not remember enough significant events before your conversion for the other person to identify with, then you may choose the thematic approach. In that case, begin by focusing on an experience, problem, issue, or feeling, such as a fear of death, a desire for success, a basic character flaw, a search for identity, or a crisis. In this case, you will use the flashback approach as follows.

- A theme, need, or problem.
- How I became a Christian.
- What being a Christian means to me.

THEMATIC

2	3	1

You may begin your testimony with your current situation, such as:
- I have discovered how not to worry.

- I have discovered a purpose for living.
- I have overcome loneliness.
- I no longer have a fear of death.
- I have discovered how to integrate my life into a meaningful whole.

State the theme and tell how you solved your problem. This flashback technique can take the place of telling your experience before conversion. Many people have full assurance that they are saved, but have trouble identifying the exact time of their conversion. The date is not as important as your personal relationship with Christ as Savior and Lord. The flashback technique allows you to give the facts without detailing when they happened. That way you can still explain the four facts of the gospel without explaining how you came to understand each one.

Regardless of which approach you use, include the following elements.

WHAT ARE THE ELEMENTS?

1. *My Life and Attitudes before I Followed Christ.* Write an interesting introduction about your life and attitudes before following Christ. Give a few brief facts to set the scene. Do not make all of it sound bad. Share good things as well. This allows others to identify with what you say.

Share enough details about yourself to help them relate to you as an ordinary person. Be prepared to talk about different aspects of your life before you became a Christian: where you lived, what you did, your interests and hobbies, your priorities, etc. Be brief. Do not reminisce too much about details that would be unimportant to a stranger. Use concrete words and word pictures to describe the situation.

Share details about your life which indicate that you needed greater meaning and purpose or the ability to overcome failings. Some examples are temper, habits, greed, and self-centeredness. Your purpose is not to confess your evil life but to tell your story.

2. *How I Realized God Was Speaking to Me.* Highlight the events that led to your salvation (how you realized your need). Explain how God began to show you His love while you were still an unbeliever. Be general enough for a person to identify with your description. How, when, and where did God get through to you? What person(s) did He use? Did He use a book, a film, or a Scripture? Did He shape events to lead you into His waiting presence? Avoid using the name of your church, your specific age, or the date of your conversion unless the person hearing your testimony has the same background.

3. *How I Became a Christian.* Summarize the facts of salvation (how you became a Christian). Share how you trusted your life to Christ. Let the Bible be your authority rather than what someone said to you. Say, "Here is a Bible verse that made me realize what Jesus did for me." Be sure to include how you prayed to surrender your life to Christ.

Be careful not to use "church language." Be sensitive to those who will not understand the meaning of words or phrases like "repented," "walked the aisle," "asked Jesus into my heart," "was saved." Also be sensitive to the fact that the person may have been frightened away by high-pressure tactics or by a zealous but tactless witness.

Be sure to include the four essential concepts of the gospel:
- Sin is an I-controlled life. It is failing or refusing to be what God wants you to be.
- Sin's penalty is separation from God both in this life and in the life to come for eternity.
- Christ paid the penalty for sin when He took your sin to the cross, accepted the judgment for it, and made it possible for you to be accepted by the Father.
- Receiving Christ is acknowledging to Him that you were a sinner, accepting forgiveness from Him, inviting Him to come into your life as Savior and Lord, and trusting Him to do for you the things you could never do for yourself.

If you do not remember how you came to realize each of these concepts in your own life, state them without a time frame. Be sure you can say with confidence that this was a personal experience of your own and that you have received Christ and are following Him as Lord.

4. *What Being a Christian Means to Me.* Share the results of knowing Christ as Lord and Savior (what being a Christian means to you). Quickly summarize the difference Christ has made in your life. Give one or two concrete examples with which the listener may identify.

Be careful not to give the impression that becoming a Christian automatically solved all of your problems. Mention the struggles of your continual pilgrimage. Say something like, "Being a Christian doesn't mean I don't have any problems, but now Christ helps me through them." Describe your lifestyle as a Christian. You may not realize how different your lifestyle is from that of an unbeliever. Many things you take for granted will be significant to a non-Christian. Describe the changes that have taken place in your relationships with family, use of money, purpose of life, attitude toward death, friendships, or how you deal with problems, frustration, and failure.

Use just one or two examples. Do not spend too much time on this point. The focus of relating will probably be in the previous section and the most important information the non-Christian needs is how you reached this point.

Close your testimony in a way that leads to further conversation about salvation. You may use leading questions such as these:

- Has anything like that ever happened to you?
- Does this make sense to you?
- Have you ever thought that you would like to have such peace, assurance, joy, etc.?
- Do you know for certain that you have eternal life and that you will go to heaven when you die?

Check your testimony by using the following criteria. Revise your rough draft as needed.

- Does it have a clear story line that ties everything together?
- Are all four parts of the testimony developed proportionally?
- Is the testimony too brief? Too long? Do details need to be added or omitted?
- Does the testimony conclude with a final sentence that will lead to further conversation?
- Does the testimony sound conversational, or is it too formal or preachy?

ADDITIONAL SUGGESTIONS FOR GIVING YOUR TESTIMONY

Keep it short so your listener will not become uncomfortable.

Tell what happened to you. It is your story that others want to hear. Use "I" and "me."

Write the way you talk. Do not worry about the formal rules of grammar. You will communicate your testimony verbally by sharing, not preaching.

Avoid negative remarks. Do not criticize religious groups or a specific church.

Ask yourself, *If I were an unbeliever, what would this mean to me?*

If you were raised in a Christian home and accepted Christ as a child, do not feel that your conversion is not dramatic enough to share. It is always significant for an unbeliever to learn the way God enters human lives.

After you have prepared, relax.

Say a brief, silent prayer before giving your testimony. Ask the Lord to give you peace and clarity and ask the Holy Spirit to speak through you. Remember, "Do not worry about what to say or how to say it. At that time you will be given what to say, for it will not be you speaking, but the Spirit of your Father speaking through you" (Matt. 10:19, 20).

The Bible says, "Always be prepared to give an answer to everyone who asks you to give the reason for the hope that you have. But do this with gentleness and respect, keeping a clear conscience" (1 Pet. 3:15, 16). Take the time to work through your personal testimony so you will always be ready to witness for Christ through the power of the Holy Spirit. He will give you the exact words you need at that time.

Part 3
THE DISCIPLE'S VICTORY

You will experience victories
over the world,
the flesh,
and the devil
in spiritual warfare.

Chapter 13
OVERCOMING THE ENEMY

When our family visited Greece on our way home from our first term of missionary service in Indonesia, I rented a Volkswagen "Bug" and crowded our four children into it for a tour of the magnificent ruins of the temples, cities, and amphitheaters of the old Greek civilization. We reached Corinth, which was situated at the base of a huge mountain. Take it from me: Don't go halfway around the world to see Corinth; it is nothing but a pile of rocks and a few pillars! Wanting to see something more interesting, we decided that we had enough time before we had to return the rental car to drive to the top of the mountain where I had heard that an impregnable fortress stood. The little Volkswagen struggled up the mountain until we reached the top. Around the entire top of the mountain was a huge wall wide enough for chariots to drive on. We walked into the fortress to see what was there.

As we went through the first gate, we saw another wall, or fortress, one hundred yards up. When we reached that one, we saw that farther up the hill was another wall completely encircling the mountain. It was becoming evident why no one had ever been able to defeat the occupants of the fortress until 1,300 years after Christ, and only twice in history had that occurred. By the time we reached the second wall, my wife Shirley and our two daughters decided to wait while our two sons and I climbed to the top of the mountain.

At the top of the mountain we looked back at Shirley and the girls, who looked about a half-inch tall. When I turned around, I was overwhelmed with the panoramic view of the Mediterranean Sea. To the left I saw the city of Athens, and if I could have seen far enough to the right, I would have seen the city of Rome. Obviously, whoever held this fortress would have held a very strong position in the ancient world. I began to understand what the apostle Paul had in mind when he wrote, "Though we live in the world, we do not wage war as the world does. The weapons we fight with are not the weapons of the world. On the contrary, they have divine power to demolish strongholds. We demolish arguments and every pretension that sets itself up against the knowledge of God, and we take captive every thought to make it obedient to Christ" (2 Cor. 10:3–5). I realized that the Christians at Corinth to whom Paul wrote would have easily understood being at war with an enemy who is buttressed in a fortress and the need to demolish that stronghold.

Who Is the Enemy?

Satan appears as a proper name in the Old Testament, referring to the superhuman enemy of God, humanity; good (1 Chron. 21:1; Job 1–2). In the New Testament, Satan is also known as the devil (Eph. 6:11), the tempter (Mark 1:13; 1 Thess. 3:5), the evil one (Matt. 13:19, 38; 1 John 5:19), the accuser of our brothers (Rev. 12:10), the god of this age (2 Cor. 4:4), and the prince of this world (John 12:31). In addition, Scripture calls Satan the wicked one, the deceiver, the destroyer, the adversary, the enemy of our souls, and the prince of the power of the air. The Bible reveals Satan's influence in worldly events: "The whole world is under the control of the evil one" (1 John 5:19).

Satan is a very powerful and highly intelligent being. Read Genesis 3:1–5 and observe Satan's cunning in tricking Adam and Eve by twisting the truth and undermining the command of God. "Did God really say?" and "You will not surely die . . . for God knows that when you eat of it your eyes will be opened, and you will be like God, knowing good and evil." When Satan tempted Jesus in Matthew 4:1–11, he did not randomly tempt Him. Satan chose three beliefs of that day about the coming Messiah: that the Messiah would bring material prosperity, that He would come dramatically to the temple, and that He would reign over earthly kingdoms and make the nation of Israel a powerful nation. Satan was inviting Jesus to reveal Himself in those ways rather than dying on the cross—to join him rather than follow God's plan.

Satan's nature is that of a liar and thief. "You belong to your father, the devil, and you want to carry out your father's desire. He was a murderer from the beginning, not holding to the truth, for there is no truth in him. When he lies, he speaks his native language, for he is a liar and the father of lies" (John 8:44). Jesus said, "I tell you the truth, the man who does not enter the sheep pen by the gate, but climbs in by some other way, is a thief and a robber. The man who enters by the gate is the shepherd of his sheep. . . . The thief comes only to steal and kill and destroy; I have come that they may have life, and have it to the full" (John 10:1, 2, 10).

What Is Spiritual Warfare?

Spiritual warfare is the conflict between the forces of God and the forces of Satan, with the goal being victory in Christ: "Our struggle is not against flesh and blood, but against the rulers, against the authorities, against the powers of this dark world and against the spiritual forces of evil in the heavenly realms" (Eph. 6:12). As a disciple you know that you are at war. You have experienced spiritual conflict in your personality between the forces of good and evil. You have discovered that no matter how many battles you win, Satan always returns to fight another day. However, you are fighting more than a private war. You are part of God's army, called to defeat Satan and his evil forces. You live and work where the enemy is still fighting; therefore, spiritual warfare takes place all around you.

When we got to Indonesia as missionaries, it was not hard to tell that we were at war. The night before we landed in the capital city of Jakarta, the Communists burned the British embassy. There were three million card-carrying Communists and eighteen million more in the front organizations. They had infiltrated most of the departments of government and communication, and they were very militant about making Indonesia into a Communist power. The first night we were there, the missionaries showed us our apartment and then told us the escape plans: A helicopter would land in Bob Stuckey's yard and whisk us out to Jakarta, where we would be flown out of the country on a jet.

Six weeks later President Sukarno pulled Indonesia out of the United Nations. At that point, the other Americans began to leave. Our escape plans were changed. There would be no helicopter; we were to get out the best way we could! When asked where we were from, we gave the street name rather than say we were Americans or their next question would be, "When are you going to leave?" There were people constantly marching, and demonstrations were

staged in which Uncle Sam was hung in effigy. It was very clear that we were behind enemy lines.

Unfortunately, many Christians today do not recognize the spiritual warfare around them. Because the final victory of our God has not yet come, we are now living in the midst of a great battle and fighting our warfare on Satan's turf. Some people do not admit that the enemy exists. But the Bible makes it plain that Satan does exist and that his main work is to oppose God's rule in the world, in your community, and in people's lives.

Spiritual warfare is a threat to everyone, even the most fervent Christian. In the spiritual battle with the kingdom of darkness, you face the forces of Satan. Therefore, you need to be armed and ready. Many strongholds need to be demolished for the kingdom of light to be established.

The battle is spiritual in nature, and your weapons are spiritual, not the weapons of the world. The weapons used in spiritual battle have divine power to demolish strongholds (2 Cor. 10:3–5). *A stronghold is an idea, a thought process, a habit, or an addiction through which Satan has set up occupancy in your life—a place where he has the advantage.* Strongholds begin in your life when Satan gets a foothold in you. Even if you do not plan to fight, Satan will wage war with you. The moment you start thinking that you are incapable of such behaviors as coveting, losing your temper, or entertaining lustful thoughts, Satan will launch a surprise attack, trying to trip you in the areas you feel most impenetrable. The greater the threat you are to him and the kingdom of darkness, the more he attacks you. Three types of spiritual strongholds define the battleground of spiritual warfare: personal strongholds (the flesh), ideological strongholds (the world), and cosmic strongholds (the devil).

Personal Strongholds

Personal strongholds are the areas of your life in which you are most vulnerable to Satan's attacks. They are areas in which Satan always seems to get advantage over you. Satan's first realm of attack is the flesh, with its inner tendency and capacity to sin. Through the flesh, Satan influences the mind, will, and the emotions. He wants you to depend on yourself and your own strength. Paul warned, "Do not give the devil a foothold" (Eph. 4:27). Satan's footholds soon become his strongholds if not defeated by spiritual weapons. In the Sermon on the Mount (Matt. 5–7), Jesus taught His disciples how to deal with several basic areas that can become strongholds of Satan: bitterness, lust, improper speech, religious ritual, greed, and pride.

Ideological Strongholds

Ideological strongholds are built around systems of thought and ideas that are embodied within cultures, and so they exert pressure on members of that culture. Through this influence, which the Bible calls "the world," a whole society begins to hold certain values. What Satan does to individuals through the flesh, he does to society through the world. Over time, personal strongholds become embodied in cultures as strongholds. "See to it that no one takes you captive through hollow and deceptive philosophy, which depends on human tradition and the basic principles of this world rather than on Christ" (Col. 2:8). Ideological strongholds include philosophical systems, value systems, economic systems, educational systems, religious systems, and political systems. Examples of these include secularism, humanism, communism, capitalism forged through greed, and such "politically correct" but scripturally incorrect thinking that calls pornography "freedom of speech," gambling "entertainment," homosexuality "an alternative lifestyle," and abortion "a choice."

Cosmic Strongholds

Satan rules a group of evil spirits that, with the aid of humanity, establishes a counterculture of sin defying God's righteous order. Its goal is to oppose God's work and to damage and defeat God's children. In the world around you are evil beings under Satan's leadership.

When I was in seminary, I learned that some scholars claim that evil spirits were psychological states of mind. The devil was dismissed as a general force or thought that represented evil, natural forces in mankind. At the same time, I met missionaries who were encountering many manifestations of Satan and his evil spirits in other cultures. When I went overseas, I did not deny the presence of evil spirits. Their influence was too widespread. When we lived in Jember, a city of seventy-five thousand people in East Java, every street except one had a three-way intersection. The people there believe spirits are everywhere but that they only move in straight lines. If the city did not have a four-way intersection, then the spirits could not turn corners to follow them and were stymied at that point. At the only four-way intersection, the police department was on one corner and the Catholic church on another.

In the midst of these errors originated by Satan, I emphasized that the Holy Spirit of God, through the victory of Jesus Christ, is more powerful than any evil spirit or satanic representative. "When you were dead in your sins and in the uncircumcision of your sinful nature, God made you alive with Christ. He forgave us all our sins, having canceled the written code, with its regulations, that was against us and that stood opposed to us; he took it away, nailing it to the cross. And having disarmed the powers and authorities, he made a public spectacle of them, triumphing over them by the cross" (Col. 2:13–15).

𝒜lert to the 𝒞nemy

During these turbulent times, Satan's forces have gained so many strongholds in the United States that Americans have begun to be more aware of evil spirits, the occult, mediums, channeling, demon possession, and satanic worship. Obviously, all of these are not mere psychological interpretations. Cosmic strongholds in the heavenlies, or the atmosphere around us, are the abodes of various kinds of spiritual beings that fight against the cause of God and Christ.

An overemphasis on spiritual warfare can sometimes cause people to become preoccupied with Satan and his forces instead of with God. Undue attention to satanic forces may make people more vulnerable or may lead people to attribute to Satan actions that result from the flesh and the world. (For example, "The devil made me do it.") It causes some Christians to put undue emphasis on directly rebuking Satan when not even Michael the archangel dared do that (Jude 9), or directly binding Satan when Jesus is the one who binds the strong man, as in Matthew 12:28, 29.

Jesus demonstrated how to confront Satan in the wilderness, in the Garden of Gethsamene, and at other critical times in His ministry. Satan can be discerned and overcome. Some Christians engage in what they call "strategic spiritual warfare," a term referring to the aggressive confrontation of Satan and his demons through intercession. But all Christians need to be alert to the reality of spiritual warfare. An awareness of spiritual warfare helps you identify major schemes of the devil, such as accusation, deception, and manipulation. You can recognize when Satan attacks churches through division, distraction, and heresy, or when he controls individuals through confusion, discouragement, and despair. It prompts you to study the Scriptures to understand and overcome Satan's temptations, persecutions, and occult practices, and it helps you depend on God for victory.

God has given Christians the authority to overcome the power of Satan in their lives. The Word of God reveals the wiles of Satan and how He can be defeated. God gives us defensive and offensive weapons to help us stand firm in the midst of warfare. He shows us how to use these to bring down strongholds.

God equips Christians to win the battle. He wants every believer to stand against Satan and all of his schemes in spiritual warfare. He wants you to stand your ground in the day of evil and then finally to conquer and to be standing when the battle is over. He warns that you are fighting not against people but against principalities and powers of a dark world and against spiritual forces of evil. One way to gain victory over evil forces is to use the spiritual armor which God provides: truth, righteousness, the gospel of peace, faith, salvation, and the Word of God. We will discuss these in the next chapter.

Questions for Meditation and Discussion

1. How do you recognize Satan and his attempts to overpower you?

2. Identify some of the schemes of Satan against God's people.

3. What is your position in the battle between God and Satan?

4. What strongholds (personal, ideological, or cosmic) do you see in your own life?

5. In what ways can you demolish those strongholds?

6. What has God provided to help you in the battle?

Chapter 14
PUTTING ON THE SPIRITUAL ARMOR

Putting on the spiritual armor is a biblical strategy to help you stand against Satan and his schemes in spiritual warfare. The apostle Paul used the equipment of a Roman soldier (to whom he may have been chained) to draw a picture of the authority, provision, and battle plans which belong to a disciple of Christ. (see Eph. 6:10–18).

When the spiritual armor is applied, your mind is protected by the helmet of salvation, your heart or will by the breastplate of righteousness, and your emotions by the belt of truth. As you march, you wear gospel shoes—prepared to share the gospel of peace. In one hand you carry the sword of the Spirit, which is the Word of God. In the other hand, you hold the shield of faith. If you study the titles "Salvation, Righteousness, Truth, Gospel of Peace, Word of God, Faith," you will discover that you are, in essence, clothing yourself with Jesus.

This armor can be used in at least three situations:

- When you seek release from Satan's dominion in a personal spiritual stronghold in your life, a stronghold such as bitterness or lack of self-control.

- When Satan attacks you through temptation, lies, or trials.
- When you attack Satan by entering his realm to claim, through intercession or witness, persons he has captured or enslaved.
  The natural person and the worldly Christian are under Satan's control and he fights to keep them there.

Each part of the spiritual armor should be donned through prayer. Each part serves a different purpose. Some of the armor is defensive and some is offensive. In this section of the book, I will explain the components of the spiritual armor, how to use them to defend yourself against the enemy, and how to take up spiritual weapons to enter the domain of darkness and establish God's kingdom on earth. "The seventh angel sounded his trumpet, and there were loud voices in heaven, which said, 'The kingdom of the world has become the kingdom of our Lord and of his Christ, and he will reign for ever and ever' " (Rev. 11:15).

Protective Armor

The first three pieces of armor I will introduce are defensive in nature. You will notice that these three pieces of armor relate directly to the areas of the disciple's personality in which Satan seeks dominion: your mind, your will, and your emotions. They are meant to protect you from Satan's direct, personal attacks. As long as your mind, will, emotions, and behavior are submitted and in line with the Spirit, Satan cannot get a foothold. Each of these armor pieces must be firmly in place before you step out to battle so that Satan's fiery arrows have no crack through which to penetrate (Eph. 6:16).

THE HELMET OF SALVATION

One of Satan's schemes is to fill your mind with doubts about your salvation, about the truth of God's Word, and about your ability to hear or to obey God when He speaks to you. Satan's words caused Eve to doubt when he said, "Did God really say?" (Gen. 3:1). He tries to convince you of your unworthiness, to remind you of past sin—even sins you have confessed, and to point out your doubts or your lack of faith. He seeks to plant his lies and evil thoughts in your mind. He uses your own passing thoughts and brings them back as temptations.

As you pray through the spiritual armor, begin by putting on the helmet of salvation. Pull it on tightly to cover your mind at all times. You put on the helmet by praising God for your salvation, for God's grace, and for Christ's death for you. Through praise you renew your mind and claim the mind of Christ: "Those who live in accordance with the Spirit have their minds set on what the Spirit desires. The mind of the sinful man is death, but the mind controlled by the Spirit is life and peace" (Rom. 8:5, 6). Let this symbol remind you to do the following:

- Thank God that you are His child: "You, dear children, are from God and have overcome them, because the one who is in you is greater than the one who is in the world" (1 John 4:4). Thank Him for your salvation.
- Praise God for eternal life. The helmet protects you at all times in any battle. Praise Him that He has covered your mind.
- Claim the mind of Christ. We have the mind of Christ and His thoughts can cover our own (see 1 Cor. 2:16).

THE BREASTPLATE OF RIGHTEOUSNESS

The second piece of armor to put on is the breastplate of righteousness. Think of it as symbolically protecting your heart and your will. It reflects the daily choice to shut the door to sin and open it to the power of the Spirit. The breastplate covers the believer with the righteousness of Christ. "I delight greatly in the LORD; my soul rejoices in my God. For he has clothed me with garments of salvation and arrayed me in a robe of righteousness, as a bridegroom adorns his head like a priest, and as a bride adorns herself with her jewels" (Isa. 61:10). To put on the breastplate of righteousness:

- Ask the Lord to search your heart to reveal any wicked ways in it. "Search me, O God, and know my heart; test me and know my anxious thoughts. See if there is any offensive way in me, and lead me in the way everlasting" (Ps. 139:23, 24).
- Confess any sin. "If we confess our sins, he is faithful and just and will forgive us our sins and purify us from all unrighteousness" (1 John 1:9).
- Claim Christ's righteousness to cover your sins and to give you right standing with Him. "God made him who had no sin to be sin for us, so that in him we might become the righteousness of God" (2 Cor. 5:21).
- Keep the breastplate of righteousness firmly fastened in place with upright character and righteous living. To the woman caught in adultery, Jesus said, "Then neither do I condemn you. . . . Go now and leave your life of sin" (John 8:11).

THE BELT OF TRUTH

Gird yourself with the belt of truth, which holds the rest of the armor in place. Truth includes integrity and moral uprightness. This piece of armor represents the protection of your emotions, or your "gut" feelings. The Bible speaks of the area of the body covered by the belt of truth as inward parts, referring to the place where feelings reside or to the feelings themselves. It also represents protection of the integrity or the moral character in your life; those things which Christ is building in you as you are molded into His image. To strap on the belt of truth:

- Determine in prayer that you want nothing but truth and integrity in your life.
- Be honest with yourself and God when you pray or fight a spiritual battle. Examine how you feel about things, words, and persons, and then surrender all of them to God in exchange for His view—truth. "Then you will know the truth and the truth will set you free" (John 8:32).
- Hold to the truth. Satan, the father of lies, would like to deceive you.
- Master your emotions. Ask God to keep your feelings from clouding the truth. The belt of truth helps you control your emotions and not compromise because of your feelings. "When you ask, you do not receive, because you ask with wrong motives, that you may spend what you get on your pleasures" (James 4:3).
- Continue to walk in the Spirit in all that you say and do. "And whatever you do, whether in word or deed, do it all in the name of the Lord Jesus, giving thanks to God the Father through him" (Col. 3:17).

Offensive Armor

When you have clothed yourself with your protective armor, it is time to take up the armor intended for moving assertively against the kingdom of Satan: the gospel shoes, the shield of faith, and the sword of the Spirit. Each of these is used while marching forward against the enemy.

GOSPEL SHOES FOR READY FEET

Picture on your feet a soldier's studded sandals that help him grip the road and move forward quickly into battle. The feet symbolize the presenting of your body for the Master's use. The gospel shoes—the readiness that comes from the gospel of peace—prepare you to go forward into the war. To put them on:

- Be prepared. Get ready before the battle begins. Pray that God will prepare you for any possibility. Prepared feet put you in a position to attack the enemy.
- Share the gospel. The readiness that comes from the gospel of peace is being ready to witness for Him. "I pray that you may be active in sharing your faith, so that you will have a full understanding of every good thing we have in Christ" (Philem. 6).
- Intercede for the lost. You are prepared to attack the enemy through prayer or through witness. Pray for lost friends on your prayer lists. Visualize the countries of the world, with their millions of lost people, and pray for their salvation. "I urge, then, first of all, that requests, prayers, intercession and thanksgiving be made for everyone. . . . This is good, and pleases God our Savior, who wants all men to be saved and to come to a knowledge of the truth" (1 Tim. 2:1, 3, 4).

THE SHIELD OF FAITH

The Roman shield was a long, oblong piece of wood that covered a great portion of the soldier's body. When enemies' fiery arrows hit it, the arrowheads became buried deep in the wood and were extinguished. Since the shield only covers the front and not the back of the person, it is obviously meant for advance, not retreat. So as the arrows of evil are aimed at you, advance with the shield of faith in your left hand and quench the fiery darts of the wicked one. To use the shield of faith:

- Claim the victory. "For everyone born of God overcomes the world. This is the victory that has overcome the world, even our faith" (1 John 5:4). "I tell you, whatever you ask for in prayer, believe that you have received it, and it will be yours" (Mark 11:24).
- Advance in faith. Put feet to your prayers. Faith without works is dead. "You see that his faith and his actions were working together, and his faith was made complete by what he did" (James 2:22).
- Quench the fiery darts of the wicked. Shut out the lies and temptations of the devil.

THE SWORD OF THE SPIRIT

Grasp the sword of the Spirit, the Word of God, in your right hand and wield it as a weapon. "For the word of God is living and active. Sharper than any double-edged sword, it penetrates even to dividing soul and spirit, joints and marrow; it judges the thoughts and attitudes of the heart" (Heb. 4:12). Spiritual victory cannot be attained apart from the

Word. As you march into Satan's territory and begin to reclaim for God the things Satan has stolen, you need marching orders from God. You need to ask for those things that God reveals through His Scripture. "Word" in this verse means "God's utterance," referring to God speaking to you about specific situations. To apply the sword of the Spirit:

- Use it whether or not the enemy acknowledges that it is the Word of God. Satan cannot withstand the Word of God. He falls back when you move in to possess God's possessions through claiming His Word by faith.
- Let the Holy Spirit use the Word. It is not the believer's sword but the sword of the Spirit.
- Pray on the basis of the Word. The Spirit will use the Word to reveal God's will to you and to help you know what to pray for. Let God impress you with Bible promises, and use them to claim that which God really wants to do. "But when he, the Spirit of truth, comes, he will guide you into all truth. He will not speak on his own; he will speak only what he hears, and he will tell you what is yet to come" (John 16:13).

Spiritual Weapons

God expects you to be wary of the tempter, but He will help you be victorious in spiritual warfare. Christ has won the battle over all evil powers and gives victory to Christians who totally depend on Him and who use the spiritual weapons which He gives. Spiritual weapons refer to the complete array of spiritual helps which God supplies for overcoming the devil's temptations. Logic, physical efforts, positive thinking, and psychological tactics will not win over Satan. Only the spiritual weapons which God gives you can win spiritual victories. One of the foremost weapons is prayer.

Spiritual battles begin with or should quickly move to prayer. It is one means which God uses to strengthen you in the power of His might. Paul concluded the list of spiritual armor with an exhortation to pray. He focused on prayer as a specific arena of warfare. He encouraged Christians to pray on all occasions; to use all kinds of prayer, but specifically supplication; to be alert; to persevere; and to pray for all the saints (Eph. 6:18).

In his book *Let the Nations Be Glad*, John Piper says, "We cannot know what prayer is for until we know that life is war. . . . Prayer is primarily a wartime walkie-talkie for the mission of the church as it advances against the powers of darkness and unbelief. It is not surprising that prayer malfunctions when we try to make it a domestic intercom to call upstairs for more comforts in the den. God has given us prayer as a wartime walkie-talkie so that we can call headquarters for everything we need as the kingdom of Christ advances in the world."[1]

A spiritual warrior begins on his or her knees. Through prayer, this warrior clothes himself or herself with articles of the spiritual armor before going out to meet the foe. When you have armed yourself with the spiritual armor, you can claim victories through prayer. Then you can move out to see those prayers answered in the battlefield of the world.

Other weapons of warfare are God's Word and the prayer of faith based on that Word. You have power when you exercise your faith, based on the Word of God, to pray about a need or a problem. I will show you more about these powerful weapons in the next chapters.

Questions for Meditation and Discussion

1. Name the pieces of spiritual armor. Which do you need to learn the most about?

2. Identify the three pieces of protective armor. In which area are you the most vulnerable?

3. Name the offensive spiritual armor that overtakes the enemy. Which do you regularly use?

4. How can you use prayer as a weapon of spiritual warfare?

Chapter 15
RELYING ON GOD'S WORD

The primary offensive weapon given to you, which you must learn to master in spiritual warfare, is the sword of the Spirit. God's truth is a powerful weapon to demolish spiritual strongholds. You can discern spiritual truth because you are born of the Spirit (John 3:6) and because God has given you His revealed Word. "Jesus answered, 'I am the way and the truth and the life. No one comes to the Father except through me'" (John 14:6). "If you hold to my teaching, you are really my disciples. Then you will know the truth, and the truth will set you free" (John 8:31, 32).

With these words, Jesus spoke to His disciples about His mission on earth: to communicate truth, the reality of God, to all people. Truth is God's revelation of Himself to you. That truth is most clearly revealed in Jesus, the incarnate Word and then in the written record of God's revelation, the Bible. You respond to the truth by following Christ and continuing in His Word. "We know that we have come to know him if we obey his commands. The man who says, 'I know him,' but does not do what he commands is a liar, and the truth is not in him. But if anyone obeys his word, God's love is truly made complete in him. This is how we know we are in him: Whoever claims to live in him must walk as Jesus did" (1 John 2:3–6).

The opposite of truth is error, and Satan is its source. Satan's assault is aimed directly at God's truth. The ungodly boast of humanity's wisdom and self-sufficiency contradict the truth. People who follow the world's ways and worship what the world offers exchange the truth of God for falsehood: "They exchanged the truth of God for a lie, and worshiped and served created things rather than the Creator—who is forever praised" (Rom. 1:25).

The Holy Spirit will help you discern truth in contrast to Satan's lies. God reveals His truth to you so that you can know His will and His way. The best way to know spiritual truth is to continue in Christ's teaching. As a disciple you are called to walk in the truth and to reveal that truth to others. "Do your best to present yourself to God as one approved, a workman who does not need to be ashamed and who correctly handles the word of truth" (2 Tim. 2:15).

God's Reliable Word

Any belief or behavior is based on truth only when it is in line with God's Word. The inspired (God-breathed) Word is the only standard that stands the test of time. Opinions and cultural priorities change, but the Word of God always endures: "All men are like grass, and all their glory is like the flowers of the field; the grass withers and the flowers fall, but the word of the Lord stands forever" (1 Pet. 1:24, 25).

God has provided His Scripture to completely equip you for every challenge of the Christian life. God's Word is profitable to teach you the ways of God and to keep you walking in them: "All Scripture is God-breathed and is useful for teaching, rebuking, correcting, and training in righteousness, so that the man of God may be thoroughly equipped for every good work" (2 Tim. 3:16, 17).

GOD'S WORD TEACHES

The first purpose of the Word of God is to teach and to prepare a person to live as a disciple. Biblical instruction and guidance are designed to prevent a problem or to help a person correct it. The Bible gives the history of God's dealing with mankind so that you can see how He seeks to deal with you. It gives the law of God so you can know God's ways. It is from Scripture that all doctrinal beliefs and standards for behavior are derived.

Sometimes false doctrines steal into our lives. Someone may say that Jesus did not really have a human nature or that He did not actually die on the cross and His resurrection was simply resuscitation. Satan can use your ignorance and false beliefs to bring you under attack. But if you are grounded in truth, you have God's Word as a point of reference when Satan attempts to deceive or mislead you.

The Scripture is also immensely practical for giving direction in daily living. It teaches you how to handle money, how to treat others, how to work at your job, and how to raise children. It keeps you from error, whether in belief or action.

GOD'S WORD REBUKES

A rebuke is a reproof that brings conviction, an awareness that you have done wrong. God's Word is useful to alert you when you are going in the wrong direction—when God intends for you to pursue one course of action, but you are pursuing another. When you have read the Scriptures in the past, has a verse ever seemed to jump out to identify a way you have rebelled against His revealed truth?

For example, you may be reading in Proverbs 10 and you see verse 19, "When words are many, sin is not absent, but he who holds his tongue is wise." Suddenly, you feel as if this verse has neon lights around it and you know the Holy Spirit is speaking to you! You remember that in a recent conversation, you revealed more than you should have when asked about a mutual friend. You realize that you not only betrayed a confidence; you implied that the friend might be unfaithful to her husband. Your excessive words have caused you to sin against both of your friends, the one spoken to and the one spoken about. When a Scripture impacts you like this, it is no coincidence. The Lord is identifying a weakness in you. This is a wake-up call from the Scriptures telling you to get back in line with God's will and God's standards.

Scriptural rebuke gives you guidance. It makes you aware that you are traveling in the opposite direction you should be going—that you have strayed from God's ways. Through the verse of Scripture the Lord seems to say, "Here is the way; turn around from the way you are going and walk in the truth." It is a call to repentance.

GOD'S WORD CORRECTS

Scripture is also useful for those who are not purposefully rebelling against God but who are straying from the path. The Lord knows that the longer they go off course, the farther they move from the right way. They need a slight change of direction to get back on course before they go so far that rebuke is necessary: "Whether you turn to the right or to the left, your ears will hear a voice behind you, saying, 'This is the way; walk in it'" (Isa. 30:21).

God's Word corrects your sins and failures. The word *correct* comes from a Greek word which means "to restore." The Phillips translation defines the term as "resetting the direction of a man's life." Correction is a word from God that shows you His perfect way so you can readjust back to Him. Perhaps you read Matthew 6:19–34 and feel that this passage is alerting you that you have begun to put your security in earthly goods instead of laying up treasures in heaven. In this case, your life direction in money management could be reset because of an encounter with God's Word.

God's correction is motivated by love. When you have Christ at the center of your life, you need to have your direction properly set. It would be impossible to be an intimate disciple of Christ if you strayed from His side. When a person delights in the Word, then the correction that springs from the Word will be welcome.

My daughter Sherrie told me of an incident in which she experienced God's correction. When she returned home from the store one day, she realized she had not been charged for an item she had bought. The price of the item was only $4.95, so the easiest thing would have been to chalk it up to clerk error and consider it her good fortune. However, in an attempt to deal honestly, she telephoned the customer service department at the store, expecting them to tell her not to worry about it. Instead, the representative informed her that if she would bring the item back in, they would be glad to let her pay for it. When she returned to do so, the woman at the service desk remarked at how unusual it was for a person to be so honest.

My daughter thanked her, paid the amount, and left. On the way home, she heard the Lord say, "Sherrie, you did the right thing to take it back. I'm glad you were honest. But next time, tell them you do it because you love Me. Don't take the glory for yourself." My daughter remarked at the gentleness and love she felt in the Lord's voice, as if He had a smile on His face, "You did well, but next time give the glory to Me."

GOD'S WORD INSTRUCTS IN RIGHTEOUSNESS

God's Word supplies ample instruction for how to live rightly. The Bible teaches moral character. The Phillips translation says the Bible is profitable for "training in good living." As a Christian, you are not left to guess which way is right. Again and again the Bible instructs you in the practical, day-to-day ways to live. It not only provides specific information on walking in holiness, it also provides answers to daily decisions.

I have learned that God most often gives me guidance as I read through a book of the Bible one chapter at a time. I usually keep a list of questions or problems I am facing to refer to during my quiet time. At one time I needed to find a successor for my associate vice president who was retiring from the International Mission Board. I had been praying about this matter for several months when I went to Brazil to speak at three meetings of missionaries. Traveling with me were Ron Wilson, the area director for Brazil and the Caribbean, and John White, the treasurer of three missionary organizations represented at the meetings.

As we traveled together during those three weeks, I became aware of John's abilities, gifts, and heart for ministry. I began to wonder if God was leading me to talk with him. Not knowing what I was thinking, Ron Wilson remarked to me that John White was so industrious that Ron continually sought ways to challenge him. Ron commented that he believed one day John would have an even more responsible position. I knew then that I needed to learn more about John White.

I found out John had been an assistant to Truett Cathy, the founder of the Chick-Fil-A restaurant chain, and he had performed the type of duties the associate vice president position would require. With a doctor's degree in law and a master's degree in business administration, John possessed the training and skills for the job. In addition, John had been a missionary for ten years and had served as a pastor in Rio de Janeiro and Belo Horizonte. Ron told me John had been the treasurer for one mission and had been given the responsibility of three missions.

I began to ask God for leadership in this very vital choice. Although John's abilities all commended him, I had planned to wait until I returned to the United States to investigate the possibility of offering him the job. I could not afford to make a mistake. God must show me His will.

On the last leg of the journey we arose very early to catch a plane. It was delayed, so I began to read the next chapter in my daily Bible reading, Luke 19. In this chapter Jesus told the parable of a royal official who was going on a journey in which he would be crowned king of that region. He called ten of his servants around him, gave them each the same amount of money, and told them to put it to work. I realized he was testing his servants to discover who could assume greater responsibility.

When the plane was further delayed, I walked in the park and talked to God about whether I should follow through on talking to John or wait. God seemed to say to me, "How clear can I make it to you? The official who gave the money to his servants knew he would be appointed king. He gave the talents so he could discern who would be his managers when he came back to establish his kingdom. John has used every opportunity given him to show that he can be trusted with even more responsibility. He is the man I have prepared for the responsibility of helping you lead the missionaries all over the world." I thanked God for the revelation and decided I did not need to wait until I had conferred with others.

Later that day I talked to Ron, his present supervisor, and then John. The more I learned, the more the Spirit confirmed His leading. Through the right Scripture at the right time, God led me to choose the right person to fill a major position. John's performance since then has confirmed that he was God's choice for the job.

Accessing the Word of God

In the spiritual armor, the Word of God was referred to as the sword of the Spirit. It is a powerful weapon against the enemy, Satan. "The word of God is living and active. Sharper than any double-edged sword" (Heb. 4:12). Imagine, though, how dangerous it would be to wield such a sharp and powerful weapon without having a good grasp of it. The more Scripture you get into your heart, the better you can use it and apply it.

Let me show you a simple illustration to help you remember how to get a grasp of the Word of God so you can use it in spiritual warfare. The original illustration came from Dawson Trotman, founder of the Navigators. It was shown to me by a friend in college and I have adapted it.

God's Word in Your Heart and Hand

You can use your hand to illustrate how to live in the Word and to get the Word into your heart. (See illustration on page 155.)

HEAR THE WORD

The simplest way to receive the Word is to hear it. Even a child or a person who cannot read can hear the Bible. "If anyone has ears to hear, let him hear" (Mark 4:23). "Faith comes from hearing the message, and the message is heard through the word of Christ" (Rom. 10:17). Matthew 13:3–23 lists four kinds of hearers of the Word: the apathetic hearer who hears the Word but is not prepared to receive and understand it (v. 19); the superficial hearer who receives the Word temporarily but does not let it take root in the heart (vv. 20, 21); the preoccupied hearer who receives the Word but lets the worries of this world and the desire for other things choke it out (v. 22); and the reproducing hearer who receives the Word, understands it, bears fruit, and brings forth results (v. 23).

THINK ABOUT THE WORD

The second way you live in the Word and the Word lives in you is to think about it or meditate on it. "His delight is in the law of the LORD, and on his law he meditates day and night" (Ps. 1:2). The thumb represents this function.

Try this experiment. Grip a Bible with your little finger (hearing the Word) and your thumb (thinking about what you hear), and ask someone to try to pull it from your grasp. You will find that you have a grasp of God's Word but not a firm enough grasp to hold it when they try to take it from you. Therefore, the next way you understand God's Word becomes important.

EXAMINE THE WORD

Examining or reading the Word is an additional way to abide in the Word; it helps you go deeper. "Blessed is the one who reads the words of this prophecy, and blessed are those who hear it and take to heart what is written in it, because the time is near" (Rev. 1:3). But even with this level added (an additional finger of strength), the truth can still be snatched from you.

ANALYZE THE WORD

When you study the Word, you go deeper into it. "The Bereans were of more noble character than the Thessalonians, for they received the message with great eagerness and examined the Scriptures every day to see if what Paul said was true" (Acts 17:11). Now you begin to have power in your handling of the Word.

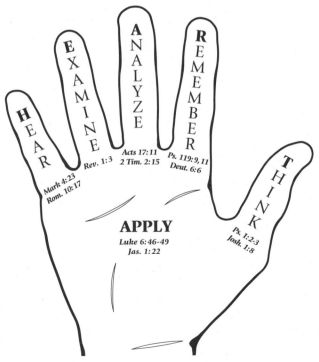

REMEMBER THE WORD

Another way to get a firm grip on God's Word and get the Word into your heart is to memorize it. When you remember the Word, it lives in you, you live in it, and God's promises become your possessions. "How can a young man keep his way pure? By living according to your word . . . I have hidden your word in my heart that I might not sin against you" (Ps. 119:9, 11). At this point, the Word is firmly in your heart and hand and will not be easily pulled from your grasp. (Try again to pull the Bible from your hand.)

APPLY THE WORD

The most effective way to get the Word into your life is to apply it. Delving into the Word and getting the Word into you are essential, but the only way to abide fully in the Word is to apply it to your life. "Do not merely listen to the word, and so deceive yourselves. Do what it says. Anyone who listens to the word but does not do what it says is like a man who looks at his face in a mirror and, after looking at himself, goes away and immediately forgets what he looks like. But the man who looks intently into the perfect law that gives freedom, and continues to do this, not forgetting what he has heard, but doing it—he will be blessed in what he does" (James 1:22–25).

Jesus told this story: "Why do you call me 'Lord, Lord' and do not do what I say? I will show you what he is like who comes to me and hears my words and puts them into practice. He is like a man building a house, who dug down deep and laid the foundation on rock. When a flood came, the torrent struck that house but could not shake it, because it was well built. But the one who hears my words and does not put them into practice is like a man who built a house on the ground without a foundation. The moment the torrent struck that house, it collapsed and its destruction was complete" (Luke 6:46–49). What was the difference between the two men who built the houses? Both of them heard, but only one acted. Only that one was able to stand firm.

You can remember these points by taking the first letter of each of the three middle fingers: Examine, Analyze, and Remember the Word, which spell EAR. If you add the little finger, you have HEAR. When you add the thumb, and think about it at each level, you have embedded it in your HEART and you have a firm grasp of it. No one, not even Satan, can take it from you. But if you also apply the Word, you have it firmly in the palm of your hand so that it can make a difference in every area of your life. Then the Word in you can demolish personal spiritual strongholds.

Now let's review specific ways to help you hear/listen, analyze/study, and think/meditate on the Scriptures. We have already learned about Scripture memory in chapter 2, and we will discuss applying Scripture to specific situations in the next chapter.

HOW TO LISTEN TO A SERMON

The key to hearing the Word accurately is to pay attention to what is said and to immediately allow the Spirit to bring a personal revelation or application of that Word. Too often you hear a sermon or taped message and either your mind may wander through part of it or there may be more information than you can retain. As a result, when you move away from the teaching and begin doing other things, it seems to "go in one ear and out the other." Sometimes by lunchtime the same day, when I have asked my family what they thought of the sermon that morning, they have to think a while to remember what it was even about. More people remember how they felt about a sermon than what was actually said.

1. Be alert for a word from God. A significant way to improve your memory is to prepare to hear before the Word is preached. Clear away all sin and pride so the Word can be planted in your heart. "Therefore, get rid of all moral filth and the evil that is so prevalent and humbly accept the word planted in you, which can save you" (James 1:21).

2. Write it down! When listening to a sermon, take notes. Write the points of the message as the speaker presents them. Under each point write explanations, illustrations, and applications that are helpful to you. Write any specific statements or thoughts the Spirit impresses on you, even if they are not the ones presented by the speaker. The Holy Spirit may have a unique word for you.

3. Personalize the message. Take a moment to hear what God would say specifically to you through this Word. Summarize as soon as possible the main point the speaker wants you to do, be, and/or feel. Then ask yourself:
   - What did God say to me through this message?
   - How does my life measure up to this Word?
   - What actions will I take to bring my life in line with this Word?
   - What truth do I need to study further?

4. Apply what you've heard. Do the Word, and you will be blessed in what you do (see James 1:25). If you keep this information in your Bible, prayer notebook, or journal for the following week, you can check yourself to see if you have done whatever the Lord may have directed of you. You may not keep all of the sermon notes over the years but if you learn to hold on to the Word long enough to obey it, then you will see its fruit in your life.

STUDYING GOD'S WORD

Bible study is an in-depth look into the Scripture, to learn and discover more than you would see in an overview or in a devotional reading. It often includes gaining additional information through commentaries and study helps. It involves comparing what the Bible says in one passage to other passages throughout the Bible. It may begin with a question and searching the Bible for its answer. Many methods of Bible study exist:

- studying a theme of the Bible;
- studying a book of the Bible;
- studying a passage of the Bible;
- studying a particular word through the Bible; and
- studying a character of the Bible.

I have put detailed instructions for each of these methods at the back of the *Disciple's Study Bible.* For now, I will simply refer you to that resource since presenting all of them here would be a book in itself.

HOW TO MEDITATE ON GOD'S WORD

You meditate on God's Word when you focus on a specific verse of Scripture such as Philippians 4:13, and chew on it and digest it until you have fully understood it. You may meditate a few minutes each day, concentrating on one verse a week. Select a verse you want to memorize or which has been a key verse in a passage you have just read. Ask the Holy Spirit for His revelation as you meditate. You may use some or all of these ideas:[1]

1. Read the verses before and after to establish the theme and setting. These will aid you in interpretation. Then write a summary of the passage.
2. Write the verse in your own words. Say your paraphrase aloud.
3. Read the verse over and over again, emphasizing a different word each time you repeat it. For example, in the verse "I can do all things through Christ which strengtheneth me" (Phil.4:13, KJV), first emphasize the word "I," then the word "can" and so on to allow each word to take on its full impact.
4. State the opposite meaning of the verse: for example, "I cannot do anything if Christ does not strengthen me." What impact does the verse have now?
5. Write at least two important words from those you have emphasized in the verse. Ask these questions about the two words to relate the Scripture to your needs: What? Why? When? Where? Who? How?

6. Personalize the verse: Let the Holy Spirit apply the verse to a need, a challenge, an opportunity, or a failure in your life. What will you *do* about this verse as it relates to your life? Be specific.

7. Pray the verse back to God. Put your own name or situation in the verse.

8. Refer to other passages that emphasize the truth of the verse. List thoughts or ideas you might not understand or might have difficulty applying in your life. Seek out instruction or help in these areas.

9. Write a way you can use the verse to help another person.

Do not underestimate the power of the Word. Having it in your heart and mind so that it is instantaneously available is like a cowboy at high noon with his holster unstrapped and his hand in ready position to draw and fire. Satan cringes and runs away. It is also a powerful tool of encouragement in this day of great discouragement. To be able to speak the Word of God readily will touch and bring change to lives all around you. "The Sovereign LORD has given me an instructed tongue, to know the word that sustains the weary. He wakens me morning by morning, wakens my ear to listen like one being taught. The Sovereign LORD has opened my ears, and I have not been rebellious; I have not drawn back" (Isa. 50:4, 5). "Preach the Word: be prepared in season and out of season; correct, rebuke and encourage—with great patience and careful instruction" (2 Tim. 4:2). The Lord declares, "As the rain and the snow come down from heaven, and do not return to it without watering the earth and making it bud and flourish, so that it yields seed for the sower and bread for the eater, so is my word that goes out from my mouth. It will not return to me empty, but will accomplish what I desire and achieve the purpose for which I sent it" (Isa. 55:10, 11).

This weapon of the Word and the weapon of prayer are both used in conjunction with the shield of faith. When you pray in faith, basing your prayer on the revealed Word of God to you for your situation, you can experience mighty victory. I will show you how to use these three weapons to pray through problems in your life in the next chapter.

Questions for Meditation and Discussion

1. How do you know what is God's truth?

2. When has God used Scripture in your life to teach, rebuke, correct, and/or train you in righteousness?

3. What type of "hearer of the Word" are you?

4. Think of a time when you have been able to speak the Word of God to bring instruction or encouragement to another person.

5. Take some time to do a Bible study or meditation exercise.

Chapter 16
PRAYING
ABOUT PROBLEMS

My longtime colleague in discipleship training, Jimmy Crowe, experienced praying in faith as he prepared to undergo his third heart surgery. His two previous heart surgeries had been successful, but they had occurred when Jimmy was younger. Now retired, Jimmy said he began to fear that his age and his seeming lack of purpose as a retiree would keep him from full recovery from another operation. He prayed, "Lord, You know that I am much older now. My life's work is finished. Those other times You had work for me to do. Can I really endure this surgery? And should I even try, now that I don't accomplish for You as much as I once did?"

A friend alerted me to Jimmy's state of mind. I called Jimmy and encouraged him to help with the new version of *MasterLife*. He also received phone calls of support from friends as far away as Australia. The night before his surgery, Jimmy heard the most important voice. The Lord revealed the answer: "I will not die but live, and will proclaim what the LORD has done" (Ps. 118:17). Jimmy said, "It was a promise but also a correction. It was as if the Father was saying to me, 'You seem to have forgotten your primary task. You still have much to do because I have commanded that you continue to tell of Me and My love for people.' Afterward, the doctor said this surgery was easy, and my recovery was quick. The time since has been one of the most fruitful periods of my ministry, with many opportunities to teach and minister."

How Does God Speak?

God provides daily guidance for you in making decisions, facing problems, and meeting needs. As He works through the indwelling presence of the Holy Spirit, God's Word becomes active, alive, and dynamic in directing your life. As you base your life on the Word by faith, it becomes a lamp to your feet and a light to your path (Ps. 119:105).

But how do you know that God is speaking to you through a specific part of the Word to apply to a specific situation in your life? How can you discern a "Bible promise" so that you can pray according to God's will in your problem or circumstance? How do you pray in faith based on that word from God? I want to introduce six steps to praying in faith. The first three involve God communicating truth to you and the last three involve you communicating faith to God.

God Communicates Truth to You

Your greatest concern as a disciple is to know and follow God's will. You cannot act on what you do not know. Faith must be based on a revealed word of truth from God. God shows you His desire for you when you do three things: abide in Christ, abide in the Word, and allow the Holy Spirit to lead you in truth.

ABIDE IN CHRIST

First of all, be sure you are abiding in Christ. "If you remain in me and my words remain in you, ask whatever you wish, and it will be given you" (John 15:7). Lay aside your own will as much as possible to seek God's will. Be sure that your fleshly desires are not standing in the way of your discovering God's will. "When you ask, you do not receive, because you ask with wrong motives, that you may spend what you get on your pleasures" (James 4:3).

ABIDE IN THE WORD

Secondly, abide in the Word. When you have a problem, first turn to God and seek His Word to find the solution to your problem. God may use some other sources to help you solve your problem, but He wants you to seek Him first. I am not suggesting that you can simply open your Bible and put your finger on a verse at random. Many abuses and misuses of Scripture occur when people use that approach.

I heard of a man who did that when he was in great desperation, and the first verse he landed on was Matthew 27:5: "Then he [Judas] went away and hanged himself." Greatly disturbed, the man tried again. This time his finger landed on Luke 10:37: "Jesus told him, 'Go and do likewise.'" Frantically, he tried once more. His Bible opened to John 13:27: "What you are about to do, do quickly." He did not meet the "God of all comfort" in those verses!

The heart of the one who abides in the Word is like the heart of Job: "He knows the way that I take; when he has tested me, I will come forth as gold. My feet have closely followed his steps; I have kept to his way without turning aside. I have not departed from the commands of his lips; I have treasured the words of his mouth more than my daily bread" (Job 23:10–12). God can speak to you as you abide in His Word if you:

- Daily spend time in the Word: reading it, meditating on it, applying it, memorizing it, and letting the Word saturate your being so you can discern the will of God.
- Read the Bible systematically and let God speak through passages He brings to mind.
- Look for specific principles and truths that apply to your situation.
- Look for a present-day application of a truth or biblical situation.
- Be willing to stay in the Word and wait for a revelation through the Word by the Holy Spirit.

In his book *Interpreting the Bible*, A. Berkley Michelson writes:

There are always two variables in personal devotional Bible study. (1) The passage being read will change from day to day. (2) The needs of the individual will change from day to day. The same passage could be read ten times during a year. If the reader is filled with the Spirit and is walking in fellowship with God on each occasion, he may apply to himself different things on each occasion. Our personal applications may be different from those of the original readers. Personal application involves the working out from the passage a principle that is true for anyone who belongs to God or a principle for individuals in parallel situations. Legitimate application by the formulation of sound principles is, in truth, what God has to say to the individual Christian.[1]

ALLOW THE HOLY SPIRIT TO LEAD YOU IN TRUTH

The third step to praying in faith is to allow the Holy Spirit to lead you in truth. "When he, the Spirit of truth, comes, he will guide you into all truth. He will not speak on his own; he will speak only what he hears, and he will tell you what is yet to come. He will bring glory to me by taking from what is mine and making it known to you" (John 16:13, 14). The Holy Spirit is the teacher in a disciple's life. One of the basic responsibilities of the Holy Spirit is to take truth and show it to you. He works both to reveal God's truth to you and to help you receive the truth. Under the Holy Spirit's guidance, the words of the Bible become a Word from the Father for you.

This is more than just reading the Bible logically or analytically and figuring out for yourself what you think God would have you do. To receive a Bible promise that is specific to your situation, read until the Spirit illuminates a verse so you know in your spirit that it is a Word for you. This may sound mystical, but it is the way of the Spirit. He is the one who inspired those who wrote the Word. Now He is working in you to interpret what is written and apply it to your life. You may have read a particular verse many times before, but this time the Spirit takes the verse and reveals to your spirit its truth for your situation. It almost seems to stand out on the page and make you catch your breath. You suddenly understand or know what God is saying to you.

After the Holy Spirit has impressed you with a Scripture, ask these questions to test your understanding.

- Is it consistent with truth revealed in the rest of the Bible?
- Is it consistent with God's character?
- Is it consistent with the meaning of the Scripture in context, or does it violate the original meaning?
- Does the Holy Spirit continue to confirm its validity as you pray more about it?

What if you do not find a Scripture that gives you direct guidance for a problem or need? Continue reading your Bible and praying until an answer comes. "Ask and it will be given to you; seek and you will find; knock and the door will be opened to you. For everyone who asks receives; he who seeks finds; and to him who knocks, the door will be opened" (Matt. 7:7, 8). "If any of you lacks wisdom, he should ask God, who gives generously to all without finding fault, and it will be given to him" (James 1:5). God may be letting you come to the end of yourself before He reveals His answer. Wait on the Lord.

What happens if you must make a decision before you get an answer? Be sure the decision must immediately be made before using your own reason.

your circumstance before it happened. Sometimes God allows problems to enter our lives to increase our dependence on and faith in Him. When this occurs, pray, "Teach me through this so that I'll know better how to walk in the Spirit by faith." Ask yourself, *How could God possibly use my problem?* Could it be:

- A platform for God to demonstrate His power? The bigger the problem, the greater the glory God receives when He solves it.
- A blessing from God for which you have not asked? God uses the problem to get your attention.
- An opportunity for God to develop another character trait in you, such as love or patience?
- An opportunity to develop a more effective prayer life? My friend Tom Elliff, who taught me this strategy of praying based on Bible promises, says, "Maybe it means the Lord has not yet given up on the fact that I might yet learn to pray."

Stop and write your problem in the form of a question so you will recognize an answer. Then, before you go to the next step, ask yourself, *Am I abiding in Christ and am I committed to His will for my life?*

2. TURN TO GOD FOR THE SOLUTION TO YOUR PROBLEM

Bring your problem to God first. God may send you to other consultants or helpers later but seek Him first. Be sure that you are systematically abiding in the Word. Be willing to wait on God for His solution.

3. ALLOW THE SPIRIT TO ILLUMINATE A SCRIPTURE AND APPLY IT TO YOUR PROBLEM

Just like different people who hear the same sermon would apply it differently in each of their lives, the Holy Spirit can apply the same Scripture in different ways to you. While biblical interpretation has very specific rules by which scholars know what that Scripture is saying to the original readers, biblical application is the Spirit taking those same truths and applying them to your life in a specific situation at a specific time. When the Holy Spirit has impressed a Scripture on you, write down the verse(s) and how you believe God is applying it to your problem.

4. ASK GOD TO ANSWER YOUR REQUEST BASED ON HIS REVEALED WORD

Write down the specific request so you will know when the answer has come.

something to believe it exists. You may not understand electricity; yet you turn on the light when you enter a dark room. The reason you can believe without seeing the source is the evidence in the result. You have never seen the Holy Spirit, but you can experience Him at work in your life and in the lives of others. You have not seen Jesus, but you know that He is present within you. Jesus told Thomas, "Blessed are those who have not seen and yet have believed" (John 20:29). You can believe because the Holy Spirit reveals truth to you through God's Word. "And without faith it is impossible to please God, because anyone who comes to him must believe that he exists and that he rewards those who earnestly seek him" (Heb. 11:6). So how do you communicate faith to God?

ASK ACCORDING TO GOD'S WILL

God is willing to give to you abundantly, but you may fail to ask for the things He wants you to have. After you discern what His will is for you, then ask on the basis of God's Word. It is not just coming with your own desires and asking the Lord to give you a verse to back it up. It is saying to the Lord, "Now that you have revealed Your will, I am going to believe it will be done as You desire."

Many incidents in the Bible illustrate times when people discerned God's will and then asked on the basis of it. When Nehemiah learned about his people in exile, he remembered the word of God to Moses: "Remember the instruction you gave your servant Moses, saying, 'If you are unfaithful, I will scatter you among the nations, but if you return to me and obey my commands, then even if your exiled people are at the farthest horizon, I will gather them from there and bring them to the place I have chosen as a dwelling for my Name'" (Neh. 1:8, 9). On the basis of that, Nehemiah prayed that God would allow him to go back to Jerusalem and rebuild the walls.

Daniel, as he studied the prophet Jeremiah, read that the desolation of Jerusalem would last seventy years. After that, God would bring His people back from exile and restore the sanctuary. It had been sixty-eight years and there was no sign that God was accomplishing this. Daniel began to pray and believe God until he saw it happen: "In the first year of his reign, I, Daniel, understood from the Scriptures, according to the word of the LORD given to Jeremiah the prophet, that the desolation of Jerusalem would last seventy years. So I turned to the Lord God and pleaded with him in prayer and petition, in fasting, and in sackcloth and ashes" (Dan. 9:2, 3; read Daniel's entire prayer in verses 4–19).

The crippled man who lay at the pool of Bethesda had been there for thirty-eight years, but when Jesus said, "Take your mat and walk," he did so based on the word of Jesus (see Mark 2:9). God will do as He has promised or will help you do as He has directed you. Remain in the verse that God reveals to you. As you read your Bible each day, God's Spirit has the power to make His will known to you. Ask God to answer, based on His Word, and be specific in your request.

ACCEPT GOD'S WILL IN FAITH

"This is the confidence—the assurance, the [privilege of] boldness—which we have in Him: [we are sure] that if we ask anything (make any request) according to his will (in agreement with His own plan), He listens to and hears us. And if (since) we [positively] know that he listens to us in whatever we ask—we also know [with settled and absolute knowledge] that we have [granted us as our present possessions] the request made of Him" (1 John 5:14–15, AMP).

The second way to communicate faith to God is to accept His will in faith. Trust what God has told you in His Word rather than your feelings or hopes. Since God said it, believe it and practice it. When the Holy Spirit puts together truth and faith in your life, the request you make will be answered. You can depend on it, not by signs or fleeces, but by faith. Begin to visualize and live as if it has already been granted. Memorize and repeat the promise to God and to yourself when doubts arise.

ACT ON THE BASIS OF GOD'S WORD TO YOU

The final step is to act on the basis of the Word from God. After you have prayed in faith, you act even when you cannot see the answer to your request. True faith acts when you cannot see. Too many Christians want to depend on physical senses and intellect for truth. Jesus often instructed persons to act first and receive the result after the act. Read His instructions to the blind man and to the lepers: "'Go,' he told him, 'wash in the Pool of Siloam' . . . So the man went and washed, and came home seeing" (John 9:7). "When he saw them, he said, 'Go, show yourselves to the priests.' And as they went, they were cleansed" (Luke 17:14).

My first mission trip required me to act in faith before I had the answer. I was serving as pastor of Inglewood Baptist Church in Grand Prairie, Texas, and the church had just been in spontaneous revival. A large contingent of volunteers was going to Japan on the first volunteer partnership my denomination had sponsored. Two volunteers from our church had been invited to go along, but I had not been asked. I really wanted to go. One morning, I was crying out to the Lord at 3:00 A.M. "Lord, why can't I go? You know I have always wanted to be a missionary." The Lord's answer was that I did not have enough faith. "Oh, if that is all I need, I'll have faith," I told Him. I sensed then the Lord's approval and affirmation and I was convinced that I would be able to go.

However, in addition to not having an invitation, the other real problem was that I did not have the fifteen hundred dollars needed to go. At that time, I was only making about four thousand dollars a year and could not spare the money. I shared with my church that I felt God wanted me to go. Eventually I received an invitation to go, and the church took an offering. After several weeks, the church had raised between five and six hundred dollars but then the money just stopped. Some of the members had decided that their pastor should not go to a foreign country but should stay and minister to them, so they had boycotted the offering.

The state evangelism director who was planning the crusade called me one day to find out if I was going to be able to go. He said he could wait no longer and needed to know now if I was going. I knew this was a test of my faith. It was not as easy to tell him "yes" as it had been to tell God that I would have the faith, but I knew it was time to exercise the faith I had proclaimed. I told him that I would go and would send him the money the following Monday.

On Sunday I told the church that this would be the last chance to give toward the mission trip. After the offering, one of the men came to the front and said, "Pastor, you are on your way to Japan. Some of the men have gotten together and decided we will borrow the money from the bank for you to go." I told them, "No, I don't believe that is God's way. I believe He has taken care of it in the offering we just received." I went on home, not even waiting for them to count the money.

A little while later, they phoned. "Brother Avery, how much do you think we got in the offering?" I told them, "$1,500." "Well," they said, "We got the $1,500 and $3.43 for coffee money." The final count had been $1,503.43!

HOW TO PRAY THROUGH A PROBLEM

Now let's use these six steps and relate them specifically to praying through a problem in your life.

1. IDENTIFY THE PROBLEM

Take a moment now and identify a problem in your life that needs a solution. One definition of a problem is "a God-acknowledged need that has entered your life." Recognize that God can and will work through your problem for your good and His glory: "We know that in all things God works for the good of those who love him, who have been called according to his purpose" (Rom. 8:28). Secondly, recognize that God is sovereign. He knew about

But if circumstances force you to make a decision before you get a specific Word from God, submit yourself to His will and make the decision in light of total biblical revelation and the Spirit's leading. "Trust in the LORD with all your heart and lean not on your understanding; in all your ways acknowledge him, and he will make your paths straight" (Prov. 3:5, 6).

𝒴ou 𝒞ommunicate 𝒡aith to 𝒢od

When you have discerned the truth of God's Word, you have something in which to put your faith. The word *faith* is often misunderstood and misused. A child once defined faith as "believing something even when you know it isn't true." That is not biblical faith. Faith is not blind allegiance that hopes against hope that something is true. Biblical faith is grounded in the truth of God's Word.

"Faith is being sure of what we hope for and certain of what we do not see" (Heb. 11:1). Faith believes God's promises as strongly as if they were already objective realities. Faith has absolute confidence in something without physical evidence. Although God is invisible, you know Him when you have faith in what He says.

Christians often try to manufacture faith by desperately trying to believe that what they desire will happen. Their "faith" is based not on God's revealed will but on the desires of their hearts. You cannot claim something in faith because you want it to be so. You can only claim in faith what you see in His Word that God wants to be so.

The account of Jesus' healing of the centurion's servant is an example of true faith. When Jesus offered to heal the servant, the centurion believed that Jesus would and could do it without even physically being there. Jesus' promise of healing was the same to the centurion as seeing the healing. He believed its reality and the servant was healed at that very moment (see Matt. 8:5–13).

Hebrews 11 records ways that many persons in the Old Testament demonstrated faith. This roll call of faith does not mention them merely because of what they thought. They are listed and praised because of their works of faith—their faith in action. Faith is not just an intellectual belief or an emotional response. Faith is acting on God's revealed will. God's will is revealed in His Word. After you have learned to use God's Word to discern His will, you walk it out in faith. "We live by faith, not by sight" (2 Cor. 5:7).

Faith pleases God because it shows you trust His promises even when they seem to be impossible. The devil would like for you to believe that if you cannot see something, you cannot believe it. But you do not have to see

5. ACCEPT GOD'S WORD IN FAITH

Believe that God is going to do it in whatever way He chooses. Accept it as a certainty, watch for it, and praise Him for it. Be open to any way God may act.

6. ACT ON THE BASIS OF GOD'S WORD TO YOU

Write down what actions you will take, based on this word. Now carry out those answers. Begin to think and act as if you can already see, feel, know, and experience God's answer. You show full faith when you act on the basis of what you believe. All through the Bible, you see God operating by covenant. In each case, God revealed His will and made a promise. When the people met the conditions of the covenant God had established, they believed God and received the blessing.

- Keep a record of God's answers to prayers. Watch your faith grow.
- If the answer is obvious, write it down.
- If the answer is long in coming, be faithful in believing prayer. "Yet he did not waver through unbelief regarding the promise of God, but was strengthened in his faith and gave glory to God, being fully persuaded that God had power to do what he had promised" (Rom. 4:20, 21).
- If the answer is not given in the way you asked, repeat the process and discern again if you correctly understood the will of God for this problem.
- When God answers the prayer differently from your request, accept it. Praise Him for His goodness.

I hope you are beginning to understand by now the precious treasures and the powerful tools you possess when you combine the sword of the Spirit (the Word of God) with the shield of faith and move forward in prayer. The Word will thoroughly equip you to be useful to the Master as you victoriously fend off the enemy's attacks. Growing in your faith to believe God's promises can help you continue to replace Satan's strongholds in your life with Christlike character traits. The more you pray, the more you will become aware of God's eagerness to give good gifts to you, His child, as you pray in faith according to His will. When you are fully armored and have a full arsenal of weapons, God will use you to achieve mighty victories, not only in your own life but also in the lives of others and in the life of your church. To help you focus the direction God will use you, I will show you in the next chapter how to write your life purpose and life goals.

Questions for Meditation and Discussion

1. Name the six "A's" of praying in faith.

2. How does God communicate truth to you?

3. How do you communicate faith to God?

4. Name a time when the Holy Spirit illumined a verse and showed you how to apply it to your life.

5. Identify a problem in your life about which you want to seek God's will and Word.

6. Which weapon (God's Word, faith, or prayer) are you the most effective in using? Which do you use the least? Who could you spend time with who would teach you more in that area?

Chapter 17
DEFINING YOUR LIFE PURPOSE

I have shared with you how God revealed to me through prayer and Scripture that He wanted me to leave the mission field of Indonesia and join the staff of my denomination's discipleship ministry. In that position I would develop *MasterLife* and LIFE courses to equip God's people to serve Him and go on mission with Him to all peoples of the world. As I was preparing to talk with the staff of my denomination's publishing house in detail, God impressed me with Exodus 18:14–27, in which Moses received helpful counsel from his father-in-law, Jethro. When I read Jethro's words to Moses in verses 19–21, I felt God was speaking to me, and I began to consider how.

The first thing He showed me was in verse 19: "Listen now to me and I will give you some advice, and may God be with you. You must be the people's representative before God and bring their disputes to him." I sensed God telling me that I should be an intercessor for His people and that I should bring their causes, or issues, before Him.

The second teaching was easy to understand, because it related to what I anticipated doing with *MasterLife*. Verse 20 says, "Teach them the decrees and laws, and show them the way to live and the duties they are to perform." "Teach them" and "show them" are discipleship. "The way to live and the duties they are to perform" are the content of discipleship and ministry.

The third point confused me. Moses was told to choose people to lead who would be rulers of thousands, hundreds, fifties, and tens (see v. 21). Although I would be supervising a few persons in this new task, that in no way compared to what this Scripture seemed to indicate. Over the next fifteen years I wondered if this referred to the numerous *MasterLife* leaders and trainers. Yet deep in my heart I believed that God had more for me to do that related to this third part of the Bible promise. I decided my responsibility was to be obedient, and if God had anything else for me, then He would reveal it and bring it to pass in His timing. I continued to yearn to return to the mission field, and every five years, I spent special times in prayer asking if this were the time. Each time God revealed to me that I was to continue to minister through publishing discipleship materials and calling for the revival of God's people.

Fifteen years later God led me to my present position at our denomination's International Mission Board. My main responsibility is to direct the work of more than 4,300 missionaries and 17,000 volunteers each year around the world by working with 14 regional leaders and the four divisions at the home office that support them. Each regional leader works with 300 to 375 missionaries. The missionaries themselves are organized as local teams, which is similar to the small unit in Moses' time.

We often do not understand what God has in mind when He begins to share with us what He wants to do with our lives. If we remain faithful to Him, He shows us how He wants to fulfill His purpose in us. Many times He opens our vision to what He is planning through a passage of Scripture that He places on our hearts.

The Importance of Staying Focused

When you are at war, you need an overarching vision to stay focused on what you need to accomplish. As a Christian, you are part of a battle with Satan. You must clearly know your life purpose if you are to be a part of God's purposes. You must define your life purpose and life goals so that in the midst of warfare Satan cannot distract you from what God wants you to do.

First, let us look at life purpose. Jesus' experience in the wilderness clarified His life purpose. He had just been baptized and had heard John the Baptist pronounce Him "the Lamb of God, who takes away the sin of the world" (John 1:29). His Father had said, "This is my Son, whom I love" (Matt. 3:17). In the wilderness, Jesus came to grips with the fact that He had the power to do everything Satan tempted Him to do. He chose instead to do things the Father's way.

$\mathcal{A}$n $\mathcal{O}$verarching $\mathcal{V}$ision

You must know your life purpose when you are in the midst of the battle. God uses His Word to teach you your life purpose and goals. When I was serving a small church as pastor while in seminary, God gave me a Scripture passage that I felt was a goal for my life: "Since my youth, O God, you have taught me, and to this day I declare your marvelous deeds. Even when I am old and gray, do not forsake me, O God, till I declare your power to the next generation, your might to all who are to come" (Ps. 71:17, 18).

I said, "Lord, You have been teaching me all my life and I have declared Your marvelous deeds ever since I was saved as a child. Even though I am still in my twenties, I am already getting gray. Can this promise be for me?" Although I did not fully understand it, I claimed those verses for the rest of my life, asking the Lord not to forsake me until I had shown His strength to this generation and His power to future generations. Those verses focused my life on glorifying God so that people now and in future generations may know Him. It seemed so audacious to claim such a promise that for over twenty-five years I told no one. But from the beginning it has been a mark of my ministry to tell others about the wonderful things God is doing.

I am beginning to see the fulfillment of that promise in many areas of my life, one of which is *MasterLife*, which God has used to help transform hundreds of thousands of lives in over a hundred countries and in fifty languages. I still don't know all that God will do in fulfilling that life purpose, but I know He is the one who gave it and He is the one who gets the glory for what He is doing.

The Bible says, "Where there is no revelation, the people cast off restraint" (Prov. 29:18). When God reveals something to you, it is His invitation to you to join Him on His mission. Great accomplishments can be traced to people with a vision, a revelation from God concerning their life purpose. A disciple's purpose and goals must be Christ-centered and come from God. One blessing of being a Christian is having a God-revealed purpose for living. Without Christ, life resembles a jigsaw puzzle. The pieces are difficult to fit together without a vision of the finished product. A believer's completed life vision should come from God and should resemble Christ Himself. In Him we discover the meaning of our lives.

Jesus did the Father's work in complete obedience. Nothing was as important to Him as doing God's will and finishing the work He was sent to do. "His disciples urged him, 'Rabbi, eat something.' But he said to them, 'I have food to eat that you know nothing about.' Then his disciples said to each other, 'Could someone have brought him food?' 'My food,' said Jesus, 'is to do the will of him who sent me and to finish his work'" (John 4:31–34).

Discovering Your Life Purpose

A life purpose is an overarching goal for you to accomplish during your lifetime. It provides direction for your everyday activities and determines your priorities. Even unspoken goals provide a driving force and direction for your life. Some people spend their lives seeking worldly success. Others desire wealth or fame. Others vainly attempt to find happiness, love, and security through human relationships.

When a scribe asked Jesus to identify the greatest commands in Scripture, Jesus' answer revealed two life purposes. "'The most important one,' answered Jesus, 'is this: "Hear, O Israel, the Lord our God, the Lord is one. Love the Lord your God with all your heart and with all your soul and with all your mind and with all your strength." The second is this: "Love your neighbor as yourself." There is no commandment greater than these'" (Mark 12:29–31). The Westminster Confession states that the ultimate purpose of mankind is to glorify God and enjoy Him forever. Loving other people is second only to loving God. Your life purpose should relate to these two love commands, regardless of your job or profession. Everything you do should glorify God.

Many people are eager to know how to "find" God's will, as if it is a deeply hidden secret. Scriptures states God's will and pleasure quite plainly. "This is good, and pleases God our Savior, who wants all men to be saved and to come to a knowledge of the truth" (1 Tim. 2:3, 4). "It is God's will that you should be sanctified" (1 Thess. 4:3). You do not have to "discover" the overarching aspects of God's will. He has revealed them. Your life purpose should relate in some way to the salvation of the world and the sanctification of God's people. If you love God, you want to be like Him. If you love those around you, you want them to have all God intended for them, including eternal life. You can bank your life on these overall objectives.

Why not take a few minutes and write a simple sentence that spells out what you believe is God's purpose for your life? If you are not sure what it is, then begin asking God to reveal His specific purpose for you. God is committed to revealing His purpose to those who earnestly seek Him.

Setting Life Goals

Personal life goals lead to the accomplishment of your life purpose. Once you settle your life purpose, then you may concentrate on life goals by asking how you can best carry out God's will in your decisions about marriage, occupation, and other areas of your life. Every time you make a decision, involve yourself in a relationship, or invest time or money, check it against your life purpose. If you question whether a particular action truly moves you toward accomplishing your life purpose, you may need to reconsider it. "Don't let the world around you squeeze you into its own mold, but let God remold your minds from within, so that you may prove in practice that the plan of God for you is good, meets all His demands, and moves toward the goal of true maturity" (Rom. 12:2, Phillips). "Live life, then, with a due sense of responsibility, not as men who do not know the meaning and purpose of life but as those who do" (Eph. 5:15, Phillips).

Life goals are necessary to accomplish God's purposes. Life goals are intermediate steps that lead to the ultimate objective. The rest of this chapter we will focus on your life goals. A life goal is a specific objective for an important area of your life. Achieving your life goals should add up to achieving your life purpose. You need life goals and convictions about what God wants you to do as you move in faith with Him to achieve His purposes. Jesus' life purposes were to glorify the Father and to accomplish God's plan for the redemption of mankind. To achieve those purposes, He set Himself to accomplish the life goals the Father had revealed to Him: making His Father known, reconciling the world to Himself, and discipling those whom the Father gave Him to carry on His work (John 17).

An Old Testament account illustrates the importance of having a life purpose and life goals. Joshua and Caleb were the two spies who gave a positive report, while the other ten spies did not believe God would defeat the people in the Promised Land. As his reward, God, through Moses, had promised Caleb that Hebron would be his land after the conquest of Canaan. "But because my servant Caleb has a different spirit and follows me wholeheartedly, I will bring him into the land he went to, and his descendants will inherit it" (Num. 14:24). He had what we are calling a Bible promise.

Caleb's life purpose was to follow the Lord wholeheartedly. His life goal was to claim the Promised Land that God had given to him and his descendants. Although Caleb had to wander in the wilderness for forty-five years with the unbelieving Israelites, he had a purpose and a life goal that kept him going. He had a mountain God wanted him to claim. When the time came to go into the Promised Land, he said,

> "Now then, just as the LORD promised, he has kept me alive for forty-five years since the time he said this to Moses, while Israel moved about in the desert. So here I am today, eight-five years old! I am still as strong today as the day Moses sent me out; I'm just as vigorous to go out to battle now as I was then. Now give me this hill country that the LORD

promised me that day. You yourself heard then that the Anakites were there and their cities were large and fortified, but, the LORD helping me, I will drive them out just as he said.". . . So Hebron has belonged to Caleb son of Jephunneh the Kenizzite ever since, because he followed the LORD, the God of Israel, wholeheartedly (Josh. 14:10–12, 14).

Characteristics of Life Goals

Caleb's goals have three important characteristics that should also characterize your goals:

1. Life goals are God-revealed rather than self-conceived. It was God who picked out the mountain for Caleb and the time when he could claim it. God's promise was the source of Caleb's faith.

2. Life goals are too big to achieve without God's power. At eighty-five years of age, Caleb could not conquer the giants in the large, fortified cities of that country by human strength. If you can accomplish a life goal by yourself, you can be sure that God didn't give it to you. God gives you goals that only He can accomplish so you will depend on Him and so only He can get the glory.

3. Life goals are life-arrangers. They arrange your life so that you can achieve your life purpose. Caleb could wait forty-five years in the desert because he was convinced of God's plan for him. If you set life goals without first determining your life purpose, you often substitute your goals for God's purposes.

Remembering your life goals helps you order your priorities. As a child and teenager, I determined that God wanted me to keep myself sexually pure for my future wife. That commitment in my youth often arranged my life. It helped me to make decisions that would ultimately keep me from yielding to temptation.

Sometimes your choices are not between good and evil but between good and best. Satan often wants you to settle for merely good things in order to keep you from waiting for God's best gifts. When you make important choices in life, such as your vocation or marriage partner, ask yourself, *Will this choice help me achieve God's purpose for my life?* If so, it is worthy of your efforts to attain it. When you set God-given goals, it is as though you put on a new set of glasses to view your future. In the long run, a God-given goal will bring you peace, will help you look at things in a long-term way, will keep you focused, and will help you measure all things in light of God's purposes.

Setting Priorities

If you aim at nothing, you are likely to hit it. Brian Tracy, in his book *The Psychology of Achievement*, claims that according to the best research, less than 3 percent of Americans have written goals. Ten percent more have goals and plans but keep them in their heads. Yet the 3 percent who have written goals accomplish 50 to 100 times more during their lifetime than the 10 percent with mental goals and plans. Imagine how much more they accomplish than the remaining 87 percent of the population who drift through life without any definite goals or plans.[1]

What is God most concerned about in your life? What is His priority for you? The diagram shows what your priorities should be. The diagram depicts basic life goals—the major items that form the framework for building a life under God's plan. A definite order exists for developing these goals. Most people make the mistake of starting at the top with mate and career before they set the previous four goals in the sequence shown in the diagram. Note how the priorities progress. As you read the explanation of each section, answer the question by writing a life goal(s) in that area of your life.

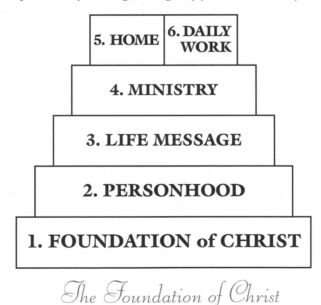

The Foundation of Christ

First is the foundation. Build and root your life in Jesus Christ. He is the foundation of your life. "No one can lay any foundation other than the one already laid, which is Jesus Christ. If any man builds on this foundation using gold, silver, costly stones, wood, hay or straw, his work will be shown for what it is, because the Day will bring it to light. It will be revealed with fire, and the fire will test the quality of each man's work" (1 Cor. 3:11–13). "Just as you received Christ Jesus as Lord, continue to live in him, rooted and built up in him, strengthened in the faith as you were taught, and overflowing with thankfulness" (Col. 2:6, 7).

The first Bible promise that I consciously claimed as a life verse was Matthew 6:33: "But seek first his kingdom and his righteousness, and all these things will be given to you as well." That promise has helped me make many right decisions about worldly possessions and life goals. Be certain that you build every aspect of your life on Jesus. The life goal that relates to this building block answers the question, *Are Christ and His kingdom my first priority?* Stop now and write one or more goals that relate to making Christ and His kingdom your first priority.

Personhood

The first building block to be placed on the foundation of Christ is you. God is more concerned about who you are than what you can do for Him. He wants to guide you to become all He intended. He is more concerned about inner qualities of character than about how you look. "The LORD does not look at the things man looks at. Man looks at the outward appearance, but the LORD looks at the heart" (1 Sam. 16:7). God begins with the task of producing in you the character of Jesus Christ. Until this happens, Christ cannot use you effectively. This second building block deals with life goals that ask, *What kind of person am I becoming?* Write a life goal that relates to developing your character.

Life Message

The next building block you place on the foundation of Christ is your life message. The life goals you write at this level answer the questions: *What do others see in my life? What does my life say to others?* You are your life message. If you are truly becoming a Christlike person, those who know you and observe your life see it. Your life message reveals to others who you really are.

In my first pastorate, I hoped people would remember the messages I preached. Then I noticed what the members said about previous pastors. They never mentioned their sermons but made comments like "Brother Jones really loved people," "Brother Smith was a great prayer warrior," and "Brother Tom was a walking Bible." Each man was a life message.

"Let your light shine before men, that they may see your good deeds and praise your Father in heaven" (Matt. 5:16). Even though people may see good qualities in you, the source of all good in you is your Father in heaven. Your life message should reflect Him and honor Him. You develop this message when you make Christ the center of your life, when you internalize God's Word, and when you develop your spiritual gifts. What is your life message? What would you like for it to be? What do you think that God wants your life to say to the world?

Ministry

Ministry flows from your person and your life message. It is a natural overflow, not a forced effort. God has called you to a life of ministry. No disciple is exempt from this call. "Each one should use whatever gift he has received to serve others, faithfully administering God's grace in its various forms" (1 Pet. 4:10).

Concentrate on walking with Christ and on becoming like Him. Learn to see people through His eyes, and He will give you a ministry. Ministry answers the question: *How can I share my life with others?* Write some ministry goals that you believe God wants to accomplish through you.

Home

Your home is a vital part of your ministry. Christ is the foundation of a disciple's home and the center of home relationships. Your home is the natural place to demonstrate what Christ is doing in your life and will do in others' lives. Your home may speak to the world more quickly than the church does. The question to ask here is, *How can I make my home a platform for my ministry?*

Both married and single people should consider how their special circumstances best contribute to their life goals. A growing disciple who is planning marriage should never consider marrying a person who does not have similar values and the concept of building a life and a relationship on Christ. For those who seek a life partner, the home building block answers the question, Who is the best person I can marry in order to have the most effective ministry together?

For Christians, marriage is a partnership, a spiritual union of two persons whose chief desire in life is to glorify God and to become like Jesus Christ. A husband and wife are "joint heirs of the grace of life" (1 Pet. 3:7, RSV). Priscilla and Aquila understood their marriage in this light and used their home as a gathering place for the church (see Rom. 16:3–5). If you are married, determine to build your marriage into a relationship that becomes a penetrating witness to the world and which demonstrates Christ's power in true love and purpose. For a married person, the question is, How does God intend to use our relationship in ministry together?

You do not have to be married to minister out of your home. If you are single, the question for you is, How can I use my singleness to increase my ministry? Stop now and write some life goals that relate to your home.

Daily Work

God can use you as an influence in your career or job. The daily-work building block answers the question, *How can I allow Christ to use my career or workplace to minister?* If you are deciding on a career or employment, it answers the question, *What career would best enable me to have an effective ministry in the world?*

"Whatever you do, work at it with all your heart, as working for the Lord, not for men, since you know that you will receive an inheritance from the Lord as a reward. It is the Lord Christ you are serving" (Col. 3:23, 24). Whatever your job, serve the Lord rather than the paycheck. Instead of goofing off or complaining, exhibit the Spirit of Christ in attitudes, relationships, work habits, and decision making. The salt can penetrate the day-by-day work world, enabling you to touch people's lives significantly by the way you work. When others see your life message, they will be open to your ministry, even in the workplace.

To help you in the workplace, you may want to pray this prayer. "Lord, as I go to work, give me a vision of what You want me to be and do to influence my coworkers for Jesus Christ. Help me live in such a way that my message will be clear yet gentle and not overbearing. Help me demonstrate genuine love and be aware of opportunities You give for ministry and verbal witness. Help me see where You are working and help me to join You. Make my job a penetrating point of my ministry for You in the world."

Do not shy away from a vocational call to full-time ministry. Most of the persons God used in the Bible didn't think they were worthy, but when they responded to what God asked them to do, God enabled them to do it. Write a life goal about the vocation God wants you in and how you believe He wants to use your vocation to accomplish His purpose in your life.

Questions for Meditation and Discussion

1. What is the difference between a life purpose and a life goal?

2. How does identifying your life purpose and life goals help you find answers to life decisions?

3. If you did not do so as you read the chapter, take some time now to write one or more life goals in each of the categories listed.

Chapter 18
STANDING VICTORIOUSLY

Although you fight an unceasing battle against the enemy, you can feel confident that you have the ultimate weapons in prayer and in the Word to deliver you. The battle against Satan and the forces of evil is fought first on your knees. God has used many of my experiences as a pastor, evangelist, missionary, and denominational leader to teach me this truth: Prayer is really involving me in God's will and basing my actions on what God wants rather than telling God what I want. I have learned that I must hear the voice of God to know the basis on which to pray.

I became pastor of a mission church of twelve members in Fort Worth, Texas. The church began to grow so rapidly that the director of the Sunday school was not able to handle the growth. So the nominating committee named another man to the director position. This naturally offended the first man, especially since he believed I was responsible for the decision. Not long after that, the pastor of the sponsoring church called me in and asked how things were going out at Sunset Heights. I told him, "Oh, fine. Just great."

"That's not what I hear," was his prompt reply. "I've had four men come visit me about the problems out there."

I was amazed. "What problems?" Then he began to tell me of how unhappy this man was and about the friends who had come with him.

"Well, I'll tell you what, we'll get that thing straightened out come Sunday!" I blustered. Operating instantly out of the flesh, I knew how I was going to settle this.

"Oh, no," the pastor counseled, "you can't do that. You've got to learn to love people and help them to grow." I left there confused and went off to spend time with the Lord in prayer. In that time of prayer, as I began to search the Word, God gave me 2 Chronicles 20, impressing it upon me like never before. Since that time, this passage has been particularly helpful in providing me with several principles of spiritual warfare.

Principle 1: Seeking God

The story begins when Jehoshaphat, king of Judah, was informed that a vast army of Moabites, Ammonites, and Meunites was on its way to make war against him.

> After this, the Moabites and Ammonites with some of the Meunites came to make war on Jehoshaphat. Some men came and told Jehoshaphat, "A vast army is coming against you from Edom, from the other side of the Sea. It is already in Hazazon Tamar" (that is, En Gedi). Alarmed, Jehoshaphat resolved to inquire of the LORD, and he proclaimed a fast for all Judah. The people of Judah came together to seek help from the LORD; indeed, they came from every town in Judah to seek him (2 Chron. 20:1–4).

Just as the people of Judah did, the first response when you realize you are at war should be to seek God. When Jehoshaphat first realized that war was inevitable, he was alarmed. He called all the people to join him in sincere pursuit of God's leadership. The seeking-God principle includes the mandate to seek Him corporately as well as individually. If you have a personal problem or a problem that involves others, such as your family or church, pray as a group for an extended time.

Jehoshaphat's heart was devoted to the ways of the Lord. Turning to God was not something he did only in an emergency. He had sought God earlier when he began his reign.

> The LORD was with Jehoshaphat because in his early years he walked in the ways his father David had followed. He did not consult the Baals but sought the God of his father and followed his commands rather than the practices of Israel. The LORD established the kingdom under his control; and all Judah brought gifts to Jehoshaphat, so that he had great wealth

and honor. His heart was devoted to the ways of the LORD (2 Chron. 17:3–6).

When you fight spiritual battles, make sure your heart is wholeheartedly devoted to the Lord. Not only had Jehoshaphat sought the Lord, but he had also sought to bring others closer to God. "In the third year of his reign, he sent his officials Ben-Hail, Obadiah, Zechariah, Nethanel and Micaiah to teach in the towns of Judah. . . . They taught throughout Judah, taking with them the Book of the Law of the LORD; they went around to all the towns of Judah and taught the people" (2 Chron. 17:7, 9).

Jehoshaphat had learned his lesson through an earlier mistake. In chapter 18, Jehoshaphat had allied himself with Ahab, king of Israel, by marriage to fight against Ramoth Gilead. By aligning himself with Ahab, he had tried to fight the battle with someone who was not of the same heart. "Jehu the seer, the son of Hanani, went out to meet him and said to the king. 'Should you help the wicked and love those who hate the Lord? Because of this, the wrath of the LORD is upon you'" (2 Chron. 19:2). You cannot solve a problem by consulting someone who does not have the same commitment to Christ that you do.

How do you go to war when the enemy surrounds you? The answer comes most clearly from Deuteronomy 20. Included in the laws of God were instructions for the nation of Israel on how they were to go to war. Not only did God tell them how to make peace treaties, how to lay seige to a city, whom to kill, and whom to leave alive; He also dealt with the issue of their heart during war. If someone had reason not to fight, be it a new house, a new vineyard, a fiancée, or a faint and fearful heart, they were to be allowed to return home. God wanted His army to be wholehearted in their purpose and in their trust of Him.

> When you go to war against your enemies and see horses and chariots and an army greater than yours, do not be afraid of them, because the LORD your God, who brought you up out of Egypt, will be with you. When you are about to go into battle, the priest shall come forward and address the army. He shall say: "Hear, O Israel, today you are going into battle against your enemies. Do not be fainthearted or afraid; do not be terrified or give way to panic before them. For the LORD your God is the one who goes with you to fight for you against your enemies to give you victory" (Deut. 20:1–4).

The people were to call the priest, who would encourage them to trust in God. When you go into battle against the enemy, make sure you are not afraid but trust God. Fear is faith in the enemy! If you believe the enemy is stronger than you and your God, you will not win the battle. God knows the enemy you are fighting, and He is able to defeat him.

Principle 2: Knowing God

Prayer is the cutting edge, the contact with God that makes everything happen. Because you know God, you can base your prayers on His person, His promises, His purposes, and His previous acts. How great is this person to whom you pray? It will take all eternity for you to know Him, but you can partially understand who He is as you read God's Word or as you look at the heavens which He spoke into being. "O LORD, God of our fathers, are you not the God who is in heaven? You rule over all the kingdoms of the nations. Power and might are in your hand, and no one can withstand you" (2 Chron. 20:6).

Because you know God, you can pray on the basis of His promises. When Jehoshaphat prayed, "O our God, did you not drive out the inhabitants of this land before your people Israel and give it forever to the descendants of Abraham your friend?" (v. 7), he was basing his prayer on God's promise to Abraham to give the Israelites the land: "On that day the LORD made a covenant with Abram and said, 'To your descendants I give this land, from the river of Egypt to the great river, the Euphrates—the land of the Kenites, Kenizzites, Kadmonites, Hittites, Perizzites, Rephaites, Amorites, Canaanites, Girgashites and Jebusites'" (Gen. 15:18).

He also based his request on the promise God made to Joshua: "'I will give you every place where you set your foot, as I promised Moses'" (Josh. 1:3). Jehoshaphat was saying in effect, "We're in the land You promised us, and now these armies are trying to take it away from us." He then cited God's promise in Solomon's prayer at the dedication of the temple (see 2 Chron. 6 and 7): "They have lived in [the land] and have built in it a sanctuary for your Name, saying 'If calamity comes upon us, whether the sword of judgment, or plague or famine, we will stand in your presence before this temple that bears your Name and will cry out to you in our distress, and you will hear us and save us'" (2 Chron. 20:8, 9). When you are praying in spiritual warfare, base your prayer not only on who God is and what He does but also on what He has promised. Jehoshaphat believed that God had promised to save the Israelites.

Pray according to God's purposes. Discover from the past what God intends to happen. Jehoshaphat reminded God that His purpose was to establish His people in the land. He identified God's overall, long-range purpose, essentially saying: "We're in the midst of Your purpose, O God. One

reason we ask You to answer our prayers is that we're doing what You wanted us to do."

Base your prayer on God's previous acts. Jeshoshaphat did this: "'Here are
men from Ammon, Moab and Mount Seir, whose territory you would not
allow Israel to invade when they came from Egypt; so they turned away from
them and did not destroy them. See how they are repaying us by coming to
drive us out of the possession you gave us as an inheritance" (2 Chron. 20:10,
11). Jehoshaphat petitioned God on the basis of His past actions, saying:
"They are coming up to destroy the land You promised to us. In the past, we
obeyed Your will concerning them. How, then, does this new development
relate to Your will for us and for them?"

This is what Henry Blackaby in *Experiencing God* calls a spiritual marker—
a time when you knew God spoke to you or led you in the past.[1] When you
are dealing with a problem in spiritual warfare, recall that time and ask,
"God, how does this present situation line up with Your prior activity in my
life?" What God does is consistent. What He tells you to do now will be consistent with what He has told you to do at other key times in your life. His
answer will continue what He has begun: "He who began a good work in you
will carry it on to completion until the day of Christ Jesus" (Phil. 1:6).

$\mathcal{P}rinciple\ 3:\ \mathcal{D}epending\ on\ \mathcal{G}od$

After you have sought God's help and have acknowledged His ability to
deal with your problem, depend on Him to show you the way. As
Jehoshaphat anticipated the siege from the three kings, the prophet Jahaziel
arrived and gave him a word from the Lord. "The Spirit of the LORD came
upon Jahaziel . . . as he stood in the assembly. He said: 'Listen, King
Jehoshaphat and all who live in Judah and Jerusalem! This is what the LORD
says to you: "Do not be afraid or discouraged because of this vast army. For
the battle is not yours, but God's"'" (2 Chron. 20:14, 15). As the prophet
reminded Jehoshaphat, God is in charge even in a desperate situation.
Although despairing at such times comes naturally, when you base your
prayers on Him and His revealed will, God can win the victory against all
human odds. The reminder that God goes to war for you and defends you in
battle assures you that you can turn over the battle to Him and let Him be the
mighty warrior rather than relying on your own strength.

The prophet then advised Jehoshaphat about the next day's events:
"Tomorrow march down against them. They will be climbing up by the Pass
of Ziz, and you will find them at the end of the gorge in the Desert of Jeruel.
You will not have to fight this battle. Take up your positions; stand firm and
see the deliverance the LORD will give you, O Judah and Jerusalem. Do not be

afraid; do not be discouraged. Go out to face them tomorrow, and the LORD will be with you" (vv. 16, 17).

As you spend time seeking the Lord, listen for His direction. Prayer leads you to God's Word and the Spirit helps you apply it to your situation in faith. God may give you very unusual instructions because He will win the battle in His way. Even fighting a seemingly insurmountable battle is no problem for Him because of His power. The Father is due glory because He is able to do immeasurably more than all we could ask or imagine. You must remain dependent on Him and base your confidence on your word from Him.

Principle 4: Believing God

God wants us to live by faith, based on God's Word. After Jehoshaphat and the people of Israel heard the promise delivered by the prophet Jahaziel, notice their response: "Jehoshaphat bowed with his face to the ground, and all the people of Judah and Jerusalem fell down in worship before the LORD. Then some Levites from the Kohathites and Korahites stood up and praised the LORD, the God of Israel, with a very loud voice" (vv. 18, 19). One way to know that a person has believed God is when he or she begins praising God for what He has promised. Jehoshaphat knew who had spoken, and he believed. Because he knew God, he had reverence for His mighty acts. Before he took any other action, he bowed before God, who was worthy of his praise. He could praise God before God acted because he knew God's Word was as certain as His deeds.

The second way you know that Jehoshaphat believed God is that he obeyed Him. What you do next after you have heard from God shows how much you believe God will do what He said. After he and the people praised God, Jehoshaphat acted on what God had told him. Early the next morning, he encouraged the troops and called on them to have faith. Even though he knew that the three kings' mighty armies were ready to overwhelm them, Jehoshaphat told the troops they must march. Then he did a strange thing: "After consulting the people, Jehoshaphat appointed men to sing to the LORD and to praise him for the splendor of his holiness as they went out at the head of the army, saying, 'Give thanks to the LORD, for his love endures forever'" (v. 21).

Jehoshaphat put the choir in front of the army because he believed his troops would not have to fight. He believed the promise he had received from God: "You will not have to fight this battle. Take up your positions; stand firm and see the deliverance the LORD will give you" (v. 17). Taking up their positions meant not only that the troops would march in formation but that the people would march in praise. This leads us to the final principle for spiritual warfare.

Principle 5: Worshiping God

> As they began to sing and praise, the LORD set ambushes against the men of Ammon and Moab and Mount Seir who were invading Judah, and they were defeated. The men of Ammon and Moab rose up against the men from Mount Seir to destroy and annihilate them. After they finished slaughtering the men from Seir, they helped to destroy one another.
>
> When the men of Judah came to the place that overlooks the desert and looked toward the vast army, they saw only dead bodies lying on the ground; no one had escaped (vv. 22–24).

At the very moment the people began to praise God, the enemy began killing one another. By the time Jehoshaphat and his people arrived, the armies were all dead. As God had promised, the Israelites did not have to fight. But it was a good thing they had brought the whole army because there was so much plunder, it took three days to collect it all!

> Jehoshaphat and his men went to carry off their plunder, and they found among them a great amount of equipment and clothing and also articles of value—more than they could take away. There was so much plunder that it took three days to collect it. On the fourth day they assembled in the Valley of Beracah, where they praised the Lord. This is why it is called the Valley of Beracah to this day.
>
> Then, led by Jehoshaphat, all the men of Judah and Jerusalem returned joyfully to Jerusalem, for the LORD had given them cause to rejoice over their enemies. They entered Jerusalem and went to the temple of the LORD with harps and lutes and trumpets (vv. 25–28).

The battle of King Jehoshaphat began and ended with the worship of God.

This account from Jehoshaphat's life does not mean that you never have to fight battles. The secret is to go to the Lord first and seek His battle plan, based on what you know about God. Then believe God no matter what it requires and depend on Him to help you through the battle. He will give obedient hearts plenty of reason to praise and glorify His name. The reason that David could kill Goliath, Gideon could defeat a host of enemies, and Samson could kill two thousand people by himself is that they had prayed first and then based their actions on what they knew from and about God. Too often

Christians try to fight the battle on their own, with their own understanding and ability, instead of learning to hear and believe God.

Personal Battles

In my situation with the offended Sunday school director who was bent on making trouble for me, I saw each of these principles played out. Just as Jehoshaphat had done (v. 3), I set myself to seek the Lord. In Jehoshaphat's prayer (v. 12), he asked God to intervene against this great company because he knew nothing else to do but to look to the Lord. I felt these four men were a great enough company against me and I certainly felt the same fear and confusion! I recognized my first answer in that verse: I had to look to God instead of to man.

When the prophet spoke to Jehoshaphat that the battle was the Lord's, I had my second answer. I knew I had not really done anything wrong in this situation and since the church belonged to the Lord, this was truly His battle. I knew I had to depend on Him. In fact, God promised me through verse 17 that I would not need to fight this battle but to set myself in a position of prayer and praise and watch to see God's solution.

The next Sunday morning came, the time I had originally planned for my "confrontation," and the four men were not there. After the service was over and I was shaking hands with people as they left, the four men drove by the church with fishing poles stuck out their window. They had gone fishing. You can imagine the credibility they had after that! God allowed us to reclaim those men and to equip them to become effective servants of God in that church. Because I believed God could deliver where I could not, standing still and depending on God helped us prevent an ugly confrontation and a foothold for the enemy to divide this new congregation.

Another time, in Indonesia, this passage and these principles guided me as we faced not just a church problem but a national problem as far as our denominational work was concerned. There came a time in Indonesia after our missionaries had been there about fifteen years that we had a strategy conference to determine what we had done, where we were going, and what God wanted to do in this land of 125 million people. We came to some conclusions that so startled us that we decided to test them by taking two surveys over the next three or four years: a church growth survey; and a joint survey by approximately thirty denominations, studying the sociological, demographic, cultural, and religious impact of Christianity in Indonesia.

Our conclusion was that we had imported an American church into the Indonesian culture, including those programs which had not functioned very well in America. The buildings, songs, and programs were, in fact, so identical that an American who did not speak the language would feel more at home there than an Indonesian from another church background who understood what was being said. To an extent, Indonesians who became Christians were cut off from their own culture and community. We had simply reproduced what we had seen, without stopping to realize its cultural impact.

We began to realize that this was not the way to reach that land for Christ. When we talked about planting a new church, the Indonesians we had trained wanted a building first. We would tell them that they didn't have to have a building to be a church; that Jesus had not had a building; and that the early church did not have buildings for three hundred years. They said, "But you always do!" They were right. We had built buildings and subsidized pastors, and now these pastors were not able to reproduce new churches.

We studied the Bible again to learn how the New Testament Christians had started churches. As we sought the Lord, He sent spiritual revival among us to empower us to move forward in what He was showing us. In 1971, we began to implement many new decisions. We wrote a document, which we circulated to our national brothers and sisters. First of all, we asked for their forgiveness for often leading them in nonspiritual ways and training them in such a way that they could not reproduce in their own culture. Then we said we would begin multiple house churches, and disciple leaders from among them to lead each house church. We would not even preach there so the leaders would set the Indonesian cultural pattern.

In order to help them trust God to provide for their own churches, we informed them that we would no longer build buildings or provide money for property except through a loan program. Our job as missionaries would be to go out into the villages to evangelize and start Bible studies. Then, instead of sending someone off to the seminary to be trained and then return on a subsidized salary, we would train them in their own villages. In our two least popular decisions, we discontinued the program of the seminary campus and re-deployed the professors into the villages to teach theological education by extension (TEE). Finally, we phased out the subsidies to the national pastors over a two-year period.

As you can imagine, these new policies were not well received, either by the Indonesian pastors or even by our own mission board. There was hurt and confusion. Some of the student pastors even threatened to burn the buildings down or to get the missionaries thrown out of the country. I told them to go ahead if that was what God told them to do. Two weeks later, a meeting was to be held by the Indonesian pastors to form a national convention. We had known about that and felt we had to make changes before burdening their new beginning with our mistakes.

The first night of that meeting some friends gathered at our home to pray after a tense opening session of the new convention. As we were praying, I opened my Bible to Jeremiah 31. (It had gotten wet once and always fell open to that passage.) I thought the Lord was going to remind me of the verse in Jeremiah 32:17, which says nothing is too hard for God, but I felt no inclination from the Spirit toward the verse. I continued to pray, and when I opened my eyes, they fell on Jeremiah 31:28: "And it shall come to pass, that like as I have watched over them, to pluck up, and to break down, and to throw down, and to destroy, and to afflict; so will I watch over them, to build, and to plant, saith the LORD" (KJV). I realized that God had led us to make the decisions we had because He was tearing down the old pattern in order to build and plant Indonesian churches that could reproduce.

That verse sustained me for five difficult years, as we struggled and the Indonesians struggled. When the missionaries considered rescinding many of the decisions, I preached on the story of Jehoshaphat and the principles we have been studying in this chapter. Since then, God has added hundreds of churches and thousands of converts to the Indonesian convention of churches. What God had to do to get ready for new growth was to clear out the old. God can speak through His Word to whatever need we have. When we obey His Word, we see Him fight battles for us so that we stand victoriously, again and again!

You have learned the power of combining prayer, God's Word, and faith in spiritual warfare. All of these stem from your vertical relationship with the Father. In the final chapters of this book, we will be exploring how to deepen your horizontal relationships, how to minister effectively to others through spiritual gifts, and how to develop disciples as you follow Christ.

Questions for Meditation and Discussion

1. Name the five principles of spiritual warfare explained in this chapter.

2. Are you more likely to experience difficulty with seeking God, knowing God, or believing God?

3. How important is it to have God's battle plan before entering the battle? How might Jehoshaphat's story have been different had he not stopped to seek God?

4. Think of a time when your job in the battle was simply to watch God act.

5. What part does worshiping God play in spiritual warfare?

Part 4

THE
DISCIPLE'S
MISSION

You will join God's mission
of making disciples
by ministering to others
in your home, church, and world.

MasterBuilder

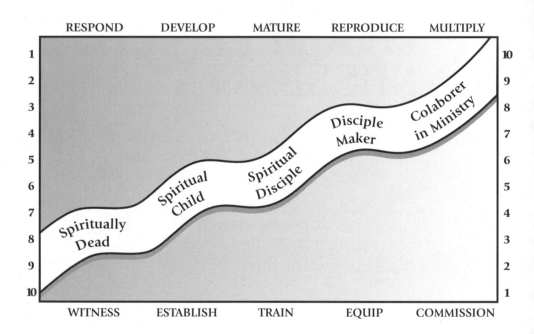

Chapter 19
MASTERBUILDER: PATH OF DISCIPLESHIP

We now come to a new phase in the process of becoming a disciple of Jesus. In part 1, I described life in Christ and used the disciplines of the Disciple's Cross as a way to develop a personal, lifelong, obedient relationship with Jesus Christ. In part 2, we explored life in the Spirit using the Disciple's Personality as the means to grow in Christlikeness. In part 3, we applied the spiritual armor as weapons in spiritual warfare to gain victory over the world, the flesh, and the devil and to exchange worldly values for kingdom values. In part 4, we will overview MasterBuilder as the process of growth so you can be on mission with God in the home, the church, and the world.

Up to now the focus has been primarily on you and your spiritual growth. However, if you are to become what Christ called you to be, then you must grow beyond yourself to care for others and their needs.

What Is Your Calling

Jesus said to His disciples, "Come, follow me" (Matt. 4:19). They did so for three years as Jesus trained them to do what the rest of His call stated, "And I will make you fishers of men." "He

appointed twelve—designating them apostles—that they might be with him"
and they were with Him for three years. After that time Jesus shifted the
responsibility to them, "that he might send them out to preach" (Mark 3:14).
As He prepared to leave them and return to heaven, He gave them the Great
Commission and the responsibility of carrying it out. You, too, are at the
place where He is shifting the responsibility to you.

When Peter made his confession that Jesus was the Christ, the Son of the
living God, Jesus said to him, "I tell you that you are Peter, and on this rock
I will build my church, and the gates of Hades will not overcome it" (Matt.
16:18). However, after three years of walking with Jesus, Peter buckled under
pressure and denied his Lord. Even after Jesus had appeared to him, he
returned to his occupation before he met Jesus—fishing—instead of allowing
Jesus to build His church on him and his confession. Jesus appeared to him
again and asked him a question that seared his soul: "'Simon son of John, do
you truly love me more than these?' 'Yes, Lord,' he said, 'you know that I love
you.' Jesus said, 'Feed my lambs.' Again Jesus said, 'Simon son of John, do you
truly love me?' He answered, 'Yes, Lord, you know that I love you.' Jesus said,
'Take care of my sheep.' The third time he said to him, 'Simon son of John,
do you love me?' Peter was hurt because Jesus asked him the third time, 'Do
you love me?' He said, 'Lord, you know all things; you know that I love you.'
Jesus said, 'Feed my sheep'" (John 21:15–17).

Are you ready to show that you love Jesus? If you do love Him, He says
to you, "Feed my lambs. Take care of my sheep. Feed my sheep." If you are to
follow Jesus, you must be on mission with Him to reach the lost of the world
and disciple them to follow Jesus. This final portion of the book will teach
you how to be a fisher of men, a caretaker of sheep, and a builder of churches.

A disciple's mission is to glorify God just as Jesus glorified Him (see John
17:1–4). You glorify God by becoming a disciple of Jesus Christ and by making disciples who are like Him. Jesus' final commission was: "Therefore go
and make disciples of all nations, baptizing them in the name of the Father
and of the Son and of the Holy Spirit, and teaching them to obey everything
I have commanded you. And surely I am with you always, to the very end of
the age" (Matt. 28:19–20). When He called you, He knew not only who you
would become as a disciple but also whom you would be able to help as a
disciple maker. What God has done in your life, He can do in others' lives
through you. Now is the time to say to Christ, "Yes, Lord, I want You to work
in me to accomplish Your purpose of making disciples of all peoples." Peter
rose to Christ's challenge and was used to multiply disciples whose descendants are alive today—including you. My prayer is that you will stop right

now and commit yourself to becoming all Christ intended for you when He called you to be His disciple and to make disciples of all nations.

Who Will You Touch?

Many people count the number of apples on a tree, but few see the number of trees in an apple. The real fruit of an apple tree is the future trees that grow from its seeds. You can be one of the few who look beyond producing disciples to discern their ultimate potential for becoming disciple makers and colaborers in ministry. Jesus saw beyond the instability and volatility of Simon and called him Peter, the rock. Barnabas saw beyond the quitter, John Mark, and dedicated his ministry to developing the future writer of the Gospel of Mark. You too can become a MasterBuilder who helps disciples produce more disciples who will minister together as colaborers.

When I was president of a seminary in Indonesia, I consciously discipled people at the five different stages of their spiritual walk shown in the MasterBuilder diagram on page 194. I witnessed to one of the groundskeepers, and led him to Christ, and then began to teach him to walk in his new faith. I was already establishing a new believer who worked in the accounting department. I helped him learn the basics of the Christian life as a spiritual child. At the same time, I was training my pastor, Suwito, to mature in his faith as a spiritual disciple. I was also equipping Sudiono, the academic dean, as a disciple maker. In addition, I was working with Marvin Leech, a colaborer in discipleship, as we worked together to develop discipleship training materials.

The Path of Spiritual Growth

Look closely at the picture of the discipling process called MasterBuilder on page 194. It overviews the stages of development in a disciple's life. It describes what happens in each stage and outlines ways a disciple maker enables disciples to move to each new stage of growth until they have become what Christ wants them to be.

The path represents your lifelong spiritual growth. Notice that the path goes up and down because spiritual growth is not a consistently upward process. In some periods you grow fast, and in others you seem to plateau. However, a disciple should have a distinctly upward growth trend. The words at the bottom of the diagram name the tasks of a disciple maker. The words at the top name the corresponding task of a disciple.

There are five stages of spiritual growth. First, people are *spiritually dead* in their sins and do not know Christ. Spiritually dead persons cannot respond to Christ except as the Holy Spirit draws them. When the Spirit of

God convicts persons and they repent, call on Jesus, and are saved, they become *spiritual children*. Spiritual children have many of the same characteristics as physical children. They require much more attention and care when they are newly born in the Spirit. As they grow, they become *spiritual disciples.* As spiritual disciples mature, they become *disciple makers*, helping others in the growth process. As disciple makers continue to develop, they finally become *colaborers in ministry* with other disciple makers as they reach the lost, make new disciples, and lead teams of disciple makers to reproduce themselves. The ultimate mission of the church is to develop disciples, as Jesus did, and to make disciples of all nations.

As you consider this process, determine your own stage of spiritual development. No matter what stage you are in, you should be able to disciple others through the stages you have completed.

Jesus' Example

Jesus' model of making disciples illustrates the work of a MasterBuilder. Jesus helped His disciples grow at each stage of development. He knew that His time on earth was limited and He had to produce fully reproducing disciples to carry on His mission when He had returned to the Father. When He first called His disciples, they were spiritually dead, so His task was to witness to them. He continually bore witness to the Father in everything He did and taught. "Anyone who has seen me has seen the Father. How can you say, 'Show us the Father'? Don't you believe that I am in the Father, and that the Father is in me? The words I say to you are not just my own. Rather, it is the Father, living in me, who is doing his work" (John 14:9–10).

After the disciples started following Jesus, He began to establish them in the faith and in relationship to the Father and to one another. However, as spiritual children, the disciples often showed childlike characteristics. They acted impulsively and made many mistakes. Yet Jesus continued to nurture them so He could present them to the Father. He continually had to teach the disciples and to correct them until they finally understood. In one of His final prayers for the disciples, Jesus said, "I have revealed you to those whom you gave me out of the world. They were yours; you gave them to me and they have obeyed your word" (John 17:6). Jesus knew before His death that He had taught the disciples how to obey.

Jesus then sent His disciples out in pairs to minister and to preach the kingdom of God. He gave them the opportunity to begin the process of becoming disciple makers. They had been with Jesus and had seen how He ministered, and now they were being sent out to put into practice all they had seen and heard. They were now able to say, "That which was from the beginning, which we have heard, which we have seen with our eyes, which we have looked at and our hands have touched—this we proclaim concerning the Word of life. The life appeared; we have seen it and testify to it, and we proclaim to you the eternal life, which was with the Father and has appeared to us. We proclaim to you what we have seen and heard, so that you also may have fellowship with us. And our fellowship is with the Father and with his Son, Jesus Christ" (1 John 1:1–3).

When Jesus called the disciples, He wanted them to be with Him. When He commissioned them to go and make disciples of all nations, His promise was to be with them. After Jesus ascended to heaven, the Holy Spirit worked in the disciples' lives to help them remember His teachings, with which they could train others. The disciples then became colaborers in ministry with Him. They became a team, continuing to multiply disciples throughout the book of Acts.

The Disciples' Example

The disciples imitated Jesus' ministry, reproducing the MasterBuilder process. First, they bore witness to spiritually dead persons (see Acts 2). They testified that they had seen Him, known Him, and experienced Him. In response, more than three thousand people came to Christ at Pentecost. The disciples immediately began to establish spiritual children. "They devoted themselves to the apostles' teaching and to the fellowship, to the breaking of bread and to prayer. Everyone was filled with awe. . . . Every day they continued to meet together in the temple courts. They broke bread in their homes and ate together with glad and sincere hearts, praising God and enjoying the favor of all the people. And the Lord added to their number daily those who were being saved" (Acts 2: 42, 43, 46).

As these spiritual disciples became "full of the Spirit and wisdom," they were selected and set apart for ministry as colaborers (see Acts 6:1–7). The apostles continued to equip the new believers until they became disciple makers. As the church became scattered, the new disciples became colaborers as they witnessed and began new churches throughout the known world. "Those who had been scattered preached the word wherever they went" (Acts 8:4).

Paul's Example

Paul held the clothes of those who stoned Stephen and then scattered the other disciples with his persecution. Stephen's death haunted him until his life-changing experience on the road to Damascus, when, as a spiritually dead person, he responded to Christ (Acts 9:1–6). God sent Ananias to help Paul understand what had happened and to begin establishing him as a spiritual child (Acts 9:17). Paul developed quickly and began witnessing and preaching. He went to Jerusalem, where Barnabas began to establish him more fully in the faith (Acts 9:27). Then Paul was sent to Tarsus, where the Lord matured and equipped him.

About ten years later, Barnabas was called to go to Antioch to help many Gentile Christians who had come to faith in Christ. Remembering Paul, Barnabas went to Tarsus to find him. He brought Paul back to Antioch, and he and Paul taught the new Christians there for a year. (Acts 11:22–26). Barnabas was training and equipping Paul to be a disciple maker. As they reproduced disciples, God blessed their ministry and called them to take the gospel to the nations. The church at Antioch commissioned them to take the gospel to those who had not heard. They went as colaborers in ministry to multiply disciples (Acts 13:1–4). Paul continued to follow this same process of developing spiritual disciples and equipping them until they were colaborers in ministry.

One person who came to Christ was a young man named Timothy, who began to develop, mature, and reproduce as Paul established, trained, and equipped him. Paul later wrote to Timothy: "The things you have heard me say in the presence of many witnesses entrust to reliable men who will also be qualified to teach others" (2 Tim. 2:2). Five generations of disciples were then established. Barnabas discipled Paul, who discipled Timothy who, in turn, was to disciple faithful people who were to teach others also.

A Modern Example

In 1963 John and Florence Griggs went to Zimbabwe (then Southern Rhodesia) to serve as missionaries. They began doing the typical missionary jobs of preaching the gospel, baptizing converts, and building churches. Then they took in a young Christian, Aaron Simon Mbulu, who lost his job and needed a home. As Aaron Simon lived with them, he coached the Griggses in the Shona language while they taught him the Scriptures.

The close relationship taught John about Jesus' relationship with His disciples. He began to understand that God's kingdom grows only as one committed believer nurtures another one to maturity. He said, "A lot of Christian leaders don't do much with discipleship because it is costly. It's like raising a baby. When it wakes up at night, you have to take care of it." The cost of discipleship is spending time with the people you are discipling.

When Southern Rhodesia declared its independence from England and war broke out, the Griggses were not able to venture far from home. So they began a home-based ministry of relationships with believers. They taught their students the importance of multiplying the kingdom in other hearts. John taught, "A disciple is more than a convert. A convert—you dip 'em, drop 'em, and that's it. But a disciple is someone you lead to the Lord and teach him to reproduce his spiritual life in someone else. It starts a multiplication process."

And the Griggses saw multiplication. When they first arrived in Masvingo, they began working with four churches, which were baptizing a handful of people every year. Once they began concentrating on discipling disciple makers, the numbers of new churches and baptized believers sharply increased. By the time they retired and returned to the United States in March 1996, the four churches had multiplied to 365 churches which were starting about 40 new churches and baptizing more than 2,000 people a year. Like Jesus, they left the ministry in the hands of faithful disciples. "I always tried to model what our leaders needed to do, then let them do it," John said. "After Jesus showed His disciples how to do it, He went back to heaven!"

Your Responsibility

You are to do what Jesus did: witness to what God has done and is doing in your life. Take every opportunity to glorify God and to emphasize that He is always working and that you are joining Him in His work. Spiritually dead persons will usually respond to your witness. Their response depends on the condition of their heart, not on your witness. The more people hear others witness of Christ, the more likely they are to respond. When persons respond to your witness for Christ, turn from their sins, and choose Him as Lord, they become new spiritual children.

Jesus wants you to establish spiritual children in the disciplines of the Christian life until they become spiritual disciples. Use the disciplines of the Disciple's Cross to help them grow. Be patient. When you train persons, you usually have to do something more than once. A MasterBuilder's task is to equip disciples to make disciples. Equipping goes beyond training. When you equip persons, they understand concepts and skills so well that they can adjust to any situation and can complete a task. Ultimately, a disciple maker should equip others to reproduce themselves so the number of disciples continues to multiply.

Paul gave some analogies to explain the process of helping others grow. He likened discipling new believers to feeding a child. Paul wrote: "I gave you milk, not solid food, for you were not ready for it. Indeed, you are still not ready" (1 Cor. 3:2). The way you can tell what stage persons are in is how they partake of spiritual food. Spiritually dead persons do not eat and assimilate God's Word. Spiritual children cannot feed themselves. Others must feed them the Word by making it simple so they can understand it. However, spiritual disciples can feed themselves. Although they continue to benefit from others, they learn to study the Bible for themselves so they grow and mature. When they become disciple makers, they want to feed others, to help them grow as they have grown. Colaborers in ministry prepare different kinds of food so the disciples of all levels can feed and grow as they need.

Paul also compared building disciples to planting a garden: "I planted the seed, Apollos watered it, but God made it grow" (1 Cor. 3:6). Someone must plant the seed by witnessing. Jesus' parable in Matthew 13:1–9 shows that the seed's growth depends on the response of the soil. God draws people to Himself so they can respond. If they receive the seed of the Word in their hearts, they have eternal life. Then you water it so that they begin to develop. As they develop, you continue to work the ground by training them until they mature. They grow and bear fruit. When this fruit has matured, it falls on the ground and dies, but in doing so, it multiplies. Jesus said, "Unless a kernel of wheat falls to the ground and dies, it remains only a single seed. But if it dies, it produces many seeds" (John 12:24). The seed begins to reproduce and multiply, and God receives glory.

HOW TO BECOME A MASTERBUILDER

1. As you develop, help someone through the stages you have already experienced. For example, even a spiritual child can witness to spiritually dead persons. A spiritual disciple can establish spiritual children. A disciple maker can train spiritual disciples. A colaborer in ministry can equip disciple makers. As you train another person in the stage you have passed through, you learn more about it and make it more a part of your life.

2. Although your ministry may focus on discipling persons at a particular stage, it is helpful to simultaneously disciple persons at different stages. If you are a disciple maker, you may spend most of your time training spiritual disciples, but you should never stop witnessing to the spiritually dead or establishing spiritual children. You are the model of the persons you train. If you do not continue to witness regularly, those you train will tend not to witness. Model all levels of spiritual discipling to encourage your disciples to reproduce at each stage they have completed.

3. Remember that you are only one component of the discipling process. God is the great MasterBuilder. He also uses the church, discipleship groups, and other colaborers to help a person grow. You are not completely responsible for failures or successes. You do not work alone. "What, after all, is Apollos? And what is Paul? Only servants, through

whom you came to believe—as the Lord has assigned to each his task. I planted the seed, Apollos watered it, but God made it grow. So neither he who plants nor he who waters is anything, but only God, who makes things grow. The man who plants and the man who waters have one purpose, and each will be rewarded according to his own labor" (1 Cor. 3:5–8).

4. Maintain a vision of what God wants to accomplish through you and through those you train. Keep looking for the needs of persons at every stage and keep looking beyond those needs to God's purpose. At each stage you ask a different question:

   - What would make this spiritually dead person open to the gospel?
   - What food would best feed the hunger of this spiritual child?
   - What would help this spiritual disciple grow to maturity?
   - How can I equip this disciple maker to be concerned with the spiritual growth of others?
   - What would keep this colaborer in ministry focused on kingdom growth and on a world vision of God's mission as he or she disciples others? What equipment does he or she need to move on into that ministry?

   As disciples show more interest, give them more time and help. The natural tendencies are to spend more time with the weak and needy and allow the growing person to continue on his own. You need to focus on those who are growing in order to produce multipliers and colaborers who can help with the spiritually dead or spiritually immature.

5. Shift the responsibility from yourself to the person you disciple as you see that person develop. Notice the numbers 1 through 10 on the sides of the MasterBuilder diagram. The numbers on the left reflect the disciple maker's responsibility level, while the numbers on the right reflect the disciple's responsibility. The discipler and disciple's responsibilities gradually shift as the disciple grows. For example, when sharing the gospel with a nonbeliever, the responsibility lies very heavily (a 9 or 10) with the discipler, but as the new disciple grows and learns to feed himself or herself, the discipler's responsibility gradually lessens until he or she shares only a small level of responsibility (1 or 2) for the colaborer in ministry.

6. Do not try to omit steps in this development process. Some people want to become leaders before they become followers. This results in colaborers in ministry who demonstrate characteristics of a spiritual child.

Keep making disciples until all people of the world have an opportunity to hear the gospel of Christ and to become His disciples. One day we will join people from every tribe, language, people, and nation to glorify God. "Be patient, then, brothers, until the Lord's coming. See how the farmer waits for the land to yield its valuable crop and how patient he is for the autumn and spring rains. You too, be patient and stand firm, because the Lord's coming is near" (James 5:7, 8). At that time Christ's mission will be accomplished.

Over the next few chapters, I will give you an in-depth look at each of the stages of the discipler-disciple relationship and how you can begin to lead others through each of the stages you have completed. Your task and your level of responsibility changes with each stage and you must learn to make the adjustment each time. Your personal journey with the Lord is the ultimate adventure, but the impact of that journey is seen in those whom you disciple along the way.

Questions for Meditation and Discussion

1. Identify the highest stage of the discipleship process through which you have developed:
   - spiritually dead,
   - spiritual child,
   - spiritual disciple,
   - disciple maker, or
   - colaborer in ministry.

2. Name a person you are helping develop through any of these stages.

3. Which of the following tasks do you spend the most time doing?
   - witnessing to unbelievers,
   - establishing spiritual children,
   - training disciples,
   - equipping disciple makers, or
   - commissioning colaborers.

4. Given your spiritual gifts, job, and the needs of a person you are discipling, rank the tasks listed above in order, according to the emphasis you feel you should be giving to each one.

5. Are there any tasks you are not yet doing? How could you get additional training in that area?

Chapter 20
RIGHTING WRONG RELATIONSHIPS

My close friend, Tom Elliff, and his wife Jeannie had just told Tom's parents that they were being called to the mission field in Africa when a chain of events began to unfold that taught Tom a powerful lesson in forgiveness and the importance of making wrong relationships right. As they shared God's call on their heart, Tom and Jeannie joyfully received support from his father and mother.

But the next thing that happened caused Tom's heart to sink into his shoes. His pastor-father, who had been his hero since childhood and who had led more than a thousand people to the Lord in his lifetime, looked at his mother and said, "I guess I had better tell everything. I don't love you anymore. I'm going to leave you."

Tom and Jeannie delayed their departure for Africa for a year as the family rallied around Tom's parents to try to help salvage their marriage of forty-three years. For a time, things seemed to improve. As Tom at last prepared to leave, his father wept and told Tom, "I'm sorry this happened. It won't happen again." Just hours later, as Tom and Jeannie prepared to board the plane for Africa, Tom called home from New York one more time. His mother greeted him with the heart-breaking news, "Tommy, your daddy has left, and this time it's for good." The family learned later that the father had lapsed into a deep moral and spiritual dementia. Within months, Tom's father remarried and moved to another state. Communication became strained and almost nonexistent as the family grieved over the breakup.

"I knew then that God was going to have to teach me how to forgive," Tom said. "I could sense a rising bitterness in my soul. Bitterness of any kind will ultimately defile a person. So I began seeking God on how to forgive."

Events that occurred after the Elliff family arrived in Africa only compounded Tom's bitterness. Nine months after their arrival, Jeannie and their four children were involved in a serious automobile accident that left their oldest daughter near death. She recovered but they needed to return to the United States to care for her medical needs. In the midst of the turmoil, Tom learned that the accident was the result of sabotage from the very people he came to serve.

Later when they were back in the States and Tom was serving as a pastor in Denver, his mother was diagnosed with Alzheimer's. Tom said, "I kept saying to God, 'This is so unfair. She never hurt anybody. She was the one who was hurt.'" Then one day his brother called to say their mother had had a cerebral hemorrhage and had only hours to live. At the end of two weeks in a coma, however, his mother stirred and stated three words, "Want. Want. Want." After family members suggested things she might want, one person asked if she desired to talk to her former husband. "It had been two and a half years since they had talked," Tom said. "But at the name of our father, she said the words, 'Forgive. Forgive. Forgive.'"

Amazingly, the next day Tom's dad called on the telephone and asked to speak to their mother. Tom told his father she was dying but finally put the telephone up to his mother's ear. As the sound of his voice, her eyes opened, tears fell down her cheeks, and she became completely lucid. In what Tom called the "awesome, restorative power of reconciliation," she replied, "Of course I forgive you. Of course I forgive you. I love you." For the next twenty-four hours she spoke often, saying to the family, "Isn't it wonderful, Dad calling? I've got to lead more people to Jesus. Isn't this wonderful?" Then she lapsed into a coma again.

For five more weeks Tom's mother lingered. His father called and asked, "What do you think she's waiting for?" Tom suggested, "Maybe you." The next day his father arrived in the hospital room. "All of us gathered at the bedside. We prayed, we read the Bible, we sang together. Within a few days she died. But I'll never forget those words—Forgive. Forgive. Forgive.'"

God used his mother's forgiving spirit to restore relationships in that family. Tom's father and wife now live back "at home" surrounded by relatives and friends. The events that led to the divorce and subsequent marriage have been openly discussed and even used by God to minister to and dissuade others who might make similar choices. The love in the family has been completely restored, because the one most hurt was willing to forgive.[1]

Discipleship is a relationship—a relationship with God and a relationship with others. Jesus said, "Love the Lord your God with all your heart and with all your soul and with all your mind and with all your strength. . . . Love your neighbor as yourself" (Mark 12:29–31). Without a relationship, there is no discipleship. As we move into the last section of the book with an emphasis on the horizontal relationships of the Disciple's Cross, I challenge you to examine your own relationships and to let your discipleship be expressed through them.

God's Purpose for Your Relationships

Relationships are essential to advancing the gospel and to making disciples of all nations. Your love for others is one of the earmarks of your discipleship. Christ is glorified through your love relationships. Love for other Christians is evidence that we have been delivered from spiritual death and given eternal life in Christ (1 John 3:14). "Dear children, let us not love with words or tongue but with actions and in truth" (1 John 3:18).

"And he has given us this command: Whoever loves God must also love his brother" (1 John 4:21). Your relationship with God through Christ binds you together with other believers as the body of Christ. The body of Christ, the church, is the vehicle through which God intends to bring His salvation to a dying world. Jesus' death on the cross paid the penalty for your sin and restored your broken relationship with God (Rom. 5:1). It also made possible right relationships among God's children.

Satan's Ploy

Satan seeks a foothold to bring destruction to your life in the area of relationships. Satan knows that if he can interfere with or cause problems in those relationships, then he can not only distract you and cause you pain, but he can also establish a root of bitterness in you which will begin to damage your relationship with the Father, to hurt others around you, and to discredit your witness to the world.

Paul wrote to the Corinthians, "If you forgive anyone, I also forgive him. And what I have forgiven—if there was anything to forgive—I have forgiven in the sight of Christ for your sake, in order that Satan might not outwit us.

For we are not unaware of his schemes" (2 Cor. 2:10–11). The number one scheme of Satan is to cause resentment and unforgiveness to build up between people because through them he can block the flow of the Spirit and the unity of Christ's body.

Damaged Relationships

Christians are not immune to relationship problems. Members of Christ's body function as a loving family, but they experience misunderstandings and hurt, just as families do. Sin still interrupts fellowship. If Christ's disciples do not deal with the strongholds of pride, greed, jealousy, covetousness, anger, and bitterness in their lives, then Satan has a powerful tool to bring hurt, confusion, and division in the church. Immaturity can cause people to take quick offense. Insensitivity, impatience, miscommunication, and misunderstanding can lead to sinful behaviors of gossip, slander, and retaliation. Differences of opinion, personality clashes, and power struggles also damage love relationships among individuals.

Jesus' disciples experienced such a struggle. The mother of James and John came to Jesus and asked that her sons be allowed to sit at the right and left of Jesus in His kingdom. "When the ten [other disciples] heard this, they were indignant with the two brothers" (Matt. 20:24).

Although this type of thing is bound to happen due to human sinfulness, relationship with Christ makes restored relationships possible. Broken relationships must be reconciled as soon as possible. By asking forgiveness, believers can be reconciled with God and with one another. "If we walk in the light, as he is in the light, we have fellowship with one another, and the blood of Jesus, his Son, purifies us from all sin" (1 John 1:7).

Reasons for Restoration

Wrong relationships affect your intimacy with God. "If anyone says, 'I love God,' yet hates his brother, he is a liar. For anyone who does not love his brother, whom he has seen, cannot love God, whom he has not seen. And he has given us this command: Whoever loves God must also love his brother" (1 John 4:20, 21). Jesus taught His disciples, "If you forgive men when they sin against you, your heavenly Father will also forgive you. But if you do not forgive men their sins, your Father will not forgive your sins" (Matt. 6:14, 15). Your relationship with God is your greatest treasure and highest value. You must not allow anything to taint or block the intimacy which Christ died to procure.

Another reason to restore relationships is that Christ commands it. Christ showed you how to love others, and you are expected to love in the same way He loved you. You are to forgive again and again. Three Scriptures command you to restore relationships, no matter who is at fault. "A new command I give you: Love one another. As I have loved you, so you must love one another. By this all men will know that you are my disciples, if you love one another" (John 13:34, 35). "If you are offering your gift at the altar and there remember that your brother has something against you, leave your gift there in front of the altar. First go and be reconciled to your brother; then come and offer your gift" (Matt. 5:23, 24). "Then Peter came to Jesus and asked, 'Lord, how many times shall I forgive my brother when he sins against me? Up to seven times?' Jesus answered, 'I tell you, not seven times, but seventy-seven times'" (Matt. 18:21, 22).

You are also to restore relationships because of your witness to a lost world. How can you tell others about God's love if you are unloving toward fellow believers? Your relationship with Christ shows in how you treat people. Others watch you model how to live the Christian life. If they hear you say you are a Christian but see you harboring bitterness, unforgiveness, or a critical spirit, your words do not matter much.

The Danger of Bitterness

Seeking out a person in order to reconcile with that individual requires a great deal of personal initiative and courage. But doing this is necessary to begin the process. You may be tempted to postpone doing anything about the estranged relationship, rationalizing that things should cool off or that you need to wait until the mood is right. The writer of Hebrews explains the danger of not immediately resolving a situation: "See to it that no one misses the grace of God and that no bitter root grows up to cause trouble and defile many" (Heb. 12:15). If you put off taking action to mend a bruised friendship, a root of bitterness will spring up.

Have you ever met a bitter person? You recognize bitter persons by the words that spew from their mouths with little provocation. You can be sure that the bitterness began with unforgiveness and resentment, which grew until they consumed his or her personality and then began to spill over on everyone. Bitterness will consume you and sap your energy. If you act quickly, the energy wasted on fretting about the broken relationship can be channeled into other areas.

The Impact of Forgiveness

As God began to work in his heart while he labored under the weight of unforgiveness, Tom Elliff said he learned several things, based on Matthew 18:21, 22:

- Forgiveness is a deliberate decision of the will. Even if the other person never asks forgiveness, you can still say in advance, "I choose to consider you no longer in debt to me."
- Satan tempts you to retry that person's case in your emotions and reminds you of how much you hurt. You can respond, "No, on July 12, I made a deliberate, volitional decision to release that person."
- Forgiveness removes you from torment. Unforgiveness can even have physical symptoms that can harm you.
- When you forgive someone, you place that person's case in God's court, saying "I trust you in your sovereign mercy to deal with this person in a better way than I can."
- Forgiveness causes you to rely on God's resources. When you do not forgive, it is as though you are saying: "God, You don't hold the ultimate key to my joy. That person does." When you forgive, you rely on God's forgiveness, which is available to you.

The Ministry of Reconciliation

Just as God reconciled the world to Himself through Christ, you have been given the ministry of reconciliation. "All this is from God, who reconciled us to himself through Christ and gave us the ministry of reconciliation" (2 Cor. 5:18). A spirit of reconciliation should be a distinguishing mark of a Christian. You are to be personally reconciled to God, reconciled to your fellow believers, and with them to bring others to a reconciled relationship with God.

Reconciling Relationships

The single most damaging obstacle to God's work and to revival among His children is unresolved sin. Unconfessed sin and unforgiveness prevent reconciliation. If you have carried this burden for years, now is the time to be free of it. This may be the most important step in your life of victory and also in the salvation of those in your circles of influence.

Prayerfully examine your relationships. List the people with whom you need to seek reconciliation. The Bible gives clear commands and instructions on how to be reconciled. Use these scriptural principles to bring about reconciliation, beginning with the most difficult situation. Continue to make reconciliation until you fulfill God's command. "If it is possible, as far as it depends on you, live at peace with everyone" (Rom. 12:18).

YOUR RESPONSIBILITY

Your responsibility is to seek peace. "Make every effort to live in peace with all men and to be holy; without holiness no one will see the Lord" (Heb. 12:14).

- Seek reconciliation with anyone you dislike, have offended, or have not forgiven.
- Try to reconcile with anyone who has something against you, whether or not you are wrong.
- Try to reconcile with anyone who has wronged you.
- Seek to be a peacemaker. "Blessed are the peacemakers, for they will be called sons of God" (Matt. 5:9).

Your responsibility is to be pure and holy (Heb. 12:14).

- Seek personal cleansing from the Lord before you attempt to be reconciled with anyone.
- Seek to have pure relationships with others so they can experience God's grace and be forgiven.
- Diligently look for opportunities to make peace rather than spread gossip or talk about others.

Your responsibility is to prevent bitterness and resentment. (see Heb. 12:15).

- Unforgiven sin puts down roots of bitterness that yield evil fruit and cause many people to be defiled (contaminated).
- Unreconciled relationships develop roots of bitterness that make a relationship continually grow worse.

YOUR RESOURCES

You have God's forgiveness (Matt. 18:21, 35).

- God has forgiven you of a greater sin than anyone has ever committed against you. Your sin sent His Son to the cross.
- You can afford to forgive others because you have been forgiven. They may not be able to forgive if they are not experiencing the grace, love, and joy that you experience.

You have fellowship with God (1 John 1:3).

- Walk openly and honestly with God in the light as Jesus did. Do not try to hide anything from God. Agree with God about the sin in your life and ask His forgiveness.
- Walk openly and honestly with others in the light. Confess your sins to other believers as well as to God. "Therefore confess your sins to each other and pray for each other so that you may be healed" (James 5:16).

- God wants you to experience full fellowship with Him and with others. Confessing your sins to God and others opens your relationship with them.

If the Holy Spirit has impressed you with a need to be reconciled to someone, you can be sure that He also is at work in the other person or that He wants to use you to help the other person to become aware of his or her sin through your confession and the conviction of the Holy Spirit.

HOW TO RECONCILE RELATIONSHIPS

1. Attempt reconciliation privately. Your need to confess sin extends only as wide as the influence of that sin. If your sin or offense extends beyond one person, you may need to confess your sin in several stages. Begin with the source. Find a place where you can talk with that person alone and uninterrupted.

2. Confess your own shortcomings first.
   - Confess your sin without rationalization. Say, "I've been thinking a lot about our relationship, and the Lord has convicted me of my [state wrong attitude] toward you and my actions when I [state wrong actions]." Some possible wrong attitudes are an unforgiving spirit, bitterness, resentment, pride, or a judgmental attitude. Possible wrong actions are ignoring you; avoiding you; talking about you; criticizing you; arguing with you; trying to tear you down; embarrassing you; teasing, annoying, provoking you; tempting you; etc. Do not qualify your sin at this point by saying, "Perhaps I have," or "If I have." Your confession should not be conditional. You are confessing a sin of which the Holy Spirit has convicted you. Do not try to lessen the conviction by getting the other person to minimize your sin or to dismiss it. The other person may have wronged you; but if you reacted wrongly in attitude or in action, confess your sin and let the Holy Spirit convict the other person of his or her sin.
   - Continue by saying: "I have asked God to forgive me, and I believe He has. Now I would like to ask you to forgive me." Use the word *forgive* and urge the other person to say that he or she forgives you if he or she does. The other person usually will try to minimize your wrong instead of taking the responsibility to forgive you. For example, the other person will say something like: "Oh, it's nothing." Or, "I've done the same thing."

Or, "Don't worry about it." Say something such as this: "It is important for me to know you forgive me. If you can forgive me, please say so." If that person does not want to forgive you, then say, "I'm sorry for what I've done, and I hope some day you can forgive me."

- Do not use the opportunity to blame the other person or point out how he or she had offended you. Do not say, "I just can't seem to relate to you." Or "I acted wrong; but you had done so and so, and I . . ." These statements suggest that the real fault lies with the other person.

3. If you were not convicted of any sin, and are unsure of the source of the problem, ask if you have offended the person in any way.

- If the person says yes, then ask him or her to tell you how. Be sure to listen and try to see the situation from the other person's point of view. If the assessment of the situation is accurate, ask the person to forgive you. If it's not true, state the truth as objectively as you can. If the facts are stated accurately but the motive that the other person interpreted in your action is not accurate, tell him or her that you did not intend to leave that impression or had never viewed the situation like that. Promise to be more careful about your actions in the future. Assure the person that you were acting from right motives.

- If the person says no, ask why he or she thinks your relationship has not been the best. Discuss underlying problems that are revealed. The person may feel that no problem exists. If so, accept that opinion and pledge to love and help each other.

4. If another Christian has sinned against you, express your feelings to that person in a spirit of love (see Matt. 18:15–17; Gal. 6:1).

- Do not ignore the problem. The tendency is to let it go. If you ignore the problem, you are not ensuring that "no one misses the grace of God" (Heb. 12:15). By facing the problem, you may help the other person to seek God's forgiveness. That person may not even be aware of the problem or may not know that anyone else is aware of it.

- Use language that expresses your feelings about the action against you rather than language that accuses. For example, begin your statement with, "I felt hurt when I learned that you had not invited me to serve on the committee again this year," or "I felt embarrassed when I learned that you made remarks about me." Beginning a conversation with "You did [state action] to me" automatically puts the other person on the defensive and dilutes the possibility that the other person will hear the depth of your feelings. However, the other person has difficulty arguing with you about the fact that you feel hurt, embarrassed, or afraid.

- If your private appeal does not resolve the conflict, ask one or two mature Christians to come with you to seek reconciliation. "If your brother sins against you, go and show him his fault, just between the two of you. If he listens to you, you have won your brother over. But if he will not listen, take one or two others along, so that 'every matter may be established by the testimony of two or three witnesses'" (Matt. 18:15, 16). When two Christians are not able to resolve a dispute, friends can be asked to step in. They should be objective, compassionate, and Spirit-led. Their role is to serve as witnesses to the fact that you have done everything possible to bring reconciliation. They can also help you hear one another and encourage reconciliation. They may have scriptural counsel that you have not considered.

- "If he refuses to listen to them, tell it to the church; and if he refuses to listen even to the church, treat him as you would a pagan or a tax collector" (Matt. 18:17). If the matter still cannot be resolved, the possibility exists that the congregation should be involved in the attempt to bring about reconciliation. Even this final effort may fail, and alienation may still be a reality. You and the congregation may have to accept the fact that, by the person's attitude and his or her refusal to be reconciled, this person has isolated himself or herself from you and from the congregation. However, the Scripture is clear that your attitude should continue to be one of deep concern, love, and a desire for reconciliation. The relationship changes, not the Christian attitude. The person does not cease to be your brother or sister in Christ. According to Scripture, neither the offended person nor the church is entitled to engage in acts of bitterness, vindictiveness, revenge, or alienation.

- Bear in mind that it is reconciliation you seek, not justification or vindication. The process outlined is valid only when you follow it because of a sincere, loving desire to restore fellowship between you and a brother or sister. Once the relationship has been restored—or once you have exhausted all of the means at your disposal, you are cleansed and free from guilt. If you, before God, have prayerfully and scripturally completed the reconciliation process, you are not at fault if the other person does not respond in a Christlike manner. Before God you are cleansed. God's forgiveness is complete, and yours is also. Forgive the other person without reservation and forgive yourself.

5. If possible, before you leave, pray together that God will help you both to walk in His light and have a pure, honest relationship in the future.

Making Restitution

After you have asked for forgiveness, you may need to go further and make restitution. Zacchaeus followed his conversion with a promise to restore fourfold what he had taken unjustly. "Zacchaeus stood up and said to the Lord, 'Look, Lord! Here and now I give half of my possessions to the poor, and if I have cheated anybody out of anything, I will pay back four times the amount'" (Luke 19:8). Making restitution goes beyond saying, "I'm sorry." It puts feet to your apologies. The purpose of restitution is to restore to the person what you have taken from them or to, as much as possible, reverse the damage of your words or actions.

For example, if you have spoken against someone, you should not only ask forgiveness of the one talked about, but you should also return to the recipient of the conversation and make any corrections or apologies there. Offering to pay for an item or help with a project or chore would make restitution only if it were related to the wrong you did. Doing an unrelated chore or project is more penance than restitution.

Being a Peacemaker

How can you be a peacemaker? First of all, pray. Prayer is a spiritual vehicle that brings spiritual solutions. Prayer enables you to see your sin and to ask forgiveness. Prayer also prepares your heart to deal with other people. The Holy Spirit prepares the way in conversations that are necessary to resolve interpersonal difficulties. Stay "caught up" in your prayer life so that the Spirit can keep you current in your relationships. "My dear brothers, take note of this: Everyone should be quick to listen, slow to speak and slow to become angry, for man's anger does not bring about the righteous life that God desires" (James 1:19, 20).

If someone does something that hurts your feelings, try not to take offense. Give them the benefit of the doubt that the offense was unintentional. Keep a Christlike attitude of love. "Love is patient, love is kind. It does not envy, it does not boast, it is not proud. It is not rude, it is not self-seeking, it is not easily angered, it keeps no record of wrongs. Love does not delight in evil but rejoices with the truth. It always protects, always trusts, always hopes, always perseveres" (1 Cor. 13:4–7).

If you see someone offend another person, go to him or her and share your perception. Paul said that persons who are spiritual should help a wrongdoer see his or her fault but should do so in a gentle way. "Brothers, if someone is caught in a sin, you who are spiritual should restore him gently. But watch yourself, or you also may be tempted" (Gal. 6:1). Love for one another involves discipline offered gently but firmly, being careful that you do not fall into the same sin as the offender. Be careful not to let pride enter your heart.

Finally, repay evil with good. "Do not pay anyone evil for evil. Be careful to do what is right in the eyes of everybody. If it is possible, as far as it depends on you, live at peace with everyone. Do not be overcome by evil, but overcome evil with good" (Rom. 12:17, 18, 21).

In each event, the key is to maintain the mind of Christ. "Your attitude should be the same as that of Christ Jesus" (Phil. 2:5). When you operate in love toward everyone around you, your life will be a dynamic and living witness to the love and power of God. You will also be able to disciple others to grow in their relationship to God and to others. In the next chapter, I will show you how to use those relationships to spread the gospel and carry out Christ's mission in the world.

Questions for Meditation and Discussion

1. Think through your relationships. Do you know of any relationship that needs restoration?

2. Why is it important to restore broken relationships?

3. What is the scriptural process of reconciliation?

4. When is restitution necessary?

5. How can you be a peacemaker?

Chapter 21
WITNESSING THROUGH RELATIONSHIPS

I began talking to the driver of a rental car in Albuquerque who was taking me from an off-site location to catch the plane. He was a college student who was working during the summer to earn extra money for college. I asked him his major, and he told me. I asked him what he wanted to do in life, and he told me. I then asked, "After that, what?" He said, "I guess I want to get married, have children, make a lot of money, and enjoy myself." I kept asking, "After that, what?" until he realized he had run out of time in this world. He said, "I guess I haven't thought about that."

I told him, "It's really important for you to think about it, because only when you have answered that question do you know how to live. Only when you are ready to die are you ready to live. In fact, I was like you one time. Then I had an experience that changed my life. May I tell you about it?" He agreed and I gave my testimony. After I finished and we had arrived at the airport, I asked, "Are you willing to turn from your sins and confess your faith in Christ right now? We can bow our heads in prayer, and you can ask Christ to come into your life." He immediately did so.

Fifteen minutes earlier, I knew nothing about this young man. Now he was my brother in Christ. I had taken the time to ask him about his life, his dreams, and his goals and I had listened. Having listened to him, I had earned the privilege of sharing my story and I was able to share Christ. We had established a relationship.

Relationships are everything. Whether you are trying to win persons to the Lord or make mature disciples, it occurs in the context of relationships. Christ provided our model, first in His relationship with God and then in His relationships with those whom God gave Him.

A Relationship with God

Eternal life is a relationship—an intimate, personal relationship with the Father and the Son. This relationship was the reason for creation. When we sin, we rebel against this relationship with God in an act that attempts to put us, instead of Him, in control. We fall short of His standard because we have gone our own way.

Jesus defined eternal life as knowing God through Jesus Christ: "Now this is eternal life: that they may know you, the only true God, and Jesus Christ, whom you have sent" (John 17:3). God calls you first into a personal relationship with Him through Jesus. As you grow in that relationship, God invites you to join Him in His reconciling work of making more disciples and extending His kingdom. *A disciple's mission is to:*

- *glorify God by being a lifelong, obedient disciple of the Lord Jesus Christ;*
- *glorify God by making disciples of all nations; and*
- *join God's mission to glorify His name, exalt Christ as Lord, reconcile the world to Himself, and establish His kingdom.*

Your purpose as a disciple is to bring people into a relationship with Christ, as Jesus brought the disciples into relationship with the Father. Henry Blackaby, author of *Experiencing God*, depicts our relationship with God as a partnership: "He's given us the partnership of revealing Him to a watching world in order to bring people into relationship with Him." In order to do this, you must first understand the condition and nature of the spiritually dead person.

The Condition of the Spiritually Dead Person

The spiritually dead person is separated from Christ and is without God. He or she is separated from the life of God, ignorant of heart, enveloped in darkness, and without hope: "Remember that at that time you were separate from Christ, excluded from citizenship in Israel and foreigners to the covenants of the promise, without hope and without God in the world" (Eph. 2:12). "They are darkened in their understanding and separated from the life of God because of the ignorance that is in them due to the hardening of their hearts. Having lost all sensitivity, they have given themselves over to sensuality so as to indulge in every kind of impurity, with a continual lust for more" (Eph. 4:18, 19). This biblical description is not meant as a statement of condemnation; rather, it is a picture of a desperate people whom God has died to save and whom Christians are called to reach.

𝒞ultivating 𝒻riends for 𝒞hrist

Take a moment to think through your relationships. These "lost" people may be members of your own family, friends, coworkers, or neighbors. If so, write their names in the appropriate circles and begin immediately to pray for their salvation. Ask God to open a door for you to share the gospel, the "much needed news" with them. Your first and natural witness will be to those with whom you are in the closest relationship because relationship is the basis for love and communication.

Do not stop there, though. Seek to enlarge your circles of influence beyond your friends and associates to include other people with whom you could form a relationship. That person (Person X) may be your mail carrier, other people regularly at your bus stop, or your pharmacist. Seek to cultivate a friendship with each contact and minister to any known needs. Unless you know they have a personal relationship with Christ and have other believers to strengthen them, assume that you are their primary contact with the person of Jesus. Be Jesus to them. Listen to them, show compassion, and care for their needs as they open up to you.

If you cannot think of any lost person among your concentric circles of influence, examine your traffic patterns. (The longer people have been church members, the fewer friends they tend to have outside the church.) Perhaps you need to become more strategic in your relationships. You may want to return to the same checkout clerk at the super-

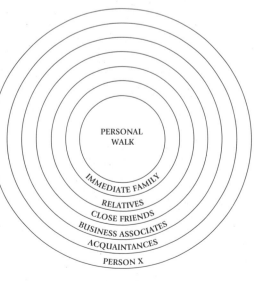

PERSONAL WALK

IMMEDIATE FAMILY

RELATIVES

CLOSE FRIENDS

BUSINESS ASSOCIATES

ACQUAINTANCES

PERSON X

market or the same hair stylist to cultivate a relationship. You may choose to walk and pray through the streets of your neighborhood so you can meet people working in their yards. You may organize a block party or invite people to your home, based on a common interest, such as sewing or crafts, books you have read, watching sports on TV, parenting, or Bible study. Consider other contacts you may have through common children's activities, such as scouts, sports, band, or school activities.

As you talk with others and listen to them, you often hear them express needs for love, healing, belonging, meaning, a sense of security, or a desire for significance. These can be avenues for ministry as well as an opportunity to share the gospel. In addition to hearing and relating to their felt need, help them to see their real need for a personal relationship with Jesus. Otherwise, they may never associate their heartache or difficulty with their need for Christ. Although you may not approve of the lifestyle they describe, maintain a spirit of love and compassion. As you deepen your relationships, share the way Christ has satisfied the deepest longings of your soul. One woman said of another, "She built a bridge from her heart to mine, and Jesus walked across." Therein lies the power of relational witnessing.

Sowing the Seed

The most effective form of witnessing comes through a combination of life witness and verbal witness over time and in the midst of relationship. However, you must always be prepared to share the gospel whenever the Spirit prompts you. Your time or opportunity to develop a relationship may be limited. You do not know what other seed has been planted, and the time you share your witness may be "harvest" time.

As I was leaving a *MasterLife* training seminar in Spartanburg, South Carolina, I prayed, "Lord help me be friendly with anyone who sits beside me on the plane. You know it is easier for me to sleep or read a book, but if You give me the chance, I'll share my faith. Help me see where You are at work and let me join You."

On the plane from Spartanburg to Atlanta, no one sat within fifteen rows of me. But when I got on the plane from Atlanta to Dallas, two men sat beside me. One was a light-heavyweight boxer, and the other was his trainer. I thought of different questions I could ask to begin to witness, but the Lord did not tell me to use any of them. So I talked with the men about other subjects for a while.

Then the boxer asked me, "What do you do?" I said something I had never said before, "I wrote a course and conduct a seminar called *MasterLife*. It helps people to master life." Both men turned toward me and asked, almost in unison, "How?"

I shared that we can know the Master and ask Him to live in and through us. The boxer said, "You know, my dad did something like that not long ago, and man, is he different!" I replied, "God is at work all around us. God is at work in your life, then, isn't He?" He said, "Yeah, I guess so." He then told me that his best buddy had recently prayed to know Christ and had been changed. "He won't go drinking with me on Saturday night. He's really different."

I said, "Do you know what I prayed before I got on this plane? I prayed, 'Lord, let me sit by somebody whose life You are working in.'"

The boxer replied, "Hey, man, that's heavy!"

Before we landed in Dallas, both of these men prayed and asked Christ to become their Savior and Lord. Did I win them to Christ? No. That was the work of the Holy Spirit. But I reaped where somebody else had sown because I took the time to cultivate relationships.

Reaping the Harvest

When Jesus prayed for His disciples, He prayed also for those who would come to salvation because of the disciples' witness (see John 17:20). He purposed for the disciples to witness to others so they, too, would believe. Part of the task Jesus has left you is to continue His work on the earth: bringing people into the saving knowledge of the Father and of the Son who gives eternal life. At the conclusion of this chapter is a simple gospel presentation that will enable you to share the whole plan of salvation by using only one verse of Scripture. You can learn it and use it as you witness.

Using an analogy of ripening wheat, Jesus told His disciples that much more work needed to be done; they needed to reap the harvest. "Do you not say, 'Four months more and then the harvest'? I tell you, open your eyes and look at the fields! They are ripe for harvest. Even now the reaper draws his wages, even now he harvests the crop for eternal life, so that the sower and the reaper may be glad together. Thus the saying, 'One sows and another reaps' is true. I sent you to reap what you have not worked for. Others have done the hard work, and you have reaped the benefits of their labor" (John 4:35–38).

Each neighborhood is a mission field of people. You must see them as people in need of the good news you have to share. In addition, people in many other nations have never heard of Jesus Christ. The gospel must be taken to them. Jesus wants you to cooperate with others in reaping the harvest. While some sow, others reap. Your responsibility is to bear witness to

God's activity in your life. When people do not respond to your witness, trust that others will reap that harvest if and when it ripens.

When you witness, you are not witnessing alone. God continues to work in these persons' lives until they are ready to respond to Him. No matter whether you sow or reap, the goal is for the sower and reaper to rejoice together. Finish what God wants you to do by sharing the gospel with those for whom Jesus died, and you will reveal God's ultimate purpose for you, which is to glorify Him.

Questions for Meditation and Discussion

1. Identify one to three people at each level of relationship in the concentric circles for whose salvation you can pray:

   - immediate family,
   - relatives,
   - close friends,
   - business associates and coworkers,
   - acquaintances, or
   - Person X.

2. Name three people with whom you will begin to cultivate a deeper relationship.

3. Can you name a time when you led someone to a commitment to Christ but you knew that others had prepared the way before you?

HOW TO PRESENT THE GOSPEL WITH ONE VERSE

The following simple presentation of the gospel uses only one verse of Scripture, Romans 6:23, to share the plan of salvation. If you will memorize this one verse and the following diagram, you can present the gospel quickly and simply. Be sure to involve the other person in thought and in dialogue about each word or concept. Write or point to the key words as you speak them. Draw a line under each word in the verse at the appropriate time in the sequence and then write the word on the drawing of the hand. Let the Holy Spirit use the questions to bring conviction. Be sure to wait for answers. The answers will reveal the person's spiritual state and will enable you to respond appropriately. Affirm each response as you can and clarify or restate any concept necessary. I will write the presentation, as you would present it to a lost person, with directions to you in parentheses. An (Answer) indicates a pause in which you should wait for a response. (Feel free to adapt the presentation with any of your own words or illustrations.)

(Open your Bible to Romans 6:23 and ask the person to read it while you write it. Then place your left hand palm up or your right hand palm down on a sheet of paper and draw an outline around it.)

I will draw a hand to illustrate what I would like to share with you. Let this be a picture of life, as God planned it, as it actually turns out, and as God recreates it. This one verse of Scripture tells us God's plan for your life. (Write *God* above the thumb; *creates, purposes,* and *loves* on the thumb; and *life* in the palm.) God has the whole world, including you and me, in His hand. The thumb represents you. God created the world and He created you. God loves you and has a purpose for your life. He wants you to have a full and meaningful life under His protection and guidance and He wants to give you eternal life, life with Him that lasts forever.

However, God does not always give the thumbs-up sign when He looks at your life. I can understand that. As I look at my own life, I see that I have never measured up to my own expectations, so I know I don't measure up to God's standards. Have you ever felt that way about yourself? (Answer) This verse explains man's situation: "The wages of sin is death." (Write *man* above the index finger and *wages, sin,* and *death* on each section of the finger as you talk.) How would you define *wages?* (Answer)

Wages are earnings for work done. How would you feel if, when payday arrived, your boss refused to pay you the wages you were due? (Answer)

We all know that it is right for a person to get what he or she deserves. We all earn wages for how we have lived our lives.

What do you think of when you hear the word *sin?* (Answer)

Sin is many things. It is breaking God's law or disobeying what He tells you to do. It is being wrong, even in attitudes and thoughts. Sin is falling short of the glory of God. The glory of God is most clearly seen in Jesus. If Jesus were standing here in the flesh, could you say you are like Him? (Answer)

Certainly not. None of us are. We all fall short of God's glory. Yet we are each responsible for our own sin. We are born with a tendency to sin. We would rather do things our own way than God's way, and that is the heart of sin. When we commit our first sin, we break the relationship with God that He intends. Imagine that a family member broke something of yours that was very expensive and precious to you. Would that create a problem or distance in your relationship? (Answer)

Has God ever seemed far away? (Answer)

Your sin creates separation between you and the holy God. What do you think of when the word *death* is mentioned? (Answer)

Death is separation from God. If you choose to reject God while you are alive, that separation will exist for eternity. You will experience separation from God, not only today, but also forever in hell.

The index finger is used for pointing. Think of how many times you have pointed at someone in an accusing way. I feel like God points His finger at me and says, "You have sinned and deserve to die."

(Underline *but* in the verse and write it on the palm below the middle finger.)

But God has good news for you. The word *but* is important because it indicates that there is hope for us even though we have sinned and deserve death and hell. Now see what God does to make up for what you have done. God comes into the picture to demonstrate His love, fulfill His purpose, and give you eternal life. This is His salvation plan.

(Write *salvation* above the ring finger. Underline *gift* in the verse and write it in the top section of the ring finger. As you speak of each one, point to the contrasting words *gift/wages, of God/ sin,* and *eternal life/ death* written on the index and ring fingers to contrast what man has done and what God does.) What is the difference between a gift and wages? (Answer)

A gift is not earned. Someone else pays for it. Some people try to earn God's favor and eternal life by doing good deeds, living moral lives, or participating in religious or charitable activities. Suppose you bought a special gift for a close friend to show how much the person means to you. How would you feel if the friend refused to accept the gift without first paying you for it? (Answer)

God feels the same way about your trying to earn eternal life. Eternal life is a gift, and you can do nothing to earn it. Suppose I want to give you this pen and I said, "I'll give you this if you pay the taxes on it?" Is that a gift? No, it may be a bargain, but it is not a gift.

God wants to give you a gift. I can't give it to you. Neither can anyone else. You can not earn it. The gift of God is eternal life. Why do you think God wants to give you this gift? (Answer)

God wants to give you the precious gift of eternal life for the same reason anyone gives a precious gift—because He loves you.

What do you think eternal life is? (Answer)

Eternal life is a relationship with God that starts now and continues forever. Nothing can separate you from Him after you receive the eternal life He offers you.

(Point to the word *in* in the verse and point to the middle finger.) Christ Jesus is represented in the middle finger. You will notice that finger stands taller than the others and is in the center of them all. Just so, Jesus is Lord of all and at the center of the purpose of God. Notice the middle finger stands between the index and ring fingers. Just so, man must go through Jesus, God's Son, to receive God's salvation and His eternal life. Jesus was God's gift to us. The only way to bring God and His people together was for God to give His only Son to die for our sins on the cross. Each name of Jesus has special meaning to those who would know Him fully.

Jesus is the earthly name of God's one and only Son. Jesus left heaven to become a human being like you in order to save you. He suffered temptations and learned to be obedient. He was like us, except that He never sinned.

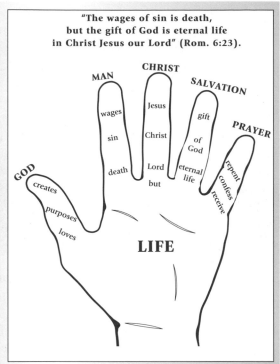

"The wages of sin is death, but the gift of God is eternal life in Christ Jesus our Lord" (Rom. 6:23).

Christ is Jesus' heavenly name. It means Messiah, King, and Anointed One. Heaven's King allowed Himself to be crucified on the cross for your sins. Imagine that a police officer writes you a ticket for speeding and takes you to court. The judge finds you guilty, but then, to your surprise, takes off his robe, comes down to the bailiff, and pays your fine out of his own pocket. In the same way, God pronounces you guilty but then pays for your sin by coming to the earth in the person of His Son Jesus to pay the price for you by His death. You should die for your sins, but He died in your place. Without bending your other fingers, bend your middle finger down to touch your palm. It hurts, doesn't it? That is just a reminder of what Christ suffered for our sins when they nailed Him to the cross.

Lord signifies that Jesus rose from the dead, defeating death, hell, and Satan. He is the first one to ever rise from the dead to live forever. The Bible says that Jesus Christ is Lord over everything and that one day everyone will bow to Him and confess Him as Lord. As Lord, He has rule over your life.

How do you get this eternal life that the Lord Jesus Christ offers you? For Jesus to be your Savior and Lord, you must trust your whole life to Him. Most people come into this new relationship through prayer. (Write *prayer* above the little finger and then *repent, confess,* and *receive* on the little finger.) The little finger is the smallest and weakest but that is like our part. You may feel small and unworthy of God's gift. We all are. But God is willing and waiting for us to accept His plan. We must simply do three things as a part of our prayer.

First, we must repent of our sin. What do you think it means to repent? (Answer)

Repent means that you turn around and go to Christ. In the past, you have gone your own way and have moved away from God. Repenting is like driving down the road and realizing you are driving in the wrong direction so you turn around and travel the other way. When you repent, you recognize that you have sinned and are headed toward death so you stop, turn to Christ, and ask Him to change the pattern of your life. You say that you are sorry for doing things your own way and commit to letting Him direct you as Lord of your life.

When you turn to Christ, you confess Him as your Savior and Lord and believe in your heart that His death and resurrection have paid the price for your sin.

Finally, when you receive Christ as your Lord and Savior, you receive eternal life. You begin a new relationship with God and start to experience a new life. When a man proposes to a woman, he usually gives her a ring as a promise of His love. What does she have to do to make the ring hers? (Answer)

The ring becomes hers only when she receives it and commits herself to be faithful to him. The gift of eternal life becomes yours when you receive Jesus as your Savior and Lord and commit to follow Him all your life. The moment you pray such a prayer, God immediately gives you new life and you are born again spiritually. (Point to the word *life* on the palm and show the hand springing open like a burst of new energy.)

Suppose my left hand represents you and this pen represents your sin. (Place the pen on your left palm and let it sink toward the ground.) According to this verse, you have to pay the wages of your sin, which is death, right? (Now lower your right hand from above and take the pen from your left.) Let my right hand represent Jesus. Jesus who had no sin came to earth. He voluntarily took your sin and mine. That meant He had to die. (Let your right hand begin to sink.) But since He is God's Son, He defeated death and was resurrected. (At this point, drop the pen and raise your right hand until you clasp the left and lift both hands above your head.) He promised that those who would turn from their sin and follow Him would be forgiven and go to heaven when they died.

Does what we have discussed make sense to you? (Answer)

Do you understand what a person must do to have a new relationship with God and receive His gift of eternal life? (Answer)

Have you ever done that? (Answer)

Would you like to turn from your sin and place your faith in Jesus? (Answer)

If so, you can do it right now. You can pray in your own words. If that is a problem, I will help you. I will pray first and then you talk to Him in your own words. God knows your heart and will understand what you mean. (Lead the person in prayer.)

If the person does receive Christ, be sure to follow up. We will talk about this in the next chapter. If the person does not receive Christ, ask if it would be all right to continue to pray for him or her. Do not try to force the decision. Leave the subject on a good note so each encounter with the gospel is positive and fruitful.

Chapter 22
ESTABLISHING SPIRITUAL CHILDREN

Imagine this scene: You are an observer in a delivery room as a child is being born into the world. You hear the groans of the mother, the encouragement of the doctors and nurses, and the supportive words of the husband. You see the medical equipment pulled close to aid the baby in any way necessary. You feel the tension and the rapt attention of everyone in the room as they wait for the entrance of this child. With one final push and a cry, the baby boy emerges to joyful cries and exclamations of delight. The parents are congratulated, the child is wrapped in a blanket, and the medical instruments are sterilized and put away. Then the nurses help the mother from the table and wheel her into another hospital room to recover. The doctor puts his arm around the father in congratulations and they walk out of the room together. They are all so pleased with the effort and the result of the birth. New life has begun.

The child, however, is left alone in the room. He is left to care for himself, to determine his own life, and to grow into a healthy adult. The parents will be nearby should he need their assistance. As soon as the child can drive himself there, the parents will meet him at the house, and they will be a family.

Take Responsibility

Would this happen? Never in the natural world! But just as the doctors, nurses, and the new parents would not leave a newborn child in the delivery room to care for itself, you should not leave a new convert, a new spiritual child, to learn and grow alone. It is not enough to pat them on the back and say, "See you at church next Sunday!" Spiritual children need attention, nourishment, and someone to help them grow and mature in Christ.

Just as God intends children to be reared in homes, He expects His spiritual children to be reared in personal, supportive, shepherding environments. Too often Christians depend on written materials and programs to disciple new believers, but programs alone do not make disciples. Someone must feel responsible for spiritual children. Only concerned disciples make worthy spiritual parents. A spiritual parent should protect, teach, be a model for, and work with the new convert until he or she can present himself or herself to Christ as a mature person. "We proclaim him, admonishing and teaching everyone with all wisdom, so that we may present everyone perfect in Christ" (Col 1:28).

In 1 Thessalonians 2, Paul described spiritual parenting. He indicated that, like a mother, the apostles ministered with care and sacrificial love (vv. 6, 7). Like a father, the apostles encouraged, comforted, and reminded them how to live lives worthy of God (vv. 11, 12). Paul addressed them also as brothers, showing how close and concerned a brother should be for other Christians. (vv. 1–4, 13, 14). Paul was not afraid to be a model. He told the Philippians, "Whatever you have learned or received or heard from me, or seen in me—put it into practice. And the God of peace will be with you" (Phil. 4:9). "Follow my example, as I follow the example of Christ" (1 Cor. 11:1).

The Importance of Follow-up

The Great Commission suggests the importance of follow-up. Jesus said, "Go and make disciples of all nations, baptizing them in the name of the Father and of the Son and of the Holy Spirit, and teaching them to obey everything I have commanded you" (Matt. 28:19, 20). The word *go* in this verse is a participle verb, literally meaning "as you go" or "while you are on your way." "Make disciples" comes from a word that means to "make learners" or "turn into disciples," which suggests a process rather than an instant occurrence. "Baptizing" speaks of a commitment to the one God who revealed Himself in three persons. Finally, "teaching to observe" can be translated "teaching to obey, guard, and keep inviolate." It communicates that discipling is not complete until the new disciples not only know the commands of Jesus but are doing them. A disciple maker can feel a sense of accomplishment only when a disciple is demonstrating his or her love for Christ by obeying Christ's commands.

Jesus surely intended for the new convert to move immediately from conversion into the process of discipleship. A church's task is not complete until the convert is baptized, taught, and trained to do the work of winning, teaching, and training others. Herschel Hobbs wrote of the Great Commission, "Evangelism is more than winning a person to Christ. It does not end with conversion any more than a full life ends with birth. It is only the beginning."[1]

Christ desires mature Christians who reflect Him and who extend His kingdom on the earth. Implicit in His Great Commission was His plan to spread the gospel through the multiplication of obedient disciples. He had established the model with His own disciples, and He asked them to continue that model out of love for Him. "When they had finished eating, Jesus said to Simon Peter, 'Simon, son of John, do you truly love me more than these?' 'Yes, Lord,' he said, 'you know that I love you.' Jesus said, 'Feed my lambs.'" Three times Jesus asked Peter that question, and three times He commanded him to demonstrate that love by feeding and taking care of His "sheep," the new spiritual children (John 21:15–17). Jesus knew that a new Christian needs the help, support, and nurture that only other Christians can give.

Nurturing a New Believer

When I lived in Nashville, Tennessee, I tried to exercise at the YMCA three times a week. I often talked with the trainer, Joe Case, about how to use the equipment. One day I saw Joe reading the Bible and immediately knew God was at work in his life. I asked Joe about his reading. He responded, "When I was in college, we used to discuss a lot of different things in the dorm. One day we were arguing about the Bible and one of the fellows asked me, 'Have you ever read the Bible?' I said, 'No.' 'Then shut up until you do!' he told me. That's been a while, but I began to think that I really ought to read it. Several months ago I started reading Genesis, and I'm about two-thirds of the way through."

I began to talk with Joe about what becoming a Christian would mean to him. He did not respond immediately but showed interest. I shared with him as opportunities came and gave him some books to read. Over time we developed a friendship. One day when I went to work out, no one but Joe was in the workout room. The Lord seemed to say that this was my opportunity to lead Joe to Christ. I began to talk to him. Then we stepped into an empty racquetball court, and Joe asked Christ to come into his life.

I began to follow up this new child of God as I came to work out. Every day was an adventure! The next week when I went into the workout room, I was surprised to learn that Joe had already been baptized. Every day Joe followed me around from one exercise machine to the other, talking to me about the Christian life. He reported, "The other day I was in a restaurant and a man pushed in front of me. I let him do it. That's not like me because I used to be a boxer, and I don't usually let people push me around. I wondered what in the world was happening to me. Then I realized that it was Jesus in me!"

The next time he told me that he had asked God to answer a prayer for him. He asked God to give him a pencil. It wasn't that Joe could not afford a pencil; he was learning to seek God in prayer. He said, "As I went to lunch, I looked along the sidewalk to see if God would give me a pencil. There wasn't one. But when I sat down in the restaurant, there on the table was a pencil someone had left. I took it home and framed it. It was my first answer to prayer."

Another time, Joe said, "I really missed a good opportunity to witness, and I'm so sorry about it. I was sitting in a restaurant, and some guys were saying things they shouldn't say. A waitress spoke up against what they were saying. I kept quiet, and now I'm sorry. I should have spoken up with her." I responded, "Don't worry. The Lord will give you another chance. Just be ready when it comes." When the next opportunity came, Joe was prepared to give a witness.

I felt privileged to watch Joe in his pilgrimage from being spiritually dead to being a joyful new believer. The follow-up with this new Christian was easy because I had a time and place to do it.

Offer Immediate Guidance

If a new believer results from your witness in a momentary relationship like the ones with the driver, boxer, and trainer in the last chapter, provide follow-up through brief and simple instructions. Encourage the person to read the Bible each day, preferably starting with one of the Gospels; to pray by simply speaking to the Lord whatever is on his or her heart; to share with others what has happened; and to find a Bible-believing church as soon as possible. If you have time, share the Disciple's Cross with them or leave some tracts on basic discipleship, such as *Welcome to God's Family*[2] Get their names and phone numbers so you can keep in contact with them until they have connected with another group of believers who can disciple them. It may feel like giving CPR until the medics arrive, but your goal is to keep them in Jesus until they can be baptized into a local body of believers, who will encourage and mature them in their new faith.

If the witnessing opportunity has come through an existing relationship such as Joe Case above, you are the natural person to follow up with this spiritual child. Follow-up is nurturing a new Christian from the time of his or her spiritual birth until this person can begin to care for himself or herself spiritually. Many times Christians do not follow up new believers because

- they do not choose to take the time;
- they do not know how;
- they assume someone else will do it ; or
- they do not remember how it is to be young in the Christian walk and how immature and helpless a new believer feels.

Immediate follow-up is essential for a new spiritual child. God used Ananias to guide Saul, later known as Paul, after he was converted on the Damascus Road. At the Lord's direction, Ananias visited Saul, told him that he came in Jesus' name, and indicated that he knew about Saul's conversion on the road to Damascus. Under Ananias's ministry performed in the name of the Lord, Paul recovered his sight, received the Holy Spirit, and was baptized (see Acts 9:15–19).

Establish a Long-term Relationship

Although Ananias was the first person to help Saul, Barnabas was the one who truly discipled him. Many times the Lord places different people in your life to help you through different stages. Barnabas was a mature, generous, obedient disciple with spiritual gifts of encouragement, teaching, and faith (Acts 4:36, 37; 11:24).

This mature disciple stepped in at a crucial time in Paul's efforts to gain credibility with the core members of the early church. Even though the disciples in Jerusalem were skeptical because Saul had persecuted the church before his conversion, Barnabas provided a character reference for him. He commended Saul to the apostles by relating Saul's conversion experience and introduced him as one whose faith was sincere. This word from Barnabas appears to be exactly what the disciples needed to receive Saul into their fold as a Christian brother (see Acts 9:26–28).

When some of the disciples who had been scattered by the persecution began sharing the good news about Jesus with the Greeks, many of them became believers, so the church in Jerusalem sent Barnabas to encourage and teach them (Acts 11:21–23): "Then Barnabas went to Tarsus to look for Saul, and when he found him, he brought him to Antioch. So for a whole year Barnabas and Saul met with the church and taught great numbers of people"

(Acts 11:25, 26). After a time, the church was instructed by the Holy Spirit to set apart Barnabas and Saul and commission them to the work to which God had called them (Acts 13:1–3).

Roles of a Discipler

Notice the roles Barnabas served in Saul's life. He introduced a new believer to mature Christians who would welcome him into the fellowship of the church and who would serve as role models of obedient disciples. He helped Saul relate his conversion experience, served as a buffer for those who would dispute or oppose him, and found support for him in the church. Barnabas then took Saul with him as he ministered so he could train him on the way. As Barnabas taught and encouraged the Christians at Antioch, Paul was not only learning the truths of Christianity for himself, he also learned how to teach others the Word of God and to encourage believers in the Christian life.

Barnabas was an important role model for Paul as he learned skills that would serve him later when he was on his own. Even when the church commissioned them together, Barnabas's name is listed first, because he was still exercising the leadership role while Paul learned and grew in the faith. In later passages, the order changes to Paul and Barnabas because Paul had become the leader. By the end of his discipleship relationship with Paul, Barnabas no longer served as disciple maker. They had become colaborers in the kingdom of God. Later, we see Barnabas repeat this process with John Mark as Paul did with Timothy. Follow this same model as you begin to disciple those who have responded to your witness.

Spiritual Children with Developmental Delays

Spiritual children are not always new Christians. They may be worldly Christians who have never been established as disciples of Christ. When I became a pastor, I discovered many people who had been Christians for years but were still spiritual children. They were not well grounded in the faith, and they did not demonstrate the lordship of Christ by their behavior. They still took their orientation from the world and were not ready for the solid food of instruction. They were prone to temptation and sin and were susceptible to harmful influences and false teaching (1 Cor. 3:11, Heb. 5:11–14).

The Surrender of Vester Roe

While I was a pastor, I visited a woman whose husband never attended church. When I visited, she would say that her husband had just left the house. She later confessed that he avoided me by slipping into a back room or out the back door because he was afraid to talk to a pastor. One evening, however, I happened to visit as they were finishing supper, so Vester, her husband, could not slip out. I just visited with him and made friends. I only mentioned coming to church as I walked out the door.

Vester became curious about a church where a pastor was more interested in him than in trying to get him to make a decision immediately. He eventually attended, became interested in the gospel, made a profession of faith, and was baptized. A few weeks later, Vester said he needed to talk to me. I told him, "Anytime. Just let me know." He did not set a time then but went on home.

That night he could not sleep because the Lord began to deal with issues in his life that he had not yet surrendered. Vester would get up after a while, go into the backyard, walk back and forth, look up at the sky, and say, "Okay, God, I'll give that up too." He told me, "It was like a game of checkers; every time I made a move, God jumped me. I would settle an issue, go back to bed, and not be able to sleep because God would bring another issue to my mind. I would go back and settle that area. This went on all night! I got up Monday morning, worked all day, came home that evening tired and sleepy, and sat down in the easy chair. Suddenly my eyes came wide open. I tried to go to bed early, but once again, it was the same thing, going back and forth in the yard and giving up things God was claiming in my life."

Finally God brought up the matter of tithing. The Lord told Vester he needed to give a tithe (a tenth of his income). Vester said, "I told Him, Lord, I've lived forty-two years and gotten along without it. I've never tithed, and I don't intend to start now. That's when God said to me, 'Burial clothes don't have pockets in them,' and I realized I needed to give that area up to God as well. I finally did and then I was able to sleep."

Vester told me this story as he voluntarily mowed the grass at the church. Then he looked at me and asked, "Pastor, why didn't someone tell me that the greatest hindrance to growth was the button on my back pocket where my wallet was?" This man later became a deacon and served well in the church. He was no longer spiritually dead; he had become a spiritual disciple who attempted to live up to his full potential in Christ.

One of the basic areas of discipleship that can either hinder spiritual growth or boost a spiritual child into spiritual maturity is learning financial partnership with God. Financial stewardship, or giving to God, is a plan God invented to keep us related to and dependent on Him. The Bible summarizes God's principles and promises in one sentence: "Seek first his kingdom and his righteousness, and all these things will be given to you as well" (Matt. 6:33). "These things" mean your physical needs. God wants to supply all of your needs (see Phil. 4:19). He wants you to depend on Him. He also wants you to demonstrate your trust, your gratitude for His grace, your compassion for others, your desire to further the work of His kingdom, and your belief that all you have comes from Him by being a willing, cheerful, and generous giver. The original language of 2 Corinthians 9:7 says that God loves a hilarious giver! You are not to give until it hurts but until you feel great.

HOW TO ENTER
INTO FINANCIAL PARTNERSHIP WITH GOD

The following guide can help you or enable you to help others to establish or renew your financial partnership with God. Learn and put into practice the following principles of godly stewardship. As you read these and evaluate your own maturity in this area, initial and date each principle by which you are currently living.

I accept the following principles of God's ownership:
- ❏ God is the sovereign Creator, owner, and ruler of everything (Ps. 24:1).
- ❏ God has made people stewards, or overseers, of all creation (Ps. 8:6).
- ❏ God meets all needs of the steward who faithfully manages all God has entrusted to him or her (Phil. 4:19).
- ❏ God will judge the steward on the basis of attitude or willingness rather than what he or she has or does not have (2 Cor. 8:12).

I believe in and rely on God's ability and desire to care for me:
- ❏ I trust God to bless the righteous (Prov. 22:4).
- ❏ I trust God to bless the person who prays (Matt. 7:7, 8; John 15:7; James 5:16).
- ❏ I trust God to bless the diligent worker (Ps. 1:3; Prov. 10:16; 11:25; 12:11; 13:4).
- ❏ I limit my desires to what God provides (Phil. 4:11, 12; 1 Tim. 6:6; Prov. 15:16).

I practice the principles of financial responsibility:
- ❏ I glorify God through how I manage the possessions He has given me to oversee (1 Cor. 10:31).
- ❏ I properly manage my finances to provide for my family (1 Tim. 5:8).
- ❏ I manage my finances in order to tithe through my church (Mal. 3:8–11).

❑ I give more than the tithe as I am led to do so (1 Cor. 16:1–2; Acts 4:32–37).

❑ I give to the government by paying taxes (Luke 20:25; Rom. 13:1–7).

I invest according to the principles of reward:

❑ I invest my possessions in God's economy because it will bring no sorrow (Prov. 10:22).

❑ I invest my material resources as a demonstration of my faith (Heb. 11:6).

❑ I rely on God to bless according to His promises (Mal 3:10; Luke 6:38).

If necessary, I repent of my current lifestyle and begin to enact the principles of restoration:

❑ I repent of failing to follow God's principles and ask for restoration (Ps. 32:1–7; Prov. 28:13).

❑ I immediately begin practicing biblical stewardship by tithing (giving 10 percent) and giving gifts through my church, paying taxes, and managing financial matters according to Scripture.

❑ I eliminate nonessentials until I can pay all overdue payments to creditors (Prov. 22:1).

❑ I arrange to pay creditors by the fairest means possible as soon as I can (Prov. 11:3; 20:18).

❑ I continue patiently to get my financial matters in order until I can live a Christian lifestyle that pleases God (Prov. 21:5; 28:6). (Remember that it may take as long to get out of financial difficulty as it did to get into it.)

Many people are trapped in personal and ideological strongholds of greed, selfishness, materialism, instant gratification, and living on credit. When this occurs, neither their heart nor their budget has room for God. However, God has stated His principles and has committed Himself to them. The way to financial and spiritual freedom is to commit yourself to living within those principles and to establishing your spiritual children to do the same.

The challenge of working with those who have been in the spiritual child stage for some time is to rekindle their original enthusiasm and the belief that they can have victorious lives. Many have given up on the possibility of experiencing the life of a disciple as you do. You can give them hope. The challenge of working with new Christians is to help them apply Christian principles in daily living. Both represent fruitful fields for disciple making:

"Then we will no longer be infants, tossed back and forth by the waves, and blown here and there by every wind of teaching and by the cunning and craftiness of men in their deceitful scheming" (Eph. 4:14).

You establish spiritual children by developing a relationship with them through which you can share the good news of Christ. After they respond, spend time with them, point them to God's Word as their guidebook for life, model for them the basic disciplines of the Christian faith, bring them into fellowship with other Christians, worship corporately with them, and continually encourage them.

Think of a new Christian who needs your help to grow. Name some Christians who have remained spiritual children for years. If you do not bear spiritual children and raise them up in the faith, you are immature, ignorant of their peril, or disobedient to Christ's command. Why not commit yourself now to establishing one or more spiritual children in their walk with Christ. In the next chapter, I will show you how Jesus loved, trained, and served His followers until they became mature disciples.

Questions for Meditation and Discussion

1. Describe the immediate follow-up you received after your decision to follow Christ.

2. What are the roles of a discipler? Who has been your discipler? (There may be several.)

3. Who have you been able to encourage or disciple to greater maturity in Christ?

4. Are you currently living by God's financial principles? If not, where are you lacking and what will you do to cultivate your economic partnership with God?

Chapter 23
PRODUCING
SPIRITUAL DISCIPLES

Elias Cuc Quim was the first president of the K'ekchi' Baptist Association and one of the first pastors in the K'ekchi' work in Guatemala. He was greatly admired for his wisdom, Bible knowledge, and faithfulness to the Lord. Although diabetes kept him homebound for many years and he almost died several times, through the grace and mercy of God he had made a remarkable recovery. Ken Sorrell, one of the Guatemalan missionaries, began to notice Elias, now able to walk again, frequently walking and talking with several younger men behind him. They would walk for a while and then stop, walk some more and stop. Each time they stopped, Elias would be speaking very intently. It was evident that these walks were more than casual strolls.

The missionaries caught up with Elias and his small group and asked him what they were doing. Elias replied, "I'm teaching my disciples." When asked to explain, Elias said, "I saw the Jesus film not long ago, and I saw that Jesus spent much of His time walking and teaching His disciples. Because I believe we should follow the example of our Lord, I began to teach these young men about the Bible and church work the same way Jesus taught the men who would continue on after He was gone." The young men then returned to their villages and repeated the process, discipling "just the way Jesus did."

Becoming a Disciple Maker

Jesus commanded each of us as His disciple to make disciples. "Therefore go and make disciples of all nations" (Matt. 28:19). As an obedient disciple of Christ, you will become a disciple maker. As a disciple maker, you will be able to train spiritual disciples as they grow into maturity. Your ultimate goal is to give them resources so they become responsible for their own growth. You want them to be able to feed themselves spiritually and to bear much fruit. You cannot cause the growth, but you can create opportunities for the disciples to grow. The disciples' responsibility is to mature to the point that they are living holy lives, developing the nature and character of Jesus, and bearing fruit for Christ. Have you identified someone or several persons you feel you could help grow as a disciple?

Jesus prayed to the Father, "I have brought you glory on earth by completing the work you gave me to do. . . . I have revealed you to those whom you gave me out of the world. They were yours; you gave them to me and they have obeyed your word. Now they know that everything you have given me comes from you" (John 17:4, 6, 7). Our ultimate model for how to disciple is Jesus. As you study the life of Jesus in Scripture, you see truths to emulate as you begin to disciple others.

Discipleship Assignments Are God-Given

Even though the New Testament describes Jesus' calling the disciples, the Father gave them to Him. Jesus did not do everything people wanted Him to do. He did only what the Father gave Him to do: to be God's Son, to teach the disciples, and to reconcile the world to Himself through His death and resurrection.

Follow this model as you make disciples. God provides persons to whom you can witness, teach, train, and serve as a role model. They are not your disciples; they are given by God. When you accept the assignment to teach a class, lead a discipleship group, or disciple someone one-on-one, make sure it is God's will for you—not your notion of someone who needs your guidance.

How Jesus Discipled

In order to disciple others effectively, study how Jesus taught His own disciples. Jesus gave three years of His life to ministry and to the training of

His disciples. He knew that because He was changing men's hearts and lives to make them like Himself, His teaching would require many repetitions over a wide variety of situations. Explanations or sermons would never be enough. He needed to model for His disciples what He desired of them in any given situation. They needed time to see, to understand, and then to practice what He had to teach them. They needed to walk with Jesus daily over a long period of time so that the nature and responses of Jesus could become their own nature.

JESUS REVEALED THE FATHER

Jesus did not take credit for anything He did or said. Scripture records Him as saying, "I gave them the words you gave me" (John 17:8). He did not just give them the information; He let them know who the source was. Jesus revealed to His disciples all that God wanted to have known about Himself (John 17:7). Every time Jesus did anything, He revealed an aspect of the Father, whether He was raising Lazarus from the dead, forgiving the sins of a paralyzed man, washing the disciples' feet, or teaching God's truth through parables.

When you are making disciples, give God credit for all you model and teach. Teach them that everything comes from God and not from you. Teach them God's Word. Teach them to obey whatever Christ asks of them. Demonstrate God's trustworthiness by keeping commitments and confidences. Show concern for the challenges they face in spiritual growth. Be patient and show forgiveness when they disappoint you.

JESUS ENCOURAGED GROWTH THROUGH EXPECTATION

Jesus used the quality of faith to encourage His disciples. His expectations of them actually influenced what they became. Jesus' first encounter with Peter was through Andrew, whom John the Baptist had pointed to Christ. "And he [Andrew] brought him [Peter] to Jesus. Jesus looked at him and said, 'You are Simon son of John. You will be called Cephas' (which, when translated, is Peter)" (John 1:42). Both Cephas and Peter mean "rock." Jesus not only knew who Simon was; He knew who he would become. A man once approached Michelangelo as he chiseled away at a huge, shapeless piece of rock. He asked the sculptor what he was making. Michelangelo responded, "I am releasing the angel imprisoned in this marble." Jesus was doing the same for Peter with His look and His words.

Jesus continued to build a relationship with Peter by healing his mother-in-law (Mark 1:30, 31), preaching from his boat (Luke 5:3), and demonstrating power through a large catch of fish (Luke 5:4–7). "When Simon Peter saw this, he fell at Jesus' knees and said, 'Go away from me, Lord; I am a sinful man!' . . . Then Jesus said to Simon, 'Don't be afraid; from now on you will catch men'" (Luke 5:8, 10). Jesus immediately stated His expectations for Peter. After Peter made his confession that Jesus was the Christ, the Son of God, Jesus addressed him again, "I tell you that you are Peter, and on this rock I will build my church, and the gates of Hades will not overcome it" (Matt. 16:18). Jesus also indicated to Peter that he would ultimately succeed even though his faith would at first be weak. After His resurrection, Jesus commissioned Peter to care for His sheep (John 21).

Although Simon may not have fully understood what Jesus was saying to him in each of these instances, the confidence Jesus expressed in him made him aware that Jesus saw potential in him and made him want to achieve that potential. As you disciple others, make your expectations clear to them, believe in them, and continue to encourage them toward those expectations.

JESUS TAUGHT OBEDIENCE

Jesus taught the disciples to obey His Word. In the Great Commission, Jesus said to make disciples, baptize them, and teach them to obey all that He had commanded. It is not enough to teach the commands themselves; the issue of discipleship is obedience to those commands. "Whoever has my commands and obeys them, he is the one who loves me. He who loves me will be loved by my Father, and I too will love him and show myself to him" (John 14:21). As a disciple maker, you must be a disciple yourself. Only those who practice what they teach are effective teachers.

No one knows all the characteristics Jesus looked for when he chose the conglomerate of twelve men to be His disciples, but they had one characteristic in common: They did what Jesus asked them to do. The disciples were superficial and impulsive at times, but even when He asked them to do something that did not make sense, they obeyed. And Jesus asked them to do some unusual and illogical things. When Jesus walked along the seashore and called the disciples to follow Him, the Scriptures say, "At once they left their nets and followed him" (Mark 1:18).

Why did they immediately drop everything and take off after Jesus? When I asked my family that question in devotions one day, my eleven-year-old son said, "I think they were tired of mending those nets!" Well, maybe, but I believe there was within the disciples a wholehearted submission to the adventure of being with Jesus. Later, they started passing out fish and loaves to the multitudes before they ever saw them multiply (Mark 6:35–44). They looked for strange men with water jugs and went to their house to prepare meals (Mark 14:13–16). They went fishing to get a gold coin out of a fish's mouth (Matt. 17:27).

Are you discipling others to be obedient? If they are to be on mission with God, they must learn to walk in obedient relationship with Him, regardless of the outcome. Those who truly belong to the Father are obedient. Obedience is the identifying mark of a disciple (John 13:34, 35). If someone is consistently disobedient, it is questionable whether this person is truly a follower of Christ.

JESUS TAUGHT SERVANTHOOD

Part of making disciples is having a servant heart. The depth of your servanthood will not really be tested until someone treats you like one! "You are not to be called 'Rabbi,' for you have only one Master and you are all brothers. And do not call anyone on earth 'father,' for you have one Father, and he is in heaven. Nor are you to be called 'teacher,' for you have one Teacher, the Christ. The greatest among you will be your servant. For whoever exalts himself will be humbled, and whoever humbles himself will be exalted" (Matt. 23:8–12).

The kingdom way is the opposite of the world's way. Even though Christ had all of the titles and riches of heaven, He left them to become a servant. You do not need titles of prestige, position, or power to have the authority to disciple. The highest status in the kingdom is that of a servant; and like Jesus, who was not exalted until after His death on the cross, you are called to be a servant for as long as you live.

One time not long after the Spirit had been teaching me these truths from Matthew 23, my family took a vacation on one of the southern beaches of the island of Java. We had rented a small bungalow for the week; in it were two bedrooms, each with two twin beds. Seven people and four beds immediately presented a problem! We had brought some sleeping bags along for the remaining family members, but now we had the task of selecting who would be using them. The five-year-old and six-year-old never stood a chance; they were immediately assigned to the floor. That left one of our three teenagers to take the other one. I told them I would leave it to them to figure out who that would be.

I passed by their door a few minutes later and listened a moment to the hullabaloo of arguing going on. Each one had a good reason why the other should be the one to sleep on the floor. I decided not to intervene and went outside. As I walked down the beach, I wondered, "What makes my children act that way?" Then it dawned on me. No one had even asked whether mom or dad would have a bed; it was assumed! We had authority, age, and position on our side. I realized that my example had taught something I had never intended to teach. The Holy Spirit needed to change more than my mind; my behavior needed to be that of a servant as well.

That night at supper, I remarked to my oldest daughter, "Sherrie, why don't you sleep with Mom tonight and I'll sleep on the floor." You would not believe the attitude change. She said, "Oh no, Dad, that's okay. You can have your bed. We've got it all worked out."

Jesus Taught through Modeling

You cannot teach what you are not practicing any more than you can come back from where you have never been. The most important thing you do to make disciples is to model the right kind of behavior. Most of what is learned is learned through imitation. Modeling will be your most effective teaching tool. It is so effective that it can also be a downfall because you may accidentally teach, through example, some things you never intended to teach.

The way Jesus taught was first to do and then to teach. Luke, the author of Acts, declared, "I wrote about all that Jesus began to do and to teach" (Acts 1:1). Jesus ministered first and then He had opportunity to teach about what He had done. For example, He fed the five thousand, then He called Himself the Bread of Life (John 6). He washed the feet of the disciples; then He talked about servanthood (John 13). He prayed for many days and hours before the disciples asked Him to teach them to pray (Luke 11).

You are not just to teach information, skills, and attitudes. You impart a lifestyle. The effect of modeling is so powerful, you can be sure that those whom you disciple will seldom go beyond your example. They may measure up to it, but they usually will not surpass it. Whatever you desire to plant in their life, you must be doing yourself. You teach more by what you do than what you say; discipleship is more "caught" than "taught." "Then Jesus said to the crowds and to his disciples: 'The teachers of the law and the Pharisees sit in Moses' seat. So you must obey them and do everything they tell you. But do not do what they do, for they do not practice what they preach" (Matt. 23:1–3).

Jesus used an obedience-based curriculum. This method includes these basic steps:

1. Model it. Perform the behavior yourself.
2. Practice it. Let them experiment alongside as you do it.

3. Ask for it. Many disciples do not perform the behavior because no one ever asked them.

4. Expect it. Have faith in their ability and in their responsibility.

5. Inspect it to see if the quality is what you desire.

6. Reinforce and praise whatever was done correctly to strengthen the behavior.

Modeling, or performing the behavior you want to teach, is particularly helpful in skill training. The disciple maker models the way something is done, and the disciple imitates the model. Imitation is the first step in learning a skill. It is difficult to believe what you cannot conceive, and it is difficult to conceive what you have never seen. Modeling follows a specific five-stage sequence.

1. I do it whether or not anybody knows it. One test of a disciple is what he or she does when alone. Whether anyone else ever sees or knows, the mature disciple will do what is right and holy in the sight of God and do those things that strengthen the relationship with the Father, Son, and Holy Spirit.

2. I do it, and you observe. This was the pattern Jesus used. Initially, the disciples simply tagged along and observed His ministry. Part of making disciples is letting people into your life and taking them with you as you minister.

3. You do it, and I observe you. Jesus let the disciples begin to minister while He was still with them. It may be only a small task or portion of a task, but the disciple begins to take part of the responsibility in the assignment. The disciple maker observes and gives feedback.

4. You do it, and report to me. Jesus did not accompany the seventy-two believers when He sent them out. They came back and told Him what happened (Luke 10). Trust disciples with responsibility and ask them to report what occurred.

5. You begin doing it even if no one else knows it. That behavior has now become a character trait as you are transformed into Christlikeness.

JESUS TAUGHT THROUGH EXPLANATION

Your modeling is not enough by itself; it needs explanation. Jesus often interpreted His parables for His disciples after the crowd had left. When they could not heal the demoniac, He taught them about the power of prayer (Mark 9:29) and faith (Matt. 17:20). When people were healed, Jesus explained how their faith had made the difference. When the disciples came back rejoicing that even the evil spirits were subject to them, Jesus reminded them of the privilege of experiencing the kingdom of God, first through salvation and then through participation (Luke 10:17–24).

JESUS COACHED THE DISCIPLES

Coaching is the third principle Jesus used to develop disciples. Through coaching, a disciple maker guides disciples to do something more skillfully until the person becomes comfortable with the new way of doing things. A wise coach knows when to let persons develop their own style and when to intervene. We see that the disciples were given opportunity to experiment and apply what they had learned as Jesus watched so that He could give positive encouragement or show them how to improve.

Brett is the youngest of my five children to whom I have tried to be a "coach for life." One Sunday, when I was away preaching, Brett shared this testimony with our church:

When I was fifteen, my family took a vacation through the mountains of Colorado. After driving for an hour, I asked my dad to stop so my sister, Krista, and I could climb a steep cliff. Krista chose the easy route up the right side, but I decided to go at the heart of the cliff to conquer the whole thing. The first third of the climb was easy. I found footholds and rock handles in the soft ridges. But soon the rocks became more scarce and footing less secure. Every time I dug a new foothold, my other foot gave way.

During the climb, my parents leaned against the front end of the car simply watching, encouraging, and cautioning. My father soon saw my precarious position and asked if I needed help. At first I told him no and continued to climb. I saw a tree limb dangling over the edge of the cliff, but realized I couldn't trust it. I was stuck! I turned to look. There were my parents still leaning on the car. They were willing to help; they were still offering, but they were unwilling to step in and take over on a climb their son had begun.

As I hung on for my life, I talked out the options that I could think of to finish what I had started. As I considered the options for one last shaking moment, I realized my only way out was to ask for help. I shouted, "OK, Dad, you can help now." I looked around and saw that Dad was already gone. Within thirty seconds I saw a large limb coming over the edge, followed by Dad's face. With sweat running down his cheek and a look of ultimate purpose, he said, "Grab the limb, son, and I will pull you up."

When I reached the top, safe and secure at last, I embraced Dad. It was then I noticed his arms and legs were scratched and bleeding from the rescue effort. He asked me, "Are you OK?" Gladly I declared, "I am now!" I realized that he had a plan to save me all along. Like a good coach, he was simply waiting for me to ask.

As the disciples demonstrated what they had learned, Jesus took a supportive role. He supported them by praying for them, teaching them, rebuking them when necessary, challenging them, and allowing them to minister while always observing Him. Finally, Jesus commissioned the disciples to minister on their own. He gave specific instructions before He sent out the seventy-two believers, and He gave specific commands before He ascended to the Father. He had trained them, validated them, and given them authority and power through the Holy Spirit. The disciples were now at the stage where they could begin another cycle of discipling. The behaviors and character of Christ were now fully a part of them, and they were able to be models for others.

When you validate others' ministries, you make them aware that someone is standing with them to serve as their cheerleader and prayer warrior. You also become accountability partners with them—someone to whom they can answer for the quality and consistency of their lives and ministries. You eventually become colaborers as you encourage each other in the Lord.

JESUS PRAYED FOR HIS DISCIPLES
Another way Jesus related to His disciples was to pray for them. John 17 records Jesus' prayer for His disciples. You may want to pause a moment to read it. Jesus made a point to say that He was not praying for the world but specifically for the disciples. He distinguished them from the world because they were God's and had knowledge of God, while the world did not. He was ready to send them into the world to carry on His ministry. His prayer shows His heart for His disciples; you must demonstrate the same compassion and earnestness of heart for those whom you disciple. Do not minimize the role of prayer to effect change in their lives. Jesus considered prayer for His followers the most—not the least—He could do for them. "But because Jesus lives forever, he has a permanent priesthood. Therefore he is able to save completely those who come to God through him, because he always lives to intercede for them" (Heb. 7:24, 25).

Notice the elements of Jesus' prayer. First, He prayed for the Father to protect His followers. The importance of this role in discipleship cannot be overstated. The disciples needed the Father's watchful care and guidance as they went into the world so they could be effective witnesses for Him. Jesus knew the Father's power could preserve the disciples on their mission with Him. Besides praying for those whom you disciple, you can teach them about the evil one and about spiritual warfare. You can describe how He has delivered you in times of temptation. Jesus told the disciples, "I have told you these things, so that in me you may have peace. In this world you will have trouble. But take heart! I have overcome the world" (John 16:33).

Jesus prayed for the sanctification of the disciples. By holding to God's Word, the disciples would be set apart, different from the world. Jesus sanctified Himself so they could be truly sanctified. If you live according to God's Word, you are different from those around you. Those whom you disciple will see you living differently from the world and will respond to what you do. Help them to understand the implications of being set apart for Christ.

Jesus also prayed for the disciples' unity. The unity of the Father, Son, and Spirit is so close that you cannot completely separate the roles. The Lord wants His followers to have the same kind of unity. You must help new believers see that they are a part of one family—past, present, and future. They will imitate the model you set for them in how you love the body of Christ, His church.

HOW TO ESTABLISH A SPIRITUAL DISCIPLE

As you disciple others, imitate Jesus. Obey as He obeyed; teach as He taught; pray as He prayed. "Your mission, should you decide to accept it," is first of all to be a disciple who glorifies God and then to establish and train others to do the same. Paul said, "Follow my example, as I follow the example of Christ" (1 Cor. 11:1). When you are teaching any skill, attitude, or behavior, use the following sequence to involve them in the disciple-making process.

1. Tell them why. The new disciples must first understand the significance of what is being taught—the reason you are taking time to explain it and the reason it is important to the Christian life. Explain its relationship to their maturing as Christ's disciples. Explain that nearly all new Christians go through predictable stages as the old nature is replaced with the new and you are providing them with tools to help them grow, to protect them, or to teach them to walk as Jesus walked. If you do not, the spiritual child may see what you are teaching as simply another activity.

2. Show them how. You can use much of what you have learned through this book as you are putting it into practice in your life. Telling the people how will not be enough; you must show them what you mean, whether it be finding Scriptures in the Bible, praying, overcoming temptation, or sharing their faith.

3. Get them started. Move them from the information stage to the action stage. Help them begin doing what you are teaching. Application—moving from the theoretical to the practical—is the step that changes a person's life.

4. Keep them going. Hold them accountable by checking what they do. Do what is necessary to help them become successful, obedient disciples. "So I will always remind you of these things, even though you know them and are firmly established in the truth you now have" (2 Pet. 1:12). Ask them to meet with you to share what they have learned that week. Ask whether they have encountered any problems. Encourage them. Keeping them going is more difficult than getting them started. Share with them your own struggle to stay disciplined. Help them become motivated to complete any work without shaming them. Remember that new Christians fight a variety of problems: unfamiliar territory, a lack of discipline, Satan's attacks, and the effort required to change from one lifestyle to another.

5. Help them reproduce. Teach them how to share with someone else what you have shared with them. All of your disciple making should be "pass-on-able." God made us to reproduce our faith. A new Christian has an innate desire to share with someone else and probably has the non-Christian friends to share with. You can teach them how to do this. Encourage them to share whatever you have taught them. "The things you have heard me say in the presence of many witnesses entrust to reliable men who will also be qualified to teach others" (2 Tim. 2:2).

Reproduction is the key to the salvation of the world. Only the making of mature, obedient, Christlike servants who glorify God and join His mission to continually reproduce more disciples will bring the kingdom of God in this generation. In the next chapter, I will show you God's plan for the multiplication of disciples who will be able to bring His gospel to all people.

Questions for Meditation and Discussion

1. What did Jesus teach?

2. How did Jesus teach?

3. What are the five steps in the modeling sequence?

4. Name four people who are watching your life. What are you modeling for them?

5. Paul said, "Follow my example, as I follow the example of Christ" (1 Cor. 11:1). What have you learned from Jesus recently that you could teach someone else?

Chapter 24
MULTIPLYING DISCIPLES

One day I asked my eighty-nine-year-old grandmother how many descendants she had.

"Sixty-two," she answered.

In jest I asked her, "Granny, how did you ever raise them all?"

"I didn't raise them all, thank goodness. I only raised six."

"What about the rest?" I asked.

"Well," she replied, "I helped some on the nineteen grandchildren; I helped some on you. But I didn't do much on the thirty-five great-grandchildren or the two great-great grandchildren. Their parents took care of them."

In the years since, those great-great grandchildren have multiplied and another generation of descendants is following the Lord. It all started when my great-grandparents did a good job of rearing their children by passing on God's truths to them. Scripture records the same to be true of Timothy: "I have been reminded of your sincere faith, which first lived in your grandmother Lois and in your mother Eunice and, I am persuaded, now lives in you also" (2 Tim. 1:5). Your job is to concentrate on the few disciples God gives you so that they can reproduce in others what you have shared with them.

Becoming a Spiritual Multiplier

The process of multiplication not only increases the number of biological descendants; it is also paramount in the reproduction of spiritual descendants. When I visited Kenya once, missionary Allan Stickney said to me, "Tell me about the persons you are discipling. Then I will know more about you than you can tell me about yourself." Allan's words, which carry significant implications for reproducing disciples, have rung in my ears ever since. Your spiritual grandchildren are a better indicator of your discipleship than are your spiritual children. The proof is not only that your disciples endure and have Christ's character but that they multiply other disciples. If your disciples are standing still and doing nothing with the truth you impart to them, either your discipling was inadequate or your life did not model your teaching.

The heart of the Great Commission focuses on multiplying disciples. The only command in Matthew 28:19 is "make disciples." Going, baptizing, and teaching are parts of that command. You may be faithful to go, baptize, and teach, but if you do not make disciples who will teach others, your effectiveness will end with one generation!

In 1976 my denomination adopted the program of Bold Mission Thrust with the objective that every person in the world would hear the gospel and have the opportunity to respond before the year 2000. Now I certainly applauded this goal to fulfill the biblical mandate of the Great Commission, but my first response was, "Do they have any idea how many people that is?" I had served in one county where there were five million lost people and in another area of Indonesia with eight to nine million people where I was the only missionary. I realized you could not even shake hands with eight or nine million people, let alone share the gospel with all of them.

When I came back to the states for furlough in 1977, I had that question on my mind and that skepticism in my heart. I wondered if anyone promoting this plan had any idea how many people a billion was. In my exasperation, I worked some figures. Do you realize that if you started baptizing people at the rate of one per minute from the time Jesus walked out of the tomb up to now, you would not yet have one billion? That is far short of the more than six billion people alive in the world in the year 2000. Even if you were able to repeat Pentecost and baptize 3,000 people every day, it would take 5,479 years to equal the world's population. That means if Abraham had begun baptizing people at the rate of 3,000 per day and others did the same all the way up to the year 2000, you would still need another thousand years just to baptize the population of the world at that date.

As hopeless as those figures sound, I am convinced that the Lord wants everyone to hear the gospel before He returns. He said so in the Great Commission! Obviously, it will take all Christians working simultaneously and side-by-side, but it will also take the process Jesus set in motion: multiplication.

God's Principle of Multiplication

Inherent in Christ's strategy for the gospel to be preached to the whole world before He returns is the principle of multiplication. If a disciple trains a disciple to train another disciple, and so on, the equation is changed from addition to multiplication. Instead of 1 plus 1 plus 1, 2 becomes 4, then 8, then 16, and so forth. If each number is doubled only 33 times, the total is over 8,159,000,000 which is more than the world's current population.

If you witness faithfully but do not teach those you win to witness, you are in the addition mode. But if you teach each person to witness—to be a disciple, and to make disciples—you become a multiplier.

As a disciple maker, your task is to equip the disciple to be a disciple maker. This is an apprenticeship relationship in which you serve as a spiritual mentor to train your apprentice and equip this person to multiply disciples. You are moving toward a partnership with this person, as Barnabas and Paul were mentor and apprentice but later became colaborers. Your goal at the end of this stage is for the disciple to be ready to help others become spiritual disciples, to move from being concerned only about his or her own growth to being concerned about others' growth. Having been equipped, they are now to reproduce. They should be able to establish a mentoring relationship that equips another apprentice to become a disciple maker.

Principles for Multiplying Disciples

There are several sound principles for multiplying disciples: "You then, my son, be strong in the grace that is in Christ Jesus. And the things you have heard me say in the presence of many witnesses entrust to reliable men who will also be qualified to teach others. Endure hardship with us like a good soldier of Christ Jesus" (2 Tim. 2:1–3).

BE A GOOD MODEL OF JESUS CHRIST

Being a good model is the single most important factor in multiplying disciples. Paul's first words in 2 Timothy 2 are, "You then, my son." The word *then* refers to the previous chapter in which Paul gave examples of two unfaithful disciples, Phygelus and Hermogenes, and one effective one, Onesiphorus. In comparison, Paul wanted Timothy to stand firm in the grace of God and to follow the model that Paul himself had set for him. Paul had demonstrated a life of obedience and endurance in the face of opposition and persecution. (A detailed account of his suffering is found in 2 Corinthians 11:23–30.)

Paul served as an encourager. He commanded Timothy to "be strong in the grace that is in Christ Jesus." "Be strong" is in the imperative mood; it is a command. It is in the passive voice; the strength does not originate with you but with Jesus Christ. It is in the present tense; it is a continuing reality. A good translation is, "Keep on being made strong by the grace of Christ." You can be a disciple only because of Christ's grace and you can accomplish only what Christ does through you. Jesus said, "If a man remains in me and I in him, he will bear much fruit; apart from me you can do nothing" (John 15:5).

Paul modeled the five essential elements of discipleship that I shared with you in the Disciple's Cross.

He modeled prayer: "I thank God, whom I serve, as my forefathers did, with a clear conscience, as night and day I constantly remember you in my prayers" (2 Tim. 1:3).

He modeled witnessing: "Do not be ashamed to testify about our Lord, or ashamed of me his prisoner. But join with me in suffering for the gospel, by the power of God" (2 Tim. 1:8).

He modeled staying in the Word: "We proclaim him, admonishing and teaching everyone with all wisdom, so that we may present everyone perfect in Christ" (Col. 1:28). "What you heard from me, keep as the pattern of sound teaching, with faith and love in Christ Jesus. Guard the good deposit that was entrusted to you—guard it with the help of the Holy Spirit who lives in us" (2 Tim. 1:13, 14).

He encouraged Timothy to take advantage of the fellowship of believers such as his mother and grandmother (2 Tim. 1:5), other reliable men (2 Tim. 2:2), or the members of the church in Ephesus (2 Tim. 4:19; 1 Tim.1:3; 3:15).

He commended Onesiphorus for his ministry to the gospel through his help to Paul: "May the Lord show mercy to the household of Onesiphorus, because he often refreshed me and was not ashamed of my chains. . . . You know very well in how many ways he helped me in Ephesus" (2 Tim. 1:16, 18).

To be centered in Christ, a disciple must keep all five of these elements in balance. Paul could only teach Timothy what he himself practiced.

Paul served to equip Timothy. Although it is God who equips you for His service through His spiritual gifts, Paul instructed Timothy in the use of his gift: "For this reason I remind you to fan into flame the gift of God, which is in you through the laying on of my hands" (2 Tim. 1:6). "Don't let anyone look down on you because you are young, but set an example for the believers in speech, in life, in love, in faith and in purity. Until I come, devote yourself to the public reading of Scripture, to preaching and to teaching. Do not neglect your gift, which was given you through a prophetic message when the body of elders laid their hands on you. Be diligent in these matters; give yourself wholly to them, so that everyone may see your progress. Watch your life and doctrine closely. Persevere in them, because if you do, you will save both yourself and your hearers" (1 Tim. 4:12–16).

ENTRUST TRUTHS TO RELIABLE DISCIPLES

Paul admonished Timothy to pass on all that he had learned (2 Tim. 2:2). Every truth you receive adds to your responsibility to pass that truth to others. Even though one-to-one discipleship is often encouraged, I have found the opposite to be more explicitly taught in the Bible. Note the plurals in this verse: "many witnesses," "men," and "others." Many years of experience have taught me that the best disciples are made in a group, as Jesus and Paul made disciples. Multiple models develop more balanced disciples. The key to making effective, multiple disciples is to select faithful and able disciples.

SELECT FAITHFUL DISCIPLES

Paul chose carefully those he invited to follow him in his ministry. He refused to take John Mark a second time because John Mark had deserted their missionary party during the first trip (see Acts 15:37–40). Paul also witnessed the unfaithfulness of Phygellus and Hermogenes (2 Tim. 1:15). He was concerned about faithfulness because he wanted every effort to count.

You may think you have an unlimited amount of time to disciple those whom God has given you. However, you can only make so many disciples in a lifetime. It is more profitable to have fewer well-trained, faithful disciples than many partially equipped disciples. Your effectiveness in making disciples will determine how they multiply. The ultimate effect of your investment will be demonstrated again and again through their spiritual descendants.

Jesus said that disciples who were faithful in a few things would be given more responsibility but unfaithful servants would lose even what they had (Luke 19:26). Faithful disciples are trustworthy and reliable. These are the kind whom God entrusts. So choose faithful persons above those with the best personalities or the most obvious gifts. You will be investing your life into them, and you desire the best return in terms of future disciples.

SELECT ABLE DISCIPLES

In addition to faithfulness, look for competence. Investing in persons who will be able to teach others is the only way to keep the chain of multiplication going. If disciples are not able to pass on what has been committed to them, each generation will reproduce itself with more difficulty. Halfhearted disciples tend to pass on their halfheartedness, which produces diminishing returns.

Invest your life in making disciples of competent, reliable, and faithful persons who will be able to teach others also. Ability appears in unexpected persons, so pray earnestly for God's leadership. Jesus' twelve disciples did not look promising to anyone else!

John and Jerry Hilbun were middle-aged when they participated in their first *MasterLife* discipleship group. Over the next five years they discipled more than thirty persons in their small-town church. These disciples then discipled more than one hundred others, who then multiplied to more than two hundred by the time the Hilbuns were appointed as missionaries to Barbados, where the chain reaction continued.

MINISTER IN SPITE OF HARDSHIPS

Ahmed (not his real name) was a former Shiite Muslim businessman who came to the Lord through encounters with a missionary and a believer in his own country. He then completed discipleship training, including *MasterLife*, and became an effective witness among his people. It was then that his life became a series of narrow escapes for Christ.

When he was invited to go to Lebanon, he determined to witness at a Shiite enclave near the airport. He was warned that it would be too dangerous. After seeking permission twice and being refused, he determined to go anyway. He was witnessing in a beach area, surrounded by a throng of Shiite Muslims, when forces arrived, indignant that a Christian was among them. Authorities took Ahmed into custody. Undaunted, Ahmed witnessed to the people in the prison and helped seven of them to know the Lord. When he was finally freed, missionaries helped him leave the country, but this merely spurred Ahmed to find a new place to witness.

Because he spoke Kurdish, he obtained a ticket to Iran and began witnessing among the Shiite Kurds. He was eventually picked up by authorities and ended up in Yemen. There he continued his lifestyle of fearless witnessing. Yemeni authorities questioned him about being a foreign spy. Some of the Yemeni Christians began to feel uncomfortable about his situation, so he left there for Cairo, Egypt, and began to witness in the mosques there.

As Ahmed continued to share the gospel, someone invited him to come to Israel. He decided to go, believing God would take care of things for him. He was detained by airport security because he had no Israeli visa. When he informed them that God wanted him to go to Israel to pray, they replied, "Your country has no diplomatic relations with Israel." "I have a higher authority; my God wants me to go," he countered. Amazingly, they let him through, and once in Tel Aviv he received a visa. In Jerusalem, he spent every free moment on the street and in coffee shops, witnessing to Arabs and Jews alike.

When Ahmed returned to Egypt, authorities were about to deport him to Syria, where he would be executed. He went, however, to another Arab country where his brother-in-law lived. He continues to live and work among the people of this country. Everywhere he travels, he asks for a supply of *MasterLife* books to use in his ministry. This colaborer believes in using his gifts of evangelism and teaching, no matter where or in what danger he finds himself.

Paul exhorted Timothy, "Endure hardship with us like a good soldier of Christ Jesus" (2 Tim. 2:3). Paul linked two key ideas: multiplying faithful, reproducing disciples and ministering in difficult times and places. Since you fight a spiritual battle against evil from the world, the flesh, and the devil, you can expect to suffer. Your goal in the midst of your struggle is to please Christ through purity, patience, and perseverance. Paul gave three illustrations in which suffering and perseverance are required to produce the desired result: fighting a battle, training for a sporting competition, and farming crops.

PUT FIRST PRIORITY ON PLEASING CHRIST

In Paul's day a commander enlisted his own soldiers. The soldier, then, had one responsibility: to please his commander. A soldier in battle cannot question the chain of command, or the result will be chaos. Paul claimed, "No one serving as a soldier gets involved in civilian affairs—he wants to please his commanding officer" (2 Tim. 2:4). The picture is one of getting your feet entangled in a net just as the bugle sounds for battle so that you are left unable to move forward or be effective. Civilian affairs can include your job, your possessions, your recreation, your goals, and even your church activities. None of these things are wrong or bad in themselves unless they distract you or keep you from following the Lord's commands. Your first priority above all other people, programs, or purposes is to please Christ.

PAY THE PRICE OF PURITY TO WIN THE PRIZE

Playing by the Lord's rules is necessary for a person who is called to multiply disciples. "If anyone competes as an athlete, he does not receive the victor's crown unless he competes according to the rules" (2 Tim. 2:5). I remember a runner who won the women's division of the Boston Marathon but was disqualified because the judges discovered that she had taken the subway on part of the twenty-six-mile route!

People pay more attention to what you do than what you say. Serving Christ during difficult times and places requires conducting yourself in a way that is above reproach so others will know your heart is completely His. "Therefore, since we are surrounded by such a great cloud of witnesses, let us throw off everything that hinders and the sin that so easily entangles, and let us run with perseverance the race marked out for us" (Heb. 12:1). "Do you not know that in a race all the runners run, but only one gets the prize? Run in such a way as to get the prize. Everyone who competes in the games goes into strict training. They do it to get a crown that will not last; but we do it to get a crown that will last forever. Therefore I do not run like a man running aimlessly; I do not fight like a man beating the air. No, I beat my body and make it my slave so that after I have preached to others, I myself will not be disqualified for the prize" (1 Cor. 9:24–27).

PERSEVERE WITH PATIENCE UNTIL THE HARVEST

Paul used the analogy of a farmer, "The hardworking farmer should be the first to receive a share of the crops" (2 Tim. 2:6). Being a farmer requires perseverance. Not only must you wait for the crop to grow, but you must also keep fertilizing it, cultivating it, and removing weeds. But if you continue, you will reap the harvest.

When I planted things as a child, I dug them up the next day to see if they were growing! Do not expect a disciple you nurture to mature too quickly. You cannot evaluate how much progress is being made in discipleship while the crop is still young. Giving up too quickly and becoming frustrated because your efforts do not seem to bear fruit are dangers that disciple makers must avoid. Even Jesus did not see instant results. He persevered and saw eternal results. If you model the life of a disciple by being strong in the grace of Jesus Christ and by persevering, you can multiply disciples.

You have studied principles Jesus used to train His disciples and which Paul used to train Timothy. You can make use of these principles as you train reproducing disciples. The disciples Jesus made were bold witnesses who were able to teach others and establish the church. You may not feel qualified or ready yet to make disciples. However, as you begin to disciple others, you will become a better disciple yourself. As you prepare, explain, model, teach, and encourage others, your own faith will be strengthened.

Remember, Christian discipleship is developing a personal, lifelong, obedient relationship with Jesus Christ in which He transforms your character into Christlikeness; changes your values into kingdom values; and involves you in His mission in the home, church, and the world. As you develop in your relationship, character, and values, and as you increase your involvement in Christ's mission, you have the blessed opportunity of bringing others along with you.

The window into your life is for many people a glimpse into Jesus. Some of those you will invite to come in and live with you a while so they will learn to go out and be windows for others. Never assume that your task is finished. After you have helped produce disciples who live like Jesus and are working in the harvest field, make sure they are bringing others with them as their own disciples. In turn, their disciples should be taking someone else through each stage they have completed. This pattern produces a long chain of continuously multiplying disciples who obey the words of Jesus to "go and make disciples of all nations" (Matt. 28:19).

Jesus said, "You are my friends if you do what I command. I no longer call you servants, because a servant does not know his master's business. Instead, I have called you friends, for everything that I learned from my Father I have made known to you. You did not choose me, but I chose you and appointed you to go and bear fruit—fruit that will last" (John 15:14–16).

Questions for Meditation and Discussion

1. What is the essence of Christ's command in the Great Commission?

2. What is the process by which Christ intended discipleship to occur?

3. What are the responsibilities of a disciple maker?

4. What are you modeling for others? Who is following you and to which stage have you brought them? Are others coming behind them?

5. Name two people whom God may be assigning to you who are faithful and able to pass on what they have learned.

6. Diagram your spiritual family tree. Look at the end disciple. Is he or she lacking any spiritual maturity? (Perhaps you need to walk alongside to correct a pattern in that genetic line.)

Chapter 25
MINISTERING AS COLABORERS

Colaborers are disciple makers who work together in ministry to multiply disciples, ministries, and churches among all peoples. Colaborers are involved in God's mission in the home, the church, and the world. God's calling on your life is to make disciples and to expand His kingdom in each of these areas of influence.

Multiplying Disciples in the Home

In the last chapter, we saw the influence in Timothy's life of the faith of his mother and grandmother. Because former generations of my family have followed the Lord and taught their children to do the same, the impact on my life has been immeasurable. I always thought my father was a powerful preacher but have since come to realize that he impacted my life more through the consistency of his walk and through the ten to fifteen minutes of family devotions each morning than through all of his preaching. At home is where my real discipling took place.

My parents prayed for my children and their spouses from the day they were born. I, too, have prayed for my children and grandchildren and raised them up in the ways of the Lord. As a result, all five of my children and their spouses are walking with the Lord and are actively ministering in their churches. All of my grandchildren are being taught to love the Lord. Beyond all of the worldwide effect of *MasterLife* and missions, my greatest responsibility and deepest joy is in the discipleship of my own family. "I have no greater joy than to hear that my children are walking in the truth" (3 John 4).

Ministering to your family is first and foremost before you prepare to minister to others. You have the greatest impact on your family, the deepest motivation to pray for them, and the most opportunities to train and instruct them in the Lord (see Eph. 6:4; Deut. 6:6–9). One way to do so is to conduct family worship in your home. Families who have faithfully honored God through daily family worship have found this practice has strengthened and enriched their home lives more than anything else.

Establishing a pattern of family worship is much like establishing a personal habit of a quiet time. Successful family worship needs a leader who recognizes its value and is committed to faithfully maintaining it in spite of obstacles. Usually, the husband and father should accept this responsibility, since he is the natural spiritual leader of the home. To ensure the best results, choose an appointed time and place which best fits the family's routine. Once it is agreed upon, the family should reserve this time to meet God in worship. Every family member should be enlisted to participate. The one who is committed to family worship should serve as encourager or facilitator, but all family members should be allowed to take turns leading the worship experience.

The Bible should be central in the worship time. In addition, many families use a devotional book or magazine. Follow the reading with a time of discussion and sharing and spend a few moments in prayer. The time need not be long or complicated; the goal is to bring the family together in the Lord.

Multiplying Disciples in the Church

Your next realm of influence is in and through the local church. God provides spiritual gifts for the building up of the church and for ministry to the world. Gifts are given to equip you to fulfill God's work through His church. As churches make disciples and operate effectively through spiritual gifts, they will begin to grow, both numerically and in maturity. As they grow and mature, God will give them vision to reach His people throughout the world.

I saw an incredible example in the body of Christ of a church that knew how to build up its members and commission them as colaborers in the kingdom when David Perrin invited me to address the church he pastored in a Maryland suburb of Washington, D.C. The church was preparing to commission its first foreign missionary. They had already sent someone to Albuquerque as a home missionary and now were sending a missionary to Guyana.

David shared with me the history of the church. It had originally been a large congregation but had dwindled in the midst of a racially changing neighborhood. Six years earlier, when the congregation consisted of twenty-four Caucasian and eight African-American members, they did a courageous thing. They called an African-American pastor. David was freshly out of seminary but had recently participated in a *MasterLife* workshop. When he arrived, he announced that the members would build the church on discipleship.

I have never seen a church that had such a disciple-making ministry. When I spoke there, the church had outgrown its present building and was holding double services in a local school auditorium to accommodate the eight hundred to nine hundred people who attended each Sunday. When I gave the invitation, about one hundred people made decisions, nearly half of them for missions. The church had already trained commitment counselors to deal with those who responded. The pastor challenged the church to send ten thousand world ambassadors from their church in some type of missions effort around the world. That number was startling because it represented more than twice what any missions agency sends, but I saw how the church was growing and realized that it was not an idle goal for these disciples. This church had changed its name to the Church of the Great Commission!

Soon the church had to rent a tent to accommodate the crowds of up to two thousand people. Members have since bought a former department store to house the congregation. The church has continued to grow and members are being commissioned as colaborers in the Lord's service. Clearly these disciples are using their spiritual gifts to bring new life and a worldwide ministry to a once-dying congregation.

Multiplying Ministries through the Church

The final stage on the path of spiritual growth is becoming a colaborer in ministry. In addition to making disciples, you must learn to work in ministry as a disciple-making team. The focus is on multiplying ministries and churches to make disciples of all peoples. One of the tasks of each disciple-making colaborer is to help others discover the spiritual gifts God has given them and the ministries in which they are to participate.

After a disciple has identified his or her spiritual gifts and how God is calling him or her to use those gifts in ministry, the disciple maker's task is to commission that disciple into ministry. Although the disciple maker is still available to encourage, help, and strengthen, the disciple now assumes almost full responsibility for his or her growth and involvement in God's mission. The disciple's task now is to multiply, using the gifts God has given in the ministry God has assigned. Equality exists now between the discipler and the disciple.

This feeling of equality characterizes the relationship among colaborers. Even if the relationship began as a disciple and disciple maker, no feeling of superiority exists. Colaborers are capable of performing the same tasks and have full authority to minister. The relationship is one of mutuality and partnership in a task greater than themselves. "The man who plants and the man who waters have one purpose, and each will be rewarded according to his own labor. For we are God's fellow workers; you are God's field, God's building" (1 Cor. 3:8, 9).

Although the task and level of authority are the same, colaborers function with a variety of spiritual gifts. In order to labor in the kingdom, you must understand the purpose and function of spiritual gifts and how they equip for ministry. You need to be able to identify your own spiritual gifts, recognize and submit to the gifts of others, and learn to work cooperatively in the unity and power of the Spirit to perform the work of the kingdom.

Paul likens the need for a variety of gifts to operate in the church to the different functions of your physical body parts. "If the whole body were an eye, where would the sense of hearing be? If the whole body were an ear, where would the sense of smell be? But in fact God has arranged the parts in the body, every one of them, just as he wanted them to be. If they were all one part, where would the body be? As it is, there are many parts, but one body" (1 Cor 12:17–20).

Ministering According to Spiritual Gifts

What is the purpose of the gifts in the church? "Since you are eager to have spiritual gifts, try to excel in gifts that build up the church" (1 Cor. 14:12). Spiritual gifts are to edify the body of Christ in order to make it stronger and help it to grow and multiply. God gives His gifts to help His body grow internally and to reach out to others. His goal is for the church to attain the whole measure of the fullness of Christ. "It was he who gave some to be apostles, some to be prophets, some to be evangelists, and some to be pastors and teachers, to prepare God's people for works of service, so that the body of Christ may be built up until we all reach unity in the faith and in the knowledge of the Son of God and become mature, attaining to the whole measure of the fullness of Christ" (Eph. 4:11–13).

The equippers in this verse are apostles, prophets, evangelists, pastors, and teachers. The word translated "to perfect or equip" literally means "to put a person in a right place or condition, to restore, to educate, to train, to guide, or to prepare a person to do a task." Their roles are to equip, train, and release all believers to do the work of the ministry. Every believer has a ministry to perform. The New Testament word for "ministry" comes for the Greek word *diakonos* which means the office and work of a servant. All Christians are to be servant ministers. Believers should function as a unit, aware of other members of the body and concerned about their well-being. God's purpose in giving different gifts to believers is to bind all Christians into one interdependent body. In this way every person can minister to someone.

HOW TO DISCOVER
AND DEVELOP YOUR SPIRITUAL GIFTS

1. Believe that you are gifted. Spiritual gifts are not special rewards for the spiritually elite. They are given to every believer.

2. Pray. Ask God to reveal to you what spiritual gifts He has given. God wants you to know so you will minister effectively.

3. Explore your gifts. Study the scriptural passages on spiritual gifts. Read books about gifts you think you may have. Talk to people about their spiritual gifts and how they use them to minister to others. Try to use different gifts you think you may have and take note of the results.

4. Consider your desires. What do you enjoy doing? What seems to come naturally to you? What are you drawn to as you pray? What motivates you? Your enjoyment of or desire for a gift may be God's way of showing you that you possess it.

5. Accept responsibility for using your gifts. All believers are called to evangelize, to show mercy, to encourage, to give, to help, to be hospitable, etc. as obedient servants. However, as you do these things, the Holy Spirit may unveil one or more of them as a spiritual gift both by your desire to do it more and by the impact it has on the one ministered to.

6. Seek the confirmation of others. They may see a gift in you long before you are aware of it. What is it, that when you do it, others tell you they have been blessed by it? In what areas do people ask for your help? What have you done in the past for which you were genuinely complimented?

7. After you have identified a potential spiritual gift, you must exercise it. Do not be afraid to use it. Paul told Timothy to stir up and use his gift as a pastor and teacher. "For this reason I remind you to fan into flame the gift of God, which is in you through the laying on of my hands" (2 Tim. 1:6).

Find someone who will mentor you in that gift and help lead you into the ministry God desires for you. Pray and ask the Holy Spirit to empower you in that gift and to show you how to use it to touch the lives of others.

God has provided your salvation through Jesus, your sanctification through His Spirit, and your equipment in the form of spiritual armor, spiritual authority, and spiritual gifts. Now He calls you to put all of these to use in the world in the ministry of reconciliation, bringing others to the saving knowledge of Jesus and making disciples of all nations.

A Mission-hearted Church

Johnny Hunt, pastor of Woodstock Baptist Church near Atlanta, Georgia, has developed a mission-hearted church. When he became pastor, the church had about two hundred members but was not really growing. About five or six men in the congregation had completed *MasterLife* training and they trained Johnny. Leaders were then invited to conduct a workshop to equip members of the congregation to disciple others. That was the beginning.

Now over four thousand people attend worship services there each Sunday, and Woodstock Baptist Church is involved in missions around the world. Johnny was ministering to a group of three hundred missionaries with me in South and Central Asia. He shared with me how missions works in their church:

When a group in our church so bonds with a person on the field that they make a long-term commitment to that area and people, we organize a team to assist. The team then takes responsibility for that people group and our church's relationship with the missionaries working among them. We have twenty-seven teams working with the current twenty-seven partnerships we have developed. Our church has adopted several whole people groups to target with prayer, giving, and going. We send volunteers for one to three weeks to help the missionaries accomplish their strategies. We commission short-term personnel for one to two years in response to requests from missionaries and we send career missionaries. Every week we have a two-hour staff prayer meeting primarily focused on missions.

Therefore, it is easy to keep missions in front of our people. Every Sunday I introduce a visiting missionary or representative of a people group, ask for prayer for specific situations, or report on what God is doing through our people overseas. It gives our people great reason to praise God and to continue to give. One man greatly blessed of God came to me recently and said, "I have five million dollars God has given me. While my hand is warm, I want to give it."

My goal for our church is to place our arms around the world. Our goal is to have ministry upon which the sun never sets—to know that, when I'm in bed asleep, they are ministering in Uganda through our dollars and through the manpower we send there, and in Kenya, and all over the world. That is really beginning to happen. The light that shines the farthest shines the brightest at home.[1]

This church has gained a vision far beyond themselves. In the past five years, eight hundred of its members have volunteered for short-term missions and fifty-five members have been commissioned to serve as career missionaries. Johnny Hunt continues to multiply his own ministry by mentoring pastors of other churches. He is consistently commissioning and training colaborers. Woodstock has started five missions with a cumulative membership of over two thousand within a thirty-five-mile radius of the church.

In addition, each year Johnny takes twenty-five pastors overseas on vision trips to experience what it is like for whole people groups to be lost and unreached for the gospel. He mentors approximately one hundred fifty pastors and their wives in his Timothy-Barnabas School three times a year so their churches will become missionary-minded churches. Although he is an immensely busy pastor/leader, he considers this mentoring process the best stewardship of his time because he can impact entire churches through mentoring their pastors.

A Multiplying Church

Some colaborers move beyond leading their churches to grow and sending their members on mission projects to become multipliers not only of ministries but also of churches. Such an example is Youtie Legoh.

I have already shared with you the struggle that occurred when we felt God leading us to reorganize the Indonesian Baptist Theological Seminary and to deploy the professors to outlying villages to teach. At that time, Youtie Legoh was a freshman seminary student, so he experienced the maximum impact of that decision. However, he came to me with a cooperative spirit and said, "Pak Willis, I like what the missionaries said, that you want to see a million of my people come to Christ. I want to be a part of that. You tell me what to do, and I'll do it."

I knew the Lord gave Youtie to me. I began to disciple him and invest time in him. He started pastoring a little house church, teaching the members everything I taught him. Members soon built another room on the house to hold about twenty-five people. Six months later Youtie asked me, "Would you come help our men know how to start Bible studies in the ten areas around the church?" I taught them a simple method of spontaneous Bible study. Many of these men were former Communists and had been Christians six months or less. But their Bibles were already tattered because Youtie had discipled the group with such fervor that they were hungry for the Word. In fact, Youtie came to me later and said, "Pak Willis, I have a problem. I'm trying to go to school as well as pastor this church. These men are staying up until daybreak in these Bible studies. I have forbidden them to go past midnight anymore!"

When Youtie's church had grown numerically and spiritually, they built a fine brick church building on top of a hill in Semarang. Later Youtie asked me to preach the triennial meeting for his home denomination which was located 1,500 miles away in Menado, Sulawesi. God sent a sweeping revival among them. The president of the convention told me, "We will invite you to come back because we must be a missionary church. God has called the Menadonese to be missionaries to the over four hundred people groups in Indonesia."

Two years later, as I preached at that missionary conference, Youtie and his wife-to-be, Ruth, surrendered to be missionaries to Kalimantan (Borneo). They led the five other families who went with them to start twenty-five churches and baptize more than two thousand people in two years!

After serving as president of the convention for a term, Youtie and his family came to the United States for further seminary work. During that time, they were in a tragic car accident. Youtie's wife, Ruth, was killed and he was badly injured. While he was still in intensive care and barely conscious, he told me on the phone, "Pak Willis, I must get back to Indonesia and reach the peoples who have never heard of Jesus." After getting out of the hospital, he visited in our home and shared with me the vision God had given him for building a school to train missionaries to go to the unreached peoples of Indonesia. Months later when he had recuperated and was ready to return, he phoned me to share that vision once more. I wondered why he repeated the whole vision again. Then I sensed that he wanted me to commission him, to encourage him, and send him forth to do what God had called him to do.

In the process of discipling, a time comes to release and commission the colaborer to do what God has called him or her to do. I told him how happy I was that he was returning and that I was convinced God was going to use him to reach the peoples who did not yet have access to the gospel. I prayed for him. He seemed satisfied with this "commissioning" over the telephone.

Youtie is not my disciple. He is the Lord's disciple. I discipled him to a relationship with the living Lord who wants to spread the kingdom. Consequently, Youtie went beyond being a disciple and a disciple maker. He became a colaborer in ministry, began to lead teams of disciple makers, and planted reproducing churches.

Through the years we have seldom seen each other, but we have written letters, called each other, and occasionally gotten together. Eighteen years after his commissioning, I responded to Youtie's invitation to return to Indonesia to lead a missions conference for him and his school. I saw him multiplying disciples there in hard places and hard times where I probably could never have gone. During that conference, eighteen more of his students responded to the missions call.

Youtie currently serves again as the president of his home convention of churches. Now more churches of his denomination exist in Kalimantan than on the island of Sulawesi from which he originally went as a missionary. The missionaries he has trained have started churches on several other islands. He has focused the work of their seminary on training missionaries to go to people groups who have never heard of Jesus. His work of spreading the gospel continues. The churches he helped to plant have become a church-planting movement.

As a disciple, you have the privilege of an eternity-long relationship with God the Father, Son, and Holy Spirit; the opportunity to be molded into God's character and to take on God's values; and the joyous task of being a blessing to others in your home, your church, and the world. As a disciple maker, you have the potential to expand God's kingdom to places you will never go, to people you will never meet, and in languages you will never speak. "Therefore go and make disciples of all nations"!

Questions for Meditation and Discussion

1. Do you have regular family worship in your home? If not, what would it take to begin?

2. What are your spiritual gifts?

3. What ministry do you feel God is calling you to? To what have you been commissioned?

4. How could you be a part of a missions project through your church?

5. In what ways does God want to use you to help plant churches in your area or in another land?

6. Look again at the MasterBuilder diagram on page 194. Have you reached the colaborer stage? Ask God to give you an equipper/mentor to instruct and commission you in ministry.

Conclusion
AN INVITATION

I began this book with a call to discipleship. I would like to end with the same. As you have read this book, I hope God has shown you areas in which you need to surrender or in which you need to mature in Christ. There were many "how-to's" I could not include in the space of this book. Because learning comes primarily through experience, the best way for you to incorporate these truths into your life is to find an accountability group or partner and take time to begin implementing each of them in your own life.

I hope this book has challenged you to become a better disciple and to make disciples. If so, I will have succeeded. But now you face a bigger decision—how to continue to grow in Christlikeness, to let Christ continually transform your values into kingdom values, and to join God on His mission in your home, church, and world. This is as far as I can take you in this book. However, large numbers of people have matured rapidly in the Lord while involved in the *MasterLife* course (LifeWay Press), and have used it to help others become productive disciples. Is God leading you to disciple one or more persons? The *MasterLife* course gives you these additional resources:

- many more "how to's" of the disciple's life;
- weekly activities to use what you are learning in real situations;
- an accountability group for sharing your discipleship experiences and challenging you to incorporate the disciplines of discipleship into your life;
- a leader's kit that includes videos of the four theme presentations (the Disciple's Cross, the Disciple's Personality, the Spiritual Armor, and MasterBuilder) and training for leading the small group with step-by-step instructions for each session;
- four workshop experiences coming at the end of each of the four sessions: Growing Disciples Workshop, Testimony Workshop, Prayer Workshop, Spiritual Gifts Workshop; and
- the cumulative effect of obeying the commands of Christ, incorporating them as habits into your life, and reaping the results as you mature in Christ.

As a final encouragement, I want to share with you a statement written by an African pastor and tacked on the wall of his home. It is one of the most stirring commitments to being a disciple I have ever read. Would you make it your own?

> I'm part of the fellowship of the unashamed. I have Holy Spirit power. The die has been cast. I have stepped over the line. The decision has been made. I'm a disciple of His. I won't look back, let up, slow down, back away, or be still.
>
> My past is redeemed, my present makes sense, my future is secure. I'm finished and done with low living, sight walking, small planning, smooth knees, colorless dreams, tamed visions, mundane talking, cheap living, and dwarfed goals.
>
> I no longer need preeminence, prosperity, position, promotions, plaudits, or popularity. I don't have to be right, first, tops, recognized, praised, regarded, or rewarded. I now live by faith, lean on His presence, walk by patience, lift by prayer, and labor by power.
>
> My face is set, my gait is fast, my goal is heaven, my road is narrow, my way is rough, my companions are few, my Guide is reliable, my mission is clear. I cannot be bought, compromised, detoured, lured away, turned back, deluded, or delayed. I will not flinch in the face of sacrifice, hesitate in the presence of the adversary, negotiate at the table of the enemy, ponder at the pool of popularity, or meander in the maze of mediocrity.
>
> I won't give up, shut up, let up, until I have stayed up, stored up, prayed up, paid up, and preached up for the cause of Christ. I am a disciple of Jesus. I must go till He comes, give till I drop, preach till all know,

and work till He stops me. And when He comes for His own, He will
have no problem recognizing me—my banner will be clear.[1]

Are you totally committed to Jesus, as this pastor has described? When Jesus comes for His own, will He recognize you as His disciple because your banner will be clear? If so, continue to grow as His disciple and He will accomplish mighty things through you. May God bless you as you pursue a lifelong, obedient relationship with your Master and experience Him transforming you into His likeness, changing your values into kingdom values, and involving you in His mission in your home, your church, and the world!

ENDNOTES

Preface

1. Avery T. Willis Jr., *Indonesian Revival: Why Two Million Came to Christ* (Pasadena, Calif.: William Carey Library, 1978).

Introduction:

1. R. A. Torrey, *Why God Used D.L. Moody* (Chicago: Moody Press, 1923), 10.
2. Taken from *The Exchanged Life*, a pamphlet reprinted from the biography of James Hudson Taylor by Dr. and Mrs. Howard Taylor. Pamphlet printed by OMF International founded in 1865 by J. Hudson Taylor as the China Inland Mission.

Chapter 5

1. Paul Eshleman, *The Touch of Jesus* (Orlando: New Life, 1995), 157-58.

Chapter 6

1. R.A. Torrey, *Why God Used D. L. Moody* (Chicago: Moody Press, 1923), 42.

Chapter 11

1. Andrew Murray, *The Full Blessing of Pentecost* (Port Washington, Pa: Christian Literature Crusade, 1954), 7.
2. L. L. Letgers, *The Simplicity of the Spirit-Filled Life* (Farmingdale, N.Y.: Christian Witness, 1968), 51-52.

Chapter 14

1. John Piper, *Let the Nations Be Glad! The Supremacy of God in Missions* (Grand Rapids: Baker Books, 1993), 41.

Chapter 15

1. Adapted from Waylon Moore, "Meditating on the Word," in *The Disciple's Study Bible* (Nashville: Holman Bible Publishers, 1988), 1755–56.

Chapter 16

1. A. Berkely Mickelsen, *Interpreting the Bible* (Grand Rapids: William B. Eerdmans Publishing Co., 1963), 357.

Chapter 17

1. Brian Tracy, *Psychology of Achievement* (Nightingale-Conant Corp., 1994).

Chapter 18

1. Henry T. Blackaby and Claude V. King, *Experiencing God: Knowing and Doing the Will of God* (Nashville: LifeWay Press, 1990), 103.

Chapter 20

1. Tom D. Elliff, *A Passion for Prayer: Experiencing Deeper Intimacy with God* (Wheaton, Ill.: Crossway, 1998), 141–44.

Chapter 21

1. Adapted from *Continuing Witness Training* (Alpharetta, Ga.: North American Mission Board of the Southern Baptist Convention).

Chapter 22

1. Herschel H. Hobbs, *The Gospel of Matthew* (Grand Rapids: Baker Book House, 1961), 134.
2. *Welcome to God's Family*. Available in Baptist Bookstores or Lifeway Christian stores or from the Baptist Sunday School Board Customer Service Center; 127 Ninth Avene, North; Nashville, TN 37234; 1-800-458-2772.

Chapter 25

1. Johnny Hunt, *Growing Churches*, Spring 1998 (Baptist Sunday School Board)

Conclusion

1. Source unknown.

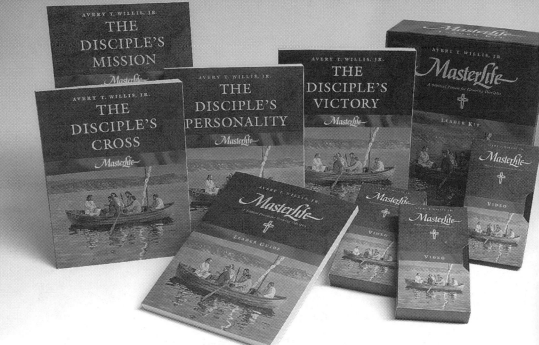

If you had to choose one course to help you grow as a disciple of Jesus, what would it be?

MasterLife is the one comprehensive discipleship course every believer needs to grow in faith and find a place of service through the church.

MasterLife helps you experience Christian victory by practicing these biblical principles:

- spending time with the Master
- fellowshipping with believers
- witnessing to the world
- living in the Word
- praying in faith
- ministering to others

MasterLife 1: The Disciple's Cross	0767325796
MasterLife 2: The Disciple's Personality	076732580X
MasterLife 3: The Disciple's Victory	0767325818
MasterLife 4: The Disciple's Mission	0767325826
MasterLife Book Set	0767326415
MasterLife Leader Guide	0767325834
MasterLife Leader Kit	0767326407

For more information or to order these resources,
WRITE Customer Service Center;
MSN 113; 127 Ninth Avenue, North; Nashville, TN 37234;
PHONE 1-800-458-2772; FAX (615) 251-5933;
EMAIL customerservice@bssb.com;
or VISIT a Baptist Book Store or Lifeway Christian Store near you.